THE NUWAUBIAN NATION

The Nuwaubian Nation takes the reader on a journey into an African-American spiritual movement. The United Nuwaubian Nation has changed shape since its inceptions in the 1970s, transforming from a Black Hebrew mystery school into a Muslim utopian community in Brooklyn, N.Y.; from an Egyptian theme park into an Amerindian reserve in rural Georgia. This book follows the extraordinary career of Dwight York, who in his teens started out in a New York street gang, but converted to Islam in prison. Emerging as a Black messiah, York proceeded to break the Paleman's "spell of Kingu" and to guide his people through a series of racial/religious identities that demanded dramatic changes in costume, gender roles and lifestyle. Dr. York's "Blackosophy" is analyzed as a new expression of that ancient mystical worldview, Gnosticism.

Referring to theories in the sociology of deviance and media studies, the author tracks the escalating hostilities against the group that climaxed in a Waco-style FBI raid on the Nuwaubian "compound" in 2002. In the ensuing legal process we witness Dr. York's dramatic reversals of fortune; he is now serving a 135-year sentence as his Black Panther lawyer prepares to take his case to the Supreme Court.

This book presents fresh and important insights into racialist spirituality and the social control of unconventional religions in America.

ASHGATE NEW RELIGIONS

Series Editors:

James R. Lewis, University of Tromsø, Norway

George D. Chryssides, University of Wolverhampton, UK

The popularity and significance of New Religious Movements is reflected in the explosion of related articles and books now being published. This Ashgate series offers an invaluable resource and lasting contribution to the field.

The Nuwaubian Nation
Black Spirituality and State Control

SUSAN PALMER

Dawson College and Concordia University, Canada

ASHGATE

Published by
Ashgate Publishing Limited
Wey Court East
Union Road
Farnham
Surrey, GU9 7PT
England

Ashgate Publishing Company
Suite 420
101 Cherry Street
Burlington
VT 05401-4405
USA

www.ashgate.com

British Library Cataloguing in Publication Data
Palmer, Susan
　　The Nuwaubian Nation : Black Spirituality and State Control. – (Ashgate new religions)
　　1. York, Dwight, 1945?– 2. United Nation of Nuwaubian Moors – History.
　　3. Unidentified flying object cults – United States.
　　I. Title II. Series
　　299.9'32'092–dc22

Library of Congress Cataloging-in-Publication Data
Palmer, Susan
　　　The Nuwaubian nation : black spirituality and state control / Susan Palmer.
　　　　　p. cm.—(Ashgate new religions)
　　　Includes bibliographical references and index.
　　　ISBN 978-0-7546-6255-6 (hardcover : alk. paper)
　　1. Nuwaubian movement. 2. York, Dwight, 1945?- I. Title.

　　BP605.N89
　　299.6'8973—dc22

2009053570

ISBN 9780754662556 (hbk)

Mixed Sources
Product group from well-managed forests and other controlled sources
www.fsc.org Cert no. SA-COC-1565
© 1996 Forest Stewardship Council
FSC

Printed and bound in Great Britain by
MPG Books Group, UK

I dedicate this book to my dear friends and pleasant colleagues who encouraged me during my research, and even accompanied me to the Nuwaubian meetings in Brooklyn, Atlanta, Philadelphia, and London: Paul Greenhouse, Michael York, Marat Shterin, Eileen Barker, Amanda Twist, Elijah Seigler, Steve Luxton, Andrew Pargellis, Tony Porcelli, and Doug Newman

Contents

List of Illustrations

All photographs are by and courtesy of Nick Oza (www.nickoza.com) with the exception of "Ansaar propagating Right Knowledge in the 1970s in New York" by Jamel Shabazz (www.jamelshabazz.com).

Acknowledgments

I would like to acknowledge the help and guidance of Paul Greenhouse, documentary filmmaker, and of the many Nuwaubians who welcomed me at their meetings and kindly took the time to explain their culture to an outsider. I would also like to thank Sheriff Howard Sills and Jacob York for sharing their fascinating stories and insights with this researcher.

List of Acronyms

AAC	Ansaaru Allah Community
ACM	Anti-cult Movement
AEO	Ancient Egiptian Order
BATF	Bureau of Alcohol, Tobacco and Firearms
BPP	Black Panther Party
DFAC	Department of Family and Children's Services
FBI	Federal Bureau of Investigation
FOI	Fruit of Islam (NOI's security force)
GBI	Georgia Bureau of Investigation
HTM	Holy Tabernacle Ministries
MSTA	Moorish Science Temple of America
NBPP	New Black Panther Party
NGE	Nation of Gods and Earths
NIH	Nubian Islamic Hebrews
NOI	Nation of Islam
NRM	New Religious Movement
NYPD	New York Police Department
NYSP	New York State Police
RICO	Racketeer Influenced and Corrupt Organizations
SWAT team	Special Weapons and Tactics team
UNIA	Universal Negro Improvement Association
UNN	United Nuwaubian Nation
UNNM	United Nuwaubian Nation of Moors

Preface
"Overstanding"[1] the Nuwaubians

The Nuwaubian movement is one of the most significant Black Nationalist spiritual movements in America, if only in terms of its longevity. For over 40 years Dr. Malachi Z. York has been directing this highly visible group, known under different titles. His disciples wear exotic costumes decorated with eclectic symbols, and they propagate "Right Knowledge" from booths set up on streets in the main cities of the U.S., Canada and the U.K. For almost two decades the group was known as the Ansaaru Allah Community (AAC), with its headquarters in Brooklyn, N.Y. The AAC was a messianic, millenarian, evangelistic and communal "Muslim" movement, well-known among Black nationalists and African-American Muslims in the 1970s and 80s. But since the late 1980s, the Nuwaubian movement has rejected Islam, embraced an eclectic range of spiritual themes—and gained considerable notoriety.

As of this writing, Dr. Malachi Z. York, the prophet-founder, is still serving his 135-year sentence in a "supermax" security federal prison in Florence, Colorado (dubbed the "Alcatraz of the Rockies"). One of Dr. York's fellow inmates is the Unabomber. Unlike the Unabomber and other fellow prisoners, York is neither a murderer nor a terrorist, but he was convicted of multiple counts of child molestation-related charges combined with "racketeering" charges, under the RICO law. His lawyers object that RICO was originally designed to prosecute organized crime and Mafia dons, not religious leaders, however unconventional their message. His disciples insist their "Master Teacher" is an innocent man who was framed, silenced and "brought down" by a conspiracy of disgruntled ex-members in collusion with the "White Power Structure." Today, they run a series of fund-raising activist organizations (*He is Innocent!* and *Free Dr .Malachi Z. York!*) lobbying for his release. Attorney Malik Shabazz, a lawyer with the New Black Panther Party, is currently working with the legal team that is preparing an appeal before the Supreme Court.

Despite (and perhaps due to) its controversial status, the United Nuwaubian Nation[2] remains one of the most enigmatic, under-researched and poorly understood spiritual groups in America. There are three sources of historical data: Dr. York's baffling, esoteric "scrolls"; sensationalistic news coverage issuing from Middle Georgia, and two books, *The Ansar Cult in America*, and

---

[1]   The Nuwaubians borrowed this term from the Rastafarians, for whom it means looking at the world from JAH's point of view.

[2]   The UNN used to be called the UNNM (United Nuwaubian Nation of Moors).

Ungodly: The True Story of Unprecedented Evil. As their titles indicate, these are hardly value-free, unbiased studies.[3]

Both authors, Bilal Phillips (a Muslim cleric) and Bill Osinski (a journalist) rely heavily on ex-members and cultural opponents of "the cult" for their material. This is the quick and easy "anticult" method—but there are four good reasons why even academic researchers would find access to this new religious movement difficult. First, the group is sectarian and adopts an oppositional stance towards society. Second, the group is elusive, almost chameleonesque in its behavior; it will vanish periodically, close down its centers, members will disperse into their urban environments—and then the group will suddenly bob up again—sometimes barely recognizable—with a new name and new symbols. A third obstacle is posed by the conflict and controversy that surrounds the leader. Many of my potential subjects have asked "whose side are you on?" and have tried to control the flow of information. I have constantly been mistaken for a journalist, whom the Nuwaubians, quite understandably, regard as hostile to their enterprise. The FBI agent responsible for the children taken during the raid on Tama Re couldn't talk to me because "there is an Eleventh Circuit appeal still pending." A fourth obstacle inhibiting access is the group's stance on race. I have often been asked if the Nuwaubians' racialist beliefs posed a problem for white researchers. The answer is—yes!

Even the African-born Nigerian researcher, Essien-Udom, author of the excellent 1962 study, *Black Nationalism: A Search for an Identity in America*, describes the obstacles he encountered when researching the Nation of Islam in the early 1960s:

> The difficulty of studying the group lies partly in its lack of appreciation for the "scientific" value of the information they would provide. Partly, it lies in the deep-seated fear of the outsider. The [Black] Muslim's sense of persecution and fear of the so-called "enemy" thus makes their cooperation difficult to secure. Sometimes, they simply do not know what information is permissible from the point of view of those in authority. Suspicion, fear and the apparent atmosphere of secrecy which surrounds the movement made it difficult for the writer to secure exact data.[4]

Essien-Udom's comments aptly describe this white researcher's situation in studying the Nuwaubians. But while the Nuwaubians resisted my plans to conduct a well-designed, formal research project, they welcomed me to their meetings, they allowed me to participate in some of their rituals, and many individuals were

---

[3]   Abu Ameenah Bilal Phillips, *The Ansar Cult in America in America*. Riyadh, Saudi Arabia: Tahweed Publications, 1988); Bill Osinski, *Ungodly: The True Story of Unprecedented Evil* (Macon, Georgia: Indigo Publishing Group, 2007).

[4]   E.U. Essien-Udom, *Black Nationalism: A Search for Identity in America* (Chicago: The University of Chicago Press, 1962), ix.

happy to engage in informal conversations.[5] Once the disciples got to know me better, some of them opened up and consented to sitting down for formal note-taking interviews.

I have been asked if researching a "black supremacist" group was perhaps foolhardy—even dangerous? The answer to that one is "no." The group's complex and shifting stance on race cannot be accurately described by the label, "black supremacist." Moreover, I never felt threatened (except for one brief moment during a meeting in Harlem, described below). In fact the Nuwaubians were friendly and impeccably courteous. They addressed me as respectfully as "Sister" and seemed to regard my presence as a bit of a joke. They evidently found something inappropriate—even silly—in having a white researcher sitting in on their meetings taking notes. My impression was they perceived me as an eccentric, slightly "crazy" person rather than as threatening figure. Later, I realized that this was a predictable cultural trait—to respond to ambiguous situations or potential conflict by joking or clowning. At times I even felt the Nuwaubians were "ganging up" on me by making me the butt of their jokes. In this way a certain tension caused by our conflicting agendas was resolved. I felt quite comfortable at the Questions&Answer meetings, jotting down notes on speeches filled with anti-white, hostile rhetoric—although sometimes I received the impression it was "toned down" when I showed up. Later on, reading sociologists Radclyffe Brown and Erving Goffman, I realized our spontaneous "joking relationship" was actually a method![6]

Suddenly at the beginning of January 2003, my access to the group seemed to open up. I received a phone call from a woman with a strong Southern accent from the legal office of Ed Garland, Dr. York's defense attorney. She was his secretary and asked if I could be available to appear as a witness in Dr. York's upcoming court case. "Will I be able to interview Dwight York in jail?" I asked. "We can arrange that," she replied. I sent them my article and notes, composed a list of questions for Dr. York, and waited excitedly for my plane ticket. But a week later she called back: "I want to thank you for agreeing to help us out, but I am happy to tell you that we won't need you to come out after all. Dwight York has agreed to a plea bargain." On 24 January Dr. York appeared in court, shackled and handcuffed, and pleaded guilty to 77 of the child molestation charges, in exchange for a promised 15-year sentence. My hopes were dashed, but York's long, convoluted legal process had only just begun.

---

[5]   Some of their rituals were restricted to initiates in the Ancient Egiptian Order.

[6]   This first came to my attention when I read Eileen Barker's published speech at the SSSR, with the witty title, "The Scientific Study of Religion? You Must be Joking!" She described how she resolved a tense situation while studying the Unificationists by resorting to humor. See Erving Goffman, *The Presentation of Self in Everyday Life* (Chicago: Chicago University Press, 1959); A.R. Radclyffe Brown, "On joking relationships" (*Africa* 13, 1950), 195-210.

While the access and design of this research has been less than satisfactory, I have persisted nonetheless—simply because the Nuwaubians fascinated me. I have researched many NRMs—the Rajneesh, the Raelians, the Twelve Tribes, Scientology, among others—but the Nuwaubians continue to baffle me. Gradually, I have come to realize that they are too sophisticated to be categorized simply as "racists" or "black supremacists." Rather, they are "racial*ists*"; radical gnostics who play with myths of race as metaphors for the veils of illusion obscuring the godlike Higher Self or Inner Man. Having read fragmentary accounts in Hans Jonas[7] of the poorly documented ancient Gnostic schools, I feel that an incomplete knowledge of this new expression of gnostic philosophy is better than no knowledge.

So, this book is the result of my efforts to understand (or "overstand") this unusual Black mystery school.

My Research Approach

In the interest of "transparency" I will recount some of my research experiences. While this may appear to be a self-indulgent exercise, I feel it is a necessary step in the pursuit of that elusive thing called "objectivity." What is objectivity? Researchers disagree. Mattias Gardell, a blonde Swedish sociologist who gained unprecedented access to Farrakhan and the Nation of Islam, actually goes so far as to deny that objectivity is possible:

> My intention is to present my findings as truthfully as possible, yet objectivity is a misleading and honorific label and inapplicable to humanistic and social research. Any human understanding of an object goes *via* the subject's mind as medium and is thus transformed into a subjective image of the object observed; it can only be grasped through filter of perception, structured by the observer's frame of reference.[8]

At the opposite end of the spectrum we find Stephen Kent and Theresa Krebs, authors of "When Scholars Know Sin."[9] They accuse several leading scholars in new religious studies (including myself) of being "kept" or duped by the cults, and insist that these scholars are a disgrace to the academy and a danger to the public, because they assist harmful NRMs in their sneaky efforts to appear respectable by writing seemingly "neutral," value-free studies of these groups. Kent and

---

[7]   Hans Jonas, *The Gnostic Religion.* (Boston: Beacon Press, 1963).

[8]   Mattias Gardell, *Countdown to Armageddon: Louis Farrakhan and the Nation of Islam* (Chicago: University of Chicago Press, 1999).

[9]   Stephen A. Kent and Theresa Krebs, "When Scholars Know Sin: Alternative Religions and Their Academic Supporters," in *Skeptic Magazine* (Vol. 6, No.3, 1998).

Krebs point to several cases of *philomandaranism*[10] (situations where scholars have received plane tickets to attend "Moonie" conferences, or had their research funded by a "cult"), and they insist that, henceforth, all scholars who do not adopt the rigorous "anticult" perspective in their writings are suspect.

For Kent and Krebs, "objectivity" is an *ontological state*, rather like grace, sainthood or perpetual virginity. This holy state can never be restored once the errant researcher has been duped or bribed by a seemingly innocuous cult. Whether the scholar is deliberately sleazy or merely misguided, he or she has succumbed to the primal "Fall" into scholarly "sin."

I happen to disagree with both extreme positions. "Objectivity," as I see it, is a valid goal, but it works as an ongoing, wobbly balancing act. It demands concentration, repetition and constant minor adjustments. Since I espouse the Pelagian view of sin (as opposed to the Augustinian one)[11] I would insist that each researcher must make his or her individual choices—and errors may be absolved through the social-scientific equivalents of soul-searching, confession, and prayer. Each researcher is their own "Adam" or "Eve" contemplating their own versions of the Fruit of Knowledge, and there are many possible endings to the myth.

But, in the interests of "objectivity," I feel it is only fair that researchers, when they present their findings, should make transparent their cultural biases and prejudicial reactions. As a "white" sociologist researching a "black" new religion, I have observed some interesting and unexpected social dynamics and emotional responses as I interacted with my Nuwaubian (and anti-Nuwaubian) subjects.

Lewis Carter, in an insightful discussion of research methods in his 1998 book, *Charisma and Control in Rajneeshpuram*, observes that obstacles to research (what he terms "research nuisances") "seem to reflect, in microcosm at least, the cultural conflicts we observed."[12] In a similar vein, by contemplating my own problems while researching the Nuwaubians, I was gaining new insights into the Nuwaubians' relationship with the surrounding "white" society.

How I Met the Nuwauabians

I first encountered the group in the late 1980s as I was rushing, late for work, through Montreal's subway in mid-winter. Two tall black men dressed in flowing

---

[10]   It is unclear whether this amusing greco-sino-neologism was invented by Thomas Robbins or by Roland Robertson. I once attended a conference where these scholars engaged in a jocular dispute over authorship.

[11]   See Elaine Pagels, *Adam, Eve and the Serpent* (New York: Vintage Books, 1989) in which she argues that Augustine introduced into Christianity the notion that every man and woman shares the consequence of the primal Fall of Adam and Eve, whereas Pelagius preached a more optimistic idea of sin, and emphasized individual choice.

[12]   Lewis Carter, *Charisma and Control in Rajneeshpuram. The Role of Shared Values in the Creation of a Community* (Cambridge University Press, 1998).

white robes handed me a religious tract with fancy Arabic script. ("What are desert sheikhs doing here, in a Canadian blizzard?" I wondered.) I categorized them as fundamentalist Muslims until, finding a seat on the train, I glanced at the tract and read about...the Mahdi...UFOs...a survivalist training camp in the Catskills (!) "Hey!" I told myself, "This group is a...cult, a *Black* cult!" (In those days I still used the "c" word, today considered "un-PC" among sociologists who study new religions.) Since I was teaching a course on new religions at the time, and writing my Ph.D. dissertation on women in NRMs, I resolved I would study them. It turned out it wasn't all that easy.

They called themselves the Ansaaru Allah Community in those days, and lived in a commune near the Bluebonnets race track in north Montreal, but their headquarters was in Brooklyn, N.Y. They peddled the teachings of their "Master Teacher" in Times Square and on the streets of many of the major U.S. and Canadian cities where they set up tables displaying African incense, oils, crafts and Dr. York's booklets, or "scrolls." But these men weren't just ordinary peddlars, they were "Propagators of the Knowledge"—a *gnosis* that concerned the true origins and spiritual identity of all dark-skinned people—whose angelic ancestors hailed from a distant star. They recruited African-American youth by day, and slept in men's barracks at night.

I would make it a point to track down the Ansaars on my trips to Toronto and New York and began collecting their "scrolls." Nestled between the incense sticks and oil bottles on a booth, I came across *The Paleman*, a book that explains how all white people have leprosy, due to the "Curse of Ham." I was amused to see Dr. Malachi Z. York turn the tables on the white Christian churches of the Southern Bible Belt. Despite my leprous condition, the Propagators seemed quite willing to stare into my blue eyes and expound "The Knowledge," or to stand around and just chat.

One day I was chatting with a friendly Propagator at his booth on 14th Street in the East Village and asked him if I could interview some of their women for my doctoral dissertation. He shook his head. "We do not allow them to speak to outsiders." So, for years I never saw their women, only photographs in the scrolls of heavily-veiled figures in white robes exposing dark eyes, hands and bare feet. They whirled in white coverings, embracing and circling around each other in mysterious Sufi dances. They served their husbands and children selflessly, emulating the folk saint, Hadrat Fatimah. They worked behind the iron gate of the Ansaar publishing office in Brooklyn, typing up Dr. York's voluminous sermons into "scrolls" to be sold in their bookstores. Some women were the plural wives of the top leaders, but most of them lived in the women's quarters, separate from their "mates." If the man was successful in fundraising, he would be rewarded by an assignation with his woman in the "Green Room" where, surrounded by murals of a jungle Eden, the couple would follow a ritual of eugenics to conceive a pure Nubian child. These children spoke no English, but were taught Hebrew, Arabic and "Nubic"—a language invented by Dr. York. They were the 144,000 pure Nuwaubian children who would Rapture their parents just before the final destruction of the planet.

As I hung out on the streets of New York observing them, I noticed that the Ansaars were part of a larger scene—what I shall refer to as the "Black cultic milieu."[13] In 1992 my friend, Steve Luxton joined me on a research trip to Manhattan to prepare our co-authored paper.[14] We noticed the "Muslim" Ansaars were on surprisingly friendly terms with members of other, rival Black nationalist religions. As I was conversing with a Propagator at his bookstall, a Rastafarian came by and chatted with him. Later, a group of Ben Ammi's Black Hebrews approached and proceeded to grasp the Ansaar's wrist in a stylized handshake. On another occasion, we were buying a copy of *The Final Call* from a Nation of Islam man in a 1950s-style overcoat and red bow tie. He and a passing Ansaar greeted each other with delighted punches and jocular insults (using the forbidden "N" word). When we asked him how the NOI regarded the Ansaars, he laughed: "We consider them our brothers. We are all working for the uplift of the people."

We also received the impression that individual Ansaars did not necessarily share Dr. York's uncompromising stance on race. We were surprised by the discrepancy between the insulting portrayal of "The Paleman" in Ansaar literature and the easygoing relationships we saw Ansaars were cultivating with "palemen" on the street. One afternoon as we were hanging out on Manhattan's 14th street, we watched a group of Hassidic boys wearing *yamukas* stop by at an Ansaar's table. On their way home from their Yeshiva, carrying their Torahs, they hailed the Ansaar, and launched into a spirited attack upon The Lamb's interpretations of Talmudic doctrine and his use of Hebrew words. The Ansaar evidently welcomed the debate and called over some of his brothers at the nearby bookstall to support him. The boys were flaunting their erudition and thumping their Torahs, reading out verses. They referred to an argument made last week, and the Ansaar promised them he would bring more "proof" from the Lamb's writings on the morrow—so it appeared that this was an ongoing relationship! On another occasion, I watched a freckled saxophonist with long red dreadlocks stop by for his favorite kind of incense which the Ansaar kept for him under the counter. The two engaged in an intense discussion about what chords should be used in certain jazz tunes, and they made a date to get together again to "jam."

One day I found, to my surprise, that it was actually "no problem" for a white person to attend their meetings. I was in Times Square conversing with a charming Propagator who was a history student at Columbia (I received the impression he was just dabbling in Ansaar spirituality over the summer holidays).

"If you are interested in The Knowledge, why don't you come on out to our Question-Answer?" he asked

---

[13]   See Chapter 1 for an explanation of the notion of the "cultic milieu."

[14]   Susan J. Palmer and Steve Luxton, "The Ansaaru Allah Community: Postmodernist Narration and the Black Jeremiad," in Peter Clarke (ed.), *New Islamic Movements in the West* (Oxford: Carfax Publications, 1996).

"Really? You allow *white* people to come to your meetings?"

"No problem," he replied.

"But, is it…safe?" (When I had invited my New York friend to accompany me to the Mosque on Bushwick Avenue, he warned me about the area. "Go there, and you'll get shot—or a knife in your back!" he said darkly.)

When I explained my hesitation, the Propagator offered to escort me personally to the mosque. I was to come back at six when his shift ended. I returned…but he was nowhere to be seen. When I came back the next day, he avoided my glance, and his brother Ansaars were teasing him. "Hey, your girlfriend's back, looking for you!"

Suddenly, in 1992, the Ansaars disappeared. I was in Toronto scouting for "cult lit" and noticed they were not at their usual spot on the corner of Bloor and Bathurst, so I went to their other post outside the Eaton Center. I saw the Hare Krishna chanting and leaping to drums, but no Ansaars. Then I noticed a lonely middle-eastern-looking man in a white *djelaba* and cap selling Arabic booklets at his stand. He looked awfully dull for an Ansaar, and his literature lacked the usual garish cartoons, but I approached him anyway and asked hesitantly, "are you with the Ansaaru Allah Community?"

"Certainly not!" he replied indignantly in a British accent. "I would never associate with them. They are not even Muslims! They are a stupid cult!" He pointed across the street to a pair of skinny teens in green and black tunics at what looked like a Bnai Brith stall with Hebrew literature. "There they are over there, see? They are crazy."

So I thanked him and crossed the street. "Yes, we *used* to be called the Ansaaru Allah, but now we are the Holy Tabernacle Ministries," explained the young man in green silk, who wore a heavy medallion of the Star of David entwined with an Ankh.

"But how can you be Jewish?" I asked. "I thought you were Muslims?"

"We still have the Right Knowledge—and we have always been Hebrews—kind of like the Falashi Jews," he replied. "We overstand *all* the world religions."

They were now called the Holy Tabernacle Ministries, and Dr. York was "The Lamb" or more simply, "Rabboni." On my next visit to the HTM bookstore in Philadelphia in August 1992, I was surprised to find a woman in charge. She was not veiled. In fact, she was wearing shorts and a tank top. She assured me they were no longer Muslims, because "we're not a religion, we study factology." When I asked her what "factology" was, she replied, "we don't *believe* in anything—we just study the facts, ma'am." I realized that women were finally visible and recognized for the *de facto* role they had held as theologians and administrators since the beginning of the movement.

After 1992 I began to show up occasionally at the Question&Answer classes, held at their *Tents of Kedar* chain of bookstores (later renamed *All Eyes on Egipt*). I attended two in Philadelphia, three in Brixton (a bleak, depressing area of London, Brixton is now considered to be a hotbed of Muslim terrorist training).

More regularly, I traveled from Montreal to Brooklyn, New York. It was there that I attended my very first Question&Answer meeting.

The Question&Answer Classes

One Sunday afternoon I took the subway from the East Village to Brooklyn and walked to the *Tents of Kedar* bookstore, located next door to the mosque on 717 Bushwick Avenue. On entering the black gold-lettered entrance, I found myself in a fantasy world, surrounded by black and gold symbols, Arabic script and Egyptian statues. The walls were lined with bookcases displaying hundreds of Dr. York's books or "scrolls," illustrated in the Ansaar's inimitable style of folk art.

I made my way to the back room behind the bookstore. There I counted 16 people sitting in unfolded metal chairs—mostly men wearing turbans or fezes, and a few women with elaborate braided hairdos or turbans. I counted three babies and five children. The walls were painted with scenes of muscular black angels flying past planets and alighting on UFOs. Statues of Egyptian gods and man-beasts of gilded *papier maché* guarded the raised platform where the Minister stood.

Some people in the front row moved over courteously to offer me a seat. I sat down and took out a notebook. The man beside me suppressed a grin, eyes dancing beneath his fez. Later I overheard a group of older disciples joking about the "white professor lady" who "spied on us." They were standing outside the temple, snorting with laughter—that stopped suddenly when they saw me.

The Minister was a young man dressed severely in black with a fez and shades. He opened with the traditional Nubic greeting, "Rahuawabbbat!"

"Rahuawabbat!" the congregation responded—and the class began.

I sat there scribbling furiously, but so was everyone else. The minister encouraged them to take notes, so I fit right in. When I reviewed my notes of that very first meeting, I can see I was having trouble recording an intense debate over the relative merits of different genres of Hip Hop. One man insisted that all recent Hip Hop music was decadent and of no spiritual benefit to the Nubian people. Then a young woman jumped to her feet: "Hip Hop exposes the no-justice, hypocrisy in Amerikahn society! That's the main business of Hiphop, and that has to be the *first step* towards Black Eye-Dent-itee!"

"Yeah! She's right!" agreed her friends.

A group of teenagers tried to defend their favorite group (that I'd never heard of) as intrinsically "spiritual," but the older adepts argued that the inspiration and uplift of '80s rap and Hiphop "got drownded" in drugs, violence and pornography. ("Have you listened to Tupac?"…"Cassius D showed us how they use the satanic symbols in Hiphop advertising!"… . "Yeah, when the Devil came out of the Pit and had sex with Jack Kennedy"…"The Central Computer Brain, 666, has digitalized those rappers you see on TV—look at Eminem, and JZ!").

"Oh! JZ!" Everyone laughed.

I had absolutely no idea what they were talking about. I was guess-spelling the names. But their radical, uncompromising stance on race really hit home on one occasion. During a Q&A meeting in Philadelphia, I boasted that in Canada we were virtually free of racial prejudice; that my students took racial integration and equality so much for granted that they were puzzled by the very concept of "racism." A woman responded by saying she had trained as a nurse in Montreal in the late 1980s, but quit after she was told by the head nurse not to wear her hair in African braids when she was on the wards because it was "too messy" and "looked dirty." "I feel sorry for all those kids in Canada," she concluded. "They are so lost. They have no idea who they are."

I suddenly realized that all my liberal attitudes were irrelevant here. The Nuwaubians did not want acceptance, equality and respect so that they could integrate more successfully into a white society. They wanted separation.[15]

I found York's ministers were talented performers, more like artists than "preachers." Some had produced their own CDs as aspiring, semi-professional Hip Hop or Rap artists, and these were on display in the bookstores. The ministers had their own style of teaching and many set up *ad hoc* "schools" of Blackosophy in the bookstores or on their websites, based loosely on Dr. York's writings.

One style, not so very different from an ordinary Sunday school class, was the Q&A I attended in August 2003 at the *All Eyes on Egipt* bookstore in Atlanta, GA.[16] People brought their Bibles and read out the verses. The presiding minister talked about serious moral and social issues. In contrast, the Sunday classes in Philadelphia in the 1990s were distinctly "New Agey"—more like study circles. The topics for discussion jumped from Theosophy, to Ancient Astronauts, to Ufology, to Edgar Cayce, to Zechariah Sitchen—punctuated by Dr. York's ever-mutating mythologies of race.

Still another style of teaching was offered by Sister Sakinah of the Brooklyn bookstore. She was a woman who insisted on audience participation. She would invite people up from the congregation to present specific topics, and would encourage audience response.

The meetings in the London suburb of Brixton, were also singular. Two skinny men in their teens or early twenties, garbed in Moorish black and gold-braided tunics, each sporting a gold-tasseled fez, were "Tutting" (a form of Break Dance based on the 90-degree angles of gods in Egyptian friezes) as they delivered long, rhythmic responses to questions about esoteric matters ("who built the pyramids?";

---

[15]   I remember as a child how my father once described a family friend who had just made a speech at the dinner table denouncing racial prejudice as "bristling with tolerance." I have noticed many "affirmative action" Hollywood films that portray deep bonding between the male white protagonists and their black sidekicks, and have wondered if African-Americans find these scenes as contrived and embarrassing as I do.

[16]   The *Tents of Kedar* bookstores were renamed *All Eyes on Egipt* once the group moved to Atlanta to build Tama Re, their Egiptian [sic] village. I was told they spell it this way because "i" is a mystical letter.

"are the Dogon people named after the Dog Star?"). The young ministers would choose a question, then launch into a Rap-style monologue, punctuated by jerky sideways head motions and weird geometrical hand-arm gestures. Their form of poetry relied heavily on word-association, I noticed. They tended to ignore Latin and Greek roots and violate the rules of semantics, relying exclusively on accidental phonetics. One example I recall went something like this:

Do your research, check the facts, be exact! "Exact" means "Eggs-Act." So, what act is done on a egg? [soliciting answers from the floor]. You *break* it, you crack it *open*, right? [Miming a cook breaking an egg over a bowl]. So, when you're making eggs for breakfast, you have to *crack* eggs! You try to be *eggs-act*, because what can happen? ["The yolk gets broke!" called out a chubby lady poetically]. That's right, Sister! Or what else can happen? ["You spill it on the floor," a little girl yelled out—then covered her mouth shyly]. You're absolutely right, Little Sister. So, we must be *eggs-act* when we *act*, in everything, 'specially when we talk about Right Knowledge, it is essential that you try to be *eggs-act* in choosing the Right Phrase, the Right Words!

This is a particularly absurd example, but in all the meetings the ministers would deconstruct the language of their European oppressors. They did this with word play, erroneous semantic links or made-up definitions. In the Nation of Islam there is a great deal of emphasis on educating oneself by expanding one's vocabulary. But NOI teachers rely on the Webster Dictionary and use the standard methods of philology. Nuwaubian teachers, in contrast, disregard the Latin and Anglo-Saxon roots, preferring to rely on accidental phonetics or spontaneous flights of fancy. I soon realized they were not "scientific" philologists, but rather poets. Their performances would often last for a good fifteen minutes to half an hour, so that the arms raised in the congregation for questions, would eventually tire and recoil.

The Challenge of Culture Shock

In the course of my research, I experienced moments of profound confusion, of culture-shock. On one trip to the Brixton meeting, I was worn out from jet lag and the morning conference, held at the London School of Economics. I nodded off, lulled by the rhythmic monologue—then suddenly awoke in a black-painted hall, flanked by gilt *papier maché* pharoahs and ankhs. I was deeply disoriented. I had absolutely no idea where I was, surrounded by young Nuwaubians wearing fezes and Egyptian headdresses, chatting away in East London/Caribbean accents.

I encountered communication problems. When I asked a Nuwaubian to describe his revered Master Teacher, he answered, "He's *bad!*" This puzzled me until I learned that *bad* meant *good*. At the motel near Tama Re, I approached Polight, a 20-year-old who had narrowly escaped being shot by a drug gang by ducking into the Nuwaubian bookstore and hiding. He ended up joining the commune and was now a minister-in-training. When I asked him for an interview, he said, "I'll bridge with you later on the Land." ("What?" I wondered.) So, I waited near the bridge outside the souvenir shop watching the exotic goldfish in the pond for at least an hour before giving up. Later, I learned that "bridge" means "talk."

The Interviews

This study draws partly from interviews, some conducted by myself, and some filmed by the documentary filmmaker, Paul Greenhouse.[17] Others are found in the books of Bilal Phillips and Bill Osinski. I interviewed non-hostile ex-members,[18] current members, and fringe members. Most of my interviews were conducted during the July 2004 "Savior's Day" pilgrimage to Tama Re.[19] In one of these interviews I confronted an unprecedented ethical dilemma.

In March 2007 I was contacted by an ex-member who had heard that I was writing a book on the Nuwaubians and offered to sell me information—for a price. This person seemed to be the spokesperson for her group, and offered put me in touch with other ex-members who were eager to be interviewed (also for a price). I had never encountered this situation before. It was an amusing twist to the more familiar pitfall of becoming what anticultists call the "cult apologist" or "kept scholar"; an academic who is paid *by* "cultists" to say nice things about them. I emailed my NRM listserve to elicit the reaction of my colleagues. I received five responses warning me not to trust "sexy data" that was bought. I was opening myself to criticism, they warned, if it were to become known that I had paid for discrediting information. So, I decided to hedge and tried to arrange a meeting with this apostate—which fell through—but I did manage to elicit some stories over the phone—for free. Since these apostates had been witnesses in the prosecution's case against Dr. York, I wondered if a less worthy motive than the pure pursuit of justice might have influenced their testimonies… .[20]

---

[17]   Greenhouse's documentary film in progress, "The Nuwaubian Story" was shown at the American Academy of Religion's regional meeting in Montreal in May 2005, and also at the meeting of the Society for the Scientific Study of Religion in October 2006.

[18]   One of the most fruitful interviews was with a second-generation member, Yusuf, a 30-year-old M.A. graduate from Cornell. His memories of communal life in a strict Muslim sect are nostalgic and utopian. He wrote his MA thesis on the significance of the Ansaaru Allah movement, available at the Africana collection at Cornell University.

[19]   These include interviews in Georgia with three top leaders; two in the "Triad" at Tama Re. These men come from interesting backgrounds; one was a former Minister for the Nation of Islam (a prison chaplain), another was a professional basketball player in Europe, and the third was a hydraulics engineer.

[20]   Abigail Washington says in her recant speech that some of the ex-members involved in the "conspiracy against Dr. York" were expecting to write books, become media stars, and get rich (see Chapter 5).

I describe my interviews with Jacob York and with Sister Sakinah below, because they reveal some of the strange, unpredictable obstacles I encountered in my research.

Interview with an Arch Apostate

I arranged to interview Jacob York on 19 August 2003 at his fashion boutique, next door to the Roxy Theatre in the Buckhead district of Atlanta, GA. Jacob York is one of the oldest of Dwight York's 100-odd children, and the son of his only legal wife. He was a heavy-set man in his early 30s with a very assertive, powerful personality. I would describe him as intellectually brilliant, witty, and charismatic.

I found Jacob presiding over his boutique in a plush armchair. We were surrounded by racks of glamorous, stagey garments suitable for nightclubs. I sat meekly at his feet on a cushion (there were no other chairs) asking him questions and scribbling down notes. Hoping to locate a critical incident that may have influenced his father's uncompromising stance on race, I asked him, "Did your father ever have a bad experience with a white person?"

Jacob didn't answer at first. His jaw dropped theatrically and he stared at me with a deadpan expression for a few long seconds. "Where are you from, Sister?" he jibed. "Are you from Mars? Oh, that's right…you're from Ca-na-*duh*. To answer your question, I can't think of a *single person* I know (like myself) who is black, who lived before Civil Rights, that *didn't* have a bad experience with white people—and I mean many, *many*, bad experiences!"

I arranged for a second interview the following evening at his recording studio and office, which was in a building complex behind high iron gates, with elaborate security systems located in a scary neighborhood. I was locked out and had to borrow a passing teenager's cell phone before they would open the gate.

A "Non-Interview"

In July 2003 Sister Sakinah, the dynamic leader who presided over the Question&Answer meetings at the bookstore in Brooklyn, after much pestering, finally granted me an interview. I was delighted. So far, I had collected only a few incoherent interviews from ex-members. The adult Nuwaubians usually deflected me—but the kids were a bit *too* eager to get interviewed. I got to know a little girl named "Harapha" quite well. She was a sprightly elf of ten, her delicate head weighed down by a massive crown of intricate beaded braids worthy of the Queen of Sheba. She would lean against my shoulder as I wrote, nudge my arm and say, Axe me *more* questions!" I overheard her boasting to her friends, "I just give a interview to the white pro-fessor lady. She goin' put me in her *book*!"

So I showed up early at the bookstore for our interview. The sister was on her cell phone and gestured towards a pair of lawn chairs in front of the mosque. It was a sweltering July afternoon in Brooklyn. I had expected to conduct the interview in the cool interior of the bookstore, next to the New Age pebble fountain trickling beside the cash register. But here we were, plunked on the treeless concrete pavement in the boiling sun, a stream of noisy traffic hurtling past us along Bushwick Avenue.

Beads of sweat slid down my face. Like most fair-skinned women well beyond their teens, I worried about sun damage. I could take a break and fetch my hat and shades from the car—but I did not want to break the spell. It had been so difficult to pin her down. If I revealed my discomfort, it might reinforce her racial stereotypes. I recalled that passage in one of the scrolls that described how, as the Millennial sun approaches Earth, the reign of Shaytan will wind down, and all Palemen will be forced to retreat into underground caves because their leprous white skin will be acting up in sun blisters, AIDS and skin cancer—leaving the noble race of Nuwaubians to rule the surface of the planet.

She snapped her cell phone shut. She sat back in the other lawn chair, and tilted her head, sphinx-like, absorbing the rays of the sun with her chocolate-gold skin. We waited in silence for a long time. I emulated the legendary stoic Indian chiefs. Finally, she sat up: "OK, Pro-fessor, you wanted to ask me some questions. Axe away."

"So, when did you first receive the Knowledge?" I began. (This was a stock opening question among the Nuwaubians, meant to put her at her ease.)

"In my dreams," she replied.

"Ok...So! Can you tell me about the time you first met Dr. York?"

"In my dreams!"

(She had decided to stall the interview. That's OK, I was used to that. I lifted my hand to shield my face from the sun, but quickly put it down again.)

"You mean you had a dream about—Him?"

My interviewee enjoyed a long silence of sun worship, then she sat up, eyes dark and alert as a cat's. "He came to me in my dreams, like maybe, like...a hundred lifetimes ago?"

"Oh, I see" (pretending to get it). "So, what year did you actually *meet* him...I mean in real time, while you were awake?"

She sat up. "Yo! Professor! You don't overstand what I'm sayin' here! I was a*sleep*, FAST asleep when he came to me. He woke me up. He took me by the hands. He *lif*-ted me up, out of my sar-*co*phagus!"

"OK...wow!" (As in the Nations of Islam and of Yahweh—the metaphor of sleep describes the mentality of the descendants of African slaves.)

"So...how do you see Dr. York?"

Silence.

"What is he to you?...I mean, who *is* Dr. York...exactly?"

She smiled.

"He is the One Who Comes Armed with The Knowledge. And look what they done to him! Or is *trying* to do (*and he's letting them do it for His own purposes*). Lyin' about him! Calling him a pe-do-phile! Lockin' him up for one hundred and thirty-five years!"

Good, I thought. She introduced this touchy topic, not I.

"So, what about the child abuse allegations…? I mean, how do *you* explain them?

Silence.

"Do you think there was a…conspiracy?" (York's supporters staunchly maintained that he was framed—that this was just another case of a great black leader being silenced and brought down.)

"*You* said it, pro-fessor. That's eggs-zackly what it was from the start—a conspiracy!"

"So, can you explain what this conspiracy was all about?"

Silence.

I decided to backtrack. "So, what were you doing before you met Dr. York?"

"I told you, I weren't doin' nothing. I was just lyin' there, a dead mummy—like most of our people in Amerikah whose consciousness is embalmed, whose time is embezzled by the white slavemasters…*and mistresses!*" (She glared at me as if I were one of the Original Slave Mistresses.)

("*But I'm only a Canadian!*" I wanted to blurt out.) Instead I stared back calmly—a trick I'd learned while researching a group that "squirreled off" from Scientology. They had called this ritual where you stare deadpan into your partner's eyes "holding the confront." But it wasn't a fair contest. Sweat beads tickled my ivory cheeks like flies, while the Minister's face deflected the sun coolly, like a copper shield. I longed for my hat in the car, but I recalled that passage in one of York's scrolls ("as reptiles shed skin, the pale creature has a sensitive skin which peels easily under the rays of the sun").

So, I dropped my gaze and skipped to the last question on the interview schedule.

"So, what have you gained from your involvement in the United Nuwaubian Nation?"

"Peace."

"What?"

"Peace. It don't cost nothing. We offer an abundance of peace. We're not worried about the shooting and robbing happening out there. We *broke* that stereotype, we *cleaned* up the neighborhood. We *provide* a peaceful environment for people seeking the Knowledge."

(Like many of my interviews in the past, this one was lapsing into PR.)

"But what have *you* gained? I mean, personally? How has it changed *your* life?"

She glared at me. "Why should I tell *you* anything?" Now she got right to the point. "Why should I tell you anything at all—especially about my personal info'mation?"

Then her cell phone rang. There had been a bureaucratic error in a book shipment. I was dismissed.

The Meeting in Harlem

Over the years I would attend the occasional meeting at the bookstores, usually accompanied by a friend or two, and would try to keep a low profile, scribbling down the discussions in my notebook.[21] Sometimes I got the impression that as soon as I showed up, the minister would downplay the anti-white rhetoric out of courtesy. But there was one minister who seemed to enjoy insulting me in public. My worst experience was when I attended a meeting at the Black National Theatre in Harlem with my old friend Tony, an Italian-American pianist (who happens to be gay).

This was a solidarity meeting for Dr. York who was in prison awaiting trial. Afrika Bombaataa's Zulu Nation, the Prince Hall Masons, the Moorish Science Temple, the New Black Panther Party, and members of various other groups had come out in support of a persecuted black leader. I was fascinated by the men's costumes, the masonic symbols, the strange hats, the fezes and turbans. Each speaker at the podium introduced himself by name, then declared…"and I am a criminal!" (meaning all black men are assumed to be criminals in Amerikah). York's disciples were handing out DVDs of Abigail Washington's recantment. She was the star witness for the prosecution in the case against Dr. York, and she had just recanted her testimony and declared he was no child molester, that it had all been a conspiracy. The Nuwaubians were full of hope… .

As I sat enjoying the speeches, my friend Tony returned from the bathroom looking distraught. "There were these tough-looking macho guys standing outside the men's, glaring at me. I hear them muttering *"Honky"*…*"Cracker."* "They were *scary*! I thought they were going to beat me up!" I asked him what those terms meant, and he explained that "honky" refers to the Caucasian protruding nose, and that "cracker" refers to the bleached color of Saltine crackers. (Later I found out, from reading Mattias Gardell, that he was quite wrong.)

"Don't worry, Tony," I said. "They were probably just joking around. Here, come sit by me, they like *me*!" Later on I went over to speak to a female minister, but she ignored my greeting and turned her chair right around so that her back was towards me. Tony commented, "She *hates* you Susan, how can you say she *likes* you?" We were the only white people in the hall, except for Paul Greenhouse, the documentary filmmaker, who was crouched on the floor in the front row, blending into his camera as he filmed the speakers. When we discussed the meeting afterwards, Paul noted that this minister had become more distant towards him also, and he thought she was disillusioned because the media showed so little interest in Abigail's recant.

---

[21]   See the dedication for their names.

Next, one of the speakers launched into a diatribe knocking homosexuals and miming "fairy" affectations, which elicited roars of appreciative laughter from the audience. Tony, who is a "gay pride" homosexual (albeit invisibly) was offended. He swore this was the last time he would ever accompany me to one of my "cult meetings."

A Nuwaubian minister was giving a speech on the podium. Suddenly she proclaimed loudly, "White people don't have no souls!" and stared down directly at me.

"White people don't have no souls!" she repeated. "They are parasites. They have no energy, no life force of their own. So they have to feed off of us! And I see one parasite *right here* sitting in the front making notes, studying how to feed off of us better!"

Every Zulu, every Black Panther, every Moor, every Mason in the room swiveled their fezes, turbans and eyeballs in my direction. I was caught—pinned—with my pencil poised over my notebook. At that moment, I felt a physical pang of pure, undiluted paranoia. I had never realized before that paranoia could be a palpable, physiological experience… .

On another occasion, when I sat in on a Q&A meeting, the minister started giving me a rough time, directing jocular insults at me. When the meeting broke up, I was slinking towards the exit behind the stragglers heading for the front room of the bookstore—but suddenly I found a chair offered to me by a smiling group of Nuwaubians, who drew up their seats to make a circle. (I'd noticed before that the more this minister insulted me in public, the friendlier the disciples became in private.)

"So, Sister, what do you think of us?" a pretty woman asked, gazing at me with golden-flecked orbs enhanced by feathery arching eyebrows.

"Yeah, what are your conclusions?" enquired her mate, an athletic man in black designer leather and a fez. "Here, little Sister, bring this lady something to eat!"

Two little girls were handing out paper plates of grilled chicken, rice, beans and salad and collecting five-dollar bills. The man in the fez kindly paid for mine.

"Well," I said, balancing my plate on my lap, "I find you very, ah…different from other spiritual movements I've studied"

"Oh yeah? How so?"

"Well, most groups I have studied borrow from Theosophy or Hinduism. I find the ideas completely unfamiliar here, and your language is so different. I guess I am pretty impressed by Dr. York's originality…his creativity!"

They laughed: "You got Our Master wrong, pro-fessor. He's an intellectual-effectual genius—and that's why *They* chose him, but he only says what *They* tell him to say."

"Who tells him?"

"The Nephelim."

"Who?"

"The Eloheem…haven't you read *The Holy Tablets*?"

"And he's got creativity, all right. She's right about cree-ay-tivity!"

(A little girl poured me a paper cup of iced peach tea.)

"So what do you *make* of us?" the golden-orbed woman kept probing. "What do you make of *The Knowledge*?"

"Well, I notice that Your Master plage…I mean *quotes* a lot of passages from Elijah Muhammad and other philosophers—but then he combines their ideas in a highly original way…so as to say something, well…new."

"You're on the right track, pro-fessor!" an older man said.

"So, what's *your* spiritual path?" the pretty girl leaned forward, her bright golden eyes seeking a chink in the sociologist's armor. "Are you a Christian or what?"

After years of studying unconventional religions, there always seems to be a critical point in my field research when the group I am scrutinizing will suddenly turn the tables, gang up and put *me* on the "hot seat." I have never enjoyed this. The Twelve Tribes subjected me to this ordeal, the Scientologists also, the Rajneeshee, the Hare Krishna, the Moonies… .

I opted to be as boring as possible, so I could get back to observing *them*. "Well, actually, I was brought up in a lapsed Mormon family. I hardly ever go to church. To tell you the truth, I am confused about my spirituality…if I have any at all. I guess that's one reason why I'm here. I'm checking it out."

"I toll you so!" piped up an older lady. "She's a pil-grim!"

"So why don't you come on *our* pilgrimage?" the golden-eyed girl asked.

"Where, when is that?"

"The Zed Festival. At Tama Re. You can sign up here at the front desk."

"Yeah. You should come!"

"*We're* all going!"

"If you really want to overstand us, you should come!"

The Pilgrimage to Tama Re

So, I did. I signed up for the June 2004 "Savior's Day" Festival in Georgia, the pilgrimage to Tama Re, the "Mecca in the West," sacred land, home to all black people in Amerikah. It involved with a four-day bus trip from Brooklyn to Georgia and back, a five-day stay at a motel with breakfast and a swimming pool, and a van that taxied us daily from the motel to "The Land." I went with my friend, Paul Greenhouse, a New York documentary filmmaker. The whole trip was a bargain, costing only two hundred dollars U.S. But I experienced moments of deep discomfort… .

I will never forget those nights—dozing, slumped against the slightly non-perpendicular seat as the bus lurched towards the Deep South. I was poking toilet paper deeper into my ear holes as it kept unfurling, trying to block out the loud blasting of dynamic preachers from the Nation of Islam. DVDs had been blaring away all night as the bus wound its way through wild farmlands of the

Carolinas. For two nights I had slept fitfully to the rap of hyper-aggressive, apocalyptic sermons.

"You ask me how I feel about the *Jewish* Holocaust," Minister Khallid Muhammad was saying right now to Phil Donahue in a voice like a volley of punches. "But no one ever mentions the *Black* Holocaust that has been going on for hundreds of years!" ("The anti-cult movement would love this," I thought sleepily..."brainwashing, sleep deprivation *and* non-stop indoctrination…thought control, mental manipulation, an "us-and-them" mentality".) Later, I asked my friend, Paul, who is Jewish, how he felt about all the anti-semitic rhetoric while he was trying to sleep. He shrugged his shoulders. "It doesn't bother me," he said.

I wrapped my pillow around my head to muffle the noise—then worried it made me look like I was trying to hide from the crimes of my forbearers (!) I peered up and down the bus aisle. No one was noticing me. The Nuwaubians were snoozing away, slumped in tortuous postures, hi-tech sneakers sticking up in incongruous bouquets from the armrests—like day-glow plastic tulips. Only the children were sleeping in comfort, tucked up in flannel blankets and quilts, cradled inside their seats, hugging teddies and brown Apple Patch dolls.

I gazed out the window as the pale dawn crept in. Ghostly grey trees dripping with moss slipped by, framing pale farmhouses guarded by tractors. Cows huddled against the dew-tipped barbed-wire.

"I tell *you* that every single *whahte* man living today is one hundred per-cent ree-*spon*sible for the torture and lynching and exe-*cu*-tion of every single black man since *tahme* imme*mor*ial!" Khallid was ranting away. ("I guess this isn't a good time to request an interview," I told myself.)

As the sun rose, I began to recognize the town names from news reports of the local "Nuwaubian nightmare"—Macon, Athens, Eatonton, Shady Lane. Suddenly *TAMA-RE* reared up on our left—a wild Disneyland of makeshift Egyptian architecture and theriomorphic idols. How incongruous it looked, set in the green, sleepy Georgian farmland! We drove past and were dropped at the motel to "freshen up" for the *Maguraj* that evening. This was a symbolic pilgrimage where we had to circle round the giant black-gilt pyramid by climbing up the ramp of the surrounding maze.

It was past midnight when I found myself walking up the cement ramps that led in wide concentric squares up the Pyramid. A loudspeaker on the tip of the pyramid chanted "OM-OM-OM-OM-OM," droning on continuously. Everyone was wading laboriously uphill, with a slow "slosh, sloosh"—we'd just experience another Georgian monsoon, so the water was, literally, up to our knees. The full moon was glowing above the towering silhouette of the pyramid. The OM-OM-OM was punctuated by a high descant of croaking frogs crouched fearlessly on the ramps, their tiny throats swelling into balloons as their round eyes fixed hypnotically on the moon.

When we reached the top of the pyramid we stood around on the edge of a large square. Two tall pharaohs in golden headdresses padded quickly along the edge of the crowd in bare feet, their hands blessing us in cryptic gestures, chanting intelligible syllables that I assumed were supposed to be ancient Egyptian. They were handsome and charismatic, and I was impressed by the power of the *Maguraj*. I had expected it to be "hokey" as a new concocted ritual. But there was something beautiful and moving about it. I felt I was on the verge of a mild, aesthetic trance-state—but I kept worrying about my new grey suede sandals, recently purchased on sale at *Arche*—the water would *ruin* them. ("What is wrong with me?" I thought. "Here is a door opening onto a mystical experience, possibly the *panenhenic* type that William James wrote about—but all I can do is obsess about fashion? Ah well, all pilgrimages demand sacrifice!")

During the week-long festival I was able to converse with many of the pilgrims, and discovered that most of them were not really "Nuwaubians." In fact, my impression was that most of the 1000-odd folks attending this festival were just plain, middle-class African-Americans with a general interest in Black Identity, who wanted to show their kids the Black History museum. In the course of the next week, I talked to schoolteachers, accountants, lawyers, doctors and engineers from all across the U.S. who had read Dr. York's writings. They didn't strike me as particularly "racialist," but they all expressed a romantic interest in their African heritage and wished to communicate "Black Pride" to their kids.

The festival was an ongoing fashion show, with hundreds of beautiful women dressed in eclectic fantasy outfits that illustrated Dr. York's shifting mythologies of their African, Arabian, Egyptian, Moorish, Amerindian origins. Masonic symbols dominated the parades, the architecture, and the men's supposedly secret meetings. The books I picked up to examine spoke of the mysteries of Freemasonry, and were often snatched from my hands. ("Excuse me, Sister, that's AEO.")

Visually, the festival was a delight, but the food was not to my taste. All they served was deep-fried chicken or fish, and fries. "Salad" meant instant macaroni with celery bits and onion. Festival events were often interrupted by a violent downpour, a kind of Georgian monsoon. We would have to halt the parade, disband the drumfest, and run for cover under the pyramid. There I would sit in the top gallery, entertaining the children.

The first morning at the motel started when I went swimming in the pool. I noticed that none of the adult Nuwaubians entered the pool (perhaps the women were too modest, since not so long ago they had been wearing Muslim robes and face veils)—but some of the kids were wading in the shallow end. A single father asked me if I could teach his kids to swim. I agreed, but I found his children surprisingly fearful of the water and mistrustful of me—although they laughed hysterically and flailed around. Then more parents asked me to watch over their kids in the pool, and I became the unofficial bodyguard. After that, the kids started following me around like a mother duck—which cramped my research efforts. A little girl liked to brush and braid my hair, and a little boy would run his hands along my arm, then stare at his palms to see if the whiteness came off. The children expressed anti-white attitudes quite openly, but they had the ability to transcend them in a twinkling of an eye.

I first noticed this when we were waiting for the bus on the pavement outside the *All Eyes on Egipt* bookstore in Brooklyn. The bus was two hours late, it was getting dark, and the children were getting brattier and brattier. One little boy bounced up to me in his thick-soled lime-green sneakers that functioned like pogo sticks.

"Why you decide come here hang out with us niggers?" he asked. [He really did say exactly that.]

I was taken aback, and responded honestly without thinking, "because I find you interesting."

He sproinged backward, considered my answer, and let out a husky laugh. He hopped forwards and threw his arms around my waist in a hug, almost throwing me off balance. Then he bounced back to his friends, his sneakers flashing red-green lights each time he landed... .

At the Zed festival, he and four other kids followed me around, constantly interfering with my work. I tried interviewing them, but found, although they exhibited a deep reverence for "Maku" or "Pops," they actually knew very little about Dr. York or their parents' religion.

One adolescent girl proved to be an exception. I asked her the standard question, "When did you receive The Knowledge?"—and she explained that her mother was a nurse who worked at the hospital, and sitting at home all alone after school, she was bored ("Nothin' to do but watch tell-lies-vision"), so she started to attend the meetings at the *All Eyes on Egipt* bookstore down the street. But her mother did not approve of this. ("My mothah won't let. She say I was getting over-involved with Nuwaupu.") So, the girl invited her friends over for a Question&Answer meeting, and they brought their sisters and brothers. Then more people started coming ("even big grownups"). The girl led the meetings ("I was *real good* at teachin' Right Knowledge!"). She even wrote a letter to Maku requesting permission to open her own bookstore, but then, "My mothah, she don't like comin' home from hospital findin' too much folks bridgin' in her livin' room. So she say, 'Stop teachin' in my house. Go back to the bookstore'!"

The Black Mud Breakthrough

One night, exhausted by the crowds and drumming, I sneaked off with my yoga mat and climbed to the top gallery of the large pyramid. I hid behind some unfinished wall panels in the peaked roof to have a nap. When I awoke, I found I was locked in. The triangular windows were almost opaque, made of a thick plexiglass. I began to feel claustrophobic. Having read a New Age book about the effects of pyramids on meat, I feared if I stayed too long I might turn into a mummy. I tapped on a plexiglass window. After half an hour or so, a passing security guard heeded me and went to fetch the keys. When he let me out he mumbled something about "a problem with the bus."

I was afraid I had missed the bus that took us back to our motel, so I ran across the cow pasture in the moonlight, skirting several temples—and was relieved to see a buslike silhouette. But was this really our bus? It was lopsided, tilted forward, nose in the mud like the last of the dinosaurs. Approaching, I heard the front wheels grinding, digging in deeper as the back wheels spun in the air. People were running in circles shouting directions, trying to right it by using pulleys and planks of wood placed under the tires. I went to the rear to help push. A fellow pusher informed me that the bus had started to leave—but then the driver decided to veer off the paved road onto the grass in order to turn around. ("They *told* us not to drive on the grass after the rain," he said. "They warned us it's a *swamp* out there.")

Suddenly, a scream split the air. As the wheels spun against the plank of wood, a splinter had flown off and pierced a man's leg. Blood was flowing copiously down his calf. Someone called for an ambulance, so there was another delay... . We kept on pushing, but I noticed that the front wheels were sinking deeper and deeper into the mud. I started running around barking orders, but so was everyone else. Finally, we got the wooden planks in the right place under the wheels, and the bus reared out of the mud like a newborn brontosaurus. We all cheered— but those pushing the bus's butt were suddenly sprayed with mud, including myself. We looked at each other, laughing, and I was reminded of that passage in *The Paleman*: "I (ALLAH) WILL CREATE A *MORTAL BEING* (ADAM) FROM *BLACK MUD* (CLAY)."[22] For Dr. York, Adam's name comes from the Hebrew root *Ah-Dam*, that means "Black Mud."[23] We didn't get back to the motel until 3:00 a.m. Every shower was going full blast and the water was cold.

It might have been my imagination, but after we de-mired the bus the Nuwaubians seemed to be more receptive towards my research efforts. I collected four fine interviews the next day—two with members of the Triad, one with a Propagator, and one with a man who turned out to be...an imposter.

The Imposter

A chubby man waddled up to me as I was wandering through the Museum of Black History and asked me if I were a journalist. He was wearing a Plains Indians feathered headdress and full Indian regalia. He said he was from Philadelphia and worked for the United Nations—and gave me his business card to prove it. He claimed he was an ambassador for the Yamassee First Nations and he was working on a project to relocate the Yamassee back to their original lands in Africa (he handed me another business card, and a flyer). We sat down on a bench in between

---

[22]   As Sayyid Issa Al Haadi Al Mahdi, *The Paleman* (Monticello, N.Y.: The Original Tents of Kedar, 1990),

[23]   It is interesting to note that the Aryan Nations translate "Ah-Dam" as "Blood in the face," to prove only the fair-skinned who blush are fully human.

Annubis and Thoth and talked. He told me about his important "humanitarian" projects, his various official "hats" (presenting appropriate business cards for each one)—but when I asked him about Dr. Malachi Z. York and Right Knowledge, I was surprised by how little he knew, and even more by his lack of passion concerning these topics. He flattered me, saying I must have African blood—that it showed up in my "beautiful red hair, like the Touareg tribe" (I decided not to mention my henna treatments). After we parted, I ran into one of the Triad and asked him about my informant: "He said *what*!?" Khunsu Hotep exploded. I showed him the man's business cards and the flyers.

"He's no Nuwaubian! He's an imposter. We get a lot of phonies who come here, pretending they received The Knowledge—just to get attention and push their own trip!"

Khunsu Hotep called the security guards over and made me describe the culprit, and they bounded off to find him and escort him off the property. I never got the cards or flyers back—but I couldn't use an interview with a fake Nuwaubian anyway.

But...Is He Really Guilty?

When I arrived home, my daughter scolded me: "Mom! I told my friends you went on a bus trip with a bunch of *Black Supremacists*! They said your Mom must be *crazy*!"

She was half joking, but by this time I had begun to realize that some serious issues were at stake.

When I started researching the Nuwaubians, it was in the spirit of fun. I even found *The Paleman* amusing. I was aware, of course, that new religious movements are stigmatized in the media and are subjected to harassment by secular authorities, mainly as a result of an overwhelming public ignorance and media-generated prejudice towards unconventional religions. But I began to realize that "Black" new religions might face an even greater weight of opposition.

This message was reinforced by an African-American woman scholar I met at a conference in Rochester, N.Y. I had just presented a paper on the Nuwaubian controversy in Georgia, using deviance amplification theory to analyze the mounting conflict. She raised her hand.

"The kind of conflicts you describe...you think it is because the group is a *new religious movement*, right?"

I nodded.

"Well, I was thinking that, coming from *Canada*, you might be unaware—that you haven't been *sensitized*—to our racial issues, to the very real race problem that exists in the U.S. today.... . The story you tell in your paper is a very *familiar* story—it's what happens every time African-American people get together and start to get organized. Then they are viewed as a threat! The leader is arrested and accused of something, their property is taken away and their community is broken up and dispersed. And it isn't because they are a 'NRM', like you argue, it's because they are *Black*!"

I thought about her statement. In the end I decided it was impossible to determine to what extent the cultural opposition to the Nuwaubian Nation was motivated by anticultism, to what extent by racism—and to what extent by Dr. York's provocative behavior—probably a mixture of all three.

The Nuwaubian story is fascinating, but it is also disturbing. It raises serious questions about justice, about the status and social control of racial and religious minorities in America, and about the steep proliferation of prophets accused of pedophilia on our new religious landscape. After returning from the pilgrimage to Tama Re, I felt someone should write a book—and perhaps I should be the one.

At the time of this writing, most of the information on the UNN's history of conflict is to be found in local newspapers from the small towns in Middle Georgia. Needless to say, journalistic portrayals of this Black utopian movement have been almost uniformly dystopian—but why should journalists have the last word on what they call the "Nuwaubian Nightmare?"

Bill Osinski, a journalist who covered the Nuwaubian story in the *Atlanta Journal Constitution*, attacks Dr. York's role as a black reformer, liberator and benefactor, accusing him of, "using the trappings of an orderly strict religious community as a cover for his wide-ranging criminal enterprises."[24] York's success, he explains, was due to his being a "gifted manipulator." He portrays York's disciples as gullible, pathetic dupes who stand by helplessly while York robs their bank accounts, seduces their wives and molests their daughters. He dismisses York's teachings as "preposterous twaddle," as "downright silly," and he insists that York's movement should not be taken seriously as a religion: "To call him a religious leader is to blaspheme the whole notion of religion as a force of good," declares Osinski.[25]

Most sociologists of religion would disagree with this statement. I would argue that the "authenticity" of a religion does not necessarily depend whether its prophet-founder measures up to twenty-first-century North American standards of morality and political correctness. Muhammad practiced polygamy, Plato was a homosexual, and Mother Ann Lee preached celibacy and denounced married life as "carnal concupiscence." Nor can this standard be applied to artists. Gesualdo, an Italian Renaissance composer of vocal polyphony, murdered his adulterous wife and his baby (whom he suspected was illegitimate). He is nevertheless universally recognized as an innovative composer. Van Gogh degenerated into schizophrenia and consorted with prostitutes. Coleridge was addicted to opium. Many great Jazz musicians have died of cirrhosis of the liver, and Rock singers of heroin overdoses—but their private vices and moral deficiencies do not diminish

---

[24]   Bill Osinski, *Ungodly: A True Story of Unprecedented Evil* (Eatonton, GA: Indigo Publishing, 2007), 269.

[25]   Osinski, 268-9.

their artistic legacy. The late James Brown was notorious as a wife-beater, but his Motown beat ruled the stage.

New religious founders are creative artists. As prophets, mystics or messiahs, they rarely conform to middle-class American standards of decorum. Thus, Osinski's notion that Dr. York concocted a series of phony, copycat "cults" simply to "control people" and facilitate his "criminal activities" is absurd. It requires raw talent and tireless effort to maintain the mantle of a prophet. Only an obsessive reader and compulsive spiritual seeker could have written, edited, and overseen the production of over 450 esoteric "scrolls." Only a preacher with extraordinary rhetorical skill and presence could inspire, excite laughter, and hold the attention of his audience for 40 years.

Tens of thousands of African-Americans have read the writings of Dr. Malachi Z. York. Over ten thousand have participated in his 40-year series of spiritual movements. Another ten thousand and more have visited Tama Re. In order for a white researcher to even begin to understand the relevance of Dr York's teachings for his Nuwaubians, it is necessary to talk to them, and to attend their meetings. Here, one can observe their rituals, see how the ideas are communicated to the congregation by York's ministers, and watch the disciples in action. In order to "overstand" York's message of "Right Knowledge," the researcher must first try to empathize with the disciples, to try to see the world through their eyes.

One of the most daunting challenges I faced in writing this manuscript was addressing the topic of child molestation. In an early draft of a paper that I submitted to an academic journal, I decided to "bracket" the issue of York's culpability and focus on how the media's treatment of the "Nuwaubian Nightmare" may have influenced his trial. The editor protested that I was "trivializing the suffering of the victims" by taking this approach. I felt strongly that this was unfair. At the time of writing, York was still on trial, and three of the witnesses for the prosecution had just recanted their testimonies, saying now that they had *not* been molested. The judge had dismissed members of the jury after finding they were "tainted" by the sensationalistic news reports that featured lurid interviews with the alleged victims of the (alleged) cult leader sexual predator. Countless news reports (and a book) have been published that broadcast the suffering of the victims—but the possibility that York may be an innocent man, or at least innocent of some of the charges laid against him, has been ignored.

Unfortunately, I cannot judge whether Dr. York is guilty or innocent of the charges of child molestation. As his lawyer, Adrian Patrick, aptly put it, "I cannot tell you what he did or did not do in the privacy of his own bedroom ten years ago." I am, however, quite convinced he did not receive a fair trial. Attorney Patrick claims that the state charges would have been dismissed for lack of evidence, except that they were "improperly combined" with the federal racketeering charges. It is also clear that the case against York was carefully planned and orchestrated by a network of cultural opponents that included ex-members, his estranged son and daughter, journalists and law-enforcement agents (although evidence that there was a "conspiracy" does not, in itself, necessarily mean the conspirators were not telling the truth).

Because of the way Dr York's court case was handled, it is possible we may never know what "really happened." As is typical of child molestation cases based on alleged crimes that may or may not have occurred years ago, there is no physical evidence, no forensic evidence. But neither is there any evidence that would prove his innocence. The case against Dr. York has rested entirely on the statements of the victims—and these cannot be examined because the court transcripts are unavailable, and the witnesses have presumably been warned by the FBI not to talk.

Moreover, there has been an extraordinary rise of allegations of child molestation or pedophilia laid against "cult leaders." As the sociologist and lawyer, James T. Richardson, notes: "child sex abuse allegations have become a new, fashionable and highly-effective strategy in the social control of unconventional religions."[26] Dr. York was already unpopular, long before he was charged with child molestation. He was a notorious "black militant" and "cult leader" of a "quasi-religious sect" with a long history of suspected arson and stockpiling arms, of violation of zoning regulations and building codes.

As of this writing, Dr. York's team of lawyers are preparing an appeal before the Supreme Court.[27] Meanwhile, Dr. York's loyal followers have been building new institutions, creating apocalyptic scenarios and hagiographies of their leader, in their efforts to mythologize the grim situation and imbue Dr. York's punishment with a higher meaning. One can only extrapolate on the possible future of this new religious movement and its imprisoned leader by drawing parallels with Sabbatai Zevi, Marcus Garvey, Elijah Muhammad, Yahweh Ben Yahweh, Clarence 13X, and other heterodox spiritual leaders who were sent to prison. My guess is that the United Nuwaubian Nation will undergo a series of schisms and then gradually subside into the Black cultic milieu, the matrix from whence it sprung. Dr. Malachi Z. York will become one of the legendary martyrs of Blackosophy in America, and his ideas will live on, as plagiarized, appropriated, uncited passages in the sacred writings of future Black Messiahs in America.

---

[26]   James T. Richardson, "Social Control of New Religions: From Brainwashing Claims to Child Sex Abuse Accusations," in *Children in New Religions*, by Susan J. Palmer and Charlotte Hardman, eds. (New Brunswick, New Jersey, Rutgers University Press. 1999), 172-86.

[27]   The Nuwaubians have dismissed the famous San Francisco attorney Robert R. Bryan, who has appeared as chief counsel in numerous murder cases and specializes in death-penalty litigation, and is the lead attorney appealing the death sentence of Mumia Abu-Jamal. They have replaced this white lawyer with Attorney Malik Shabazz of the New Black Panther Party.

Chapter 1

"Don't Believe Me, Check it Out for Yourself!"

Who is Dr. Malachi Zador York?

Forty years ago in New York City, a young man of 22 named Dwight York was released from jail and founded a spiritual circle with his close friends called "Ansar Pure Sufi." Since then it has grown, changed names, and mutated rapidly. Over the years York has led his movement through its many phases, trying on and then discarding charismatic titles as if they were masks. His prison wardens know him as Inmate #17911, serving a 135-year sentence in the "supermax" security federal prison in Florence, Colorado, known as the "Alcatraz of the Rockies." Sheriff Howard Sills of Eatonton G.A., who assisted in York's arrest, brands him, "the most heinous criminal in the history of the United States." Journalists portray York as a "cult leader" or "con artist" who exploits the gullible members of his "black militant," "quasi-religious" "sect." Orthodox Sunnis denounce York as a fake Muslim, as a Mahdi "pretender" and "blasphemer."

But Dr. York's African-African supporters insist he is an innocent man who was framed, silenced, and "brought down" by a "conspiracy" of disgruntled ex-members who colluded with the "White Power Structure." Malik Zulu Shabazz of the New Black Panther Party (who is York's lawyer) calls him "a great leader of our people...a victim of an open conspiracy by our enemy." And as for his disciples, he is their "Master Teacher," their "Savior," come to awaken the sleeping African-Americans, to help them break the "Spell of Kingu," to arm them with "Right Knowledge."

Despite these conflicting perceptions, Dr. York's critics and supporters have one thing in common—passion.

It is difficult to get a sense of who Dwight York is through reading his writings. Visitors to the *All Eyes on Egipt* bookstores[1] can browse through the 450-odd booklets ("scrolls") that are authored, edited, or plagiarized under various *noms de plumes*. In these pages, the curious reader will encounter a bewildering array of esoteric topics culled from seemingly incompatible sources—mystical Islam, "scientific" theories in UFO lore, American Blackosophy, Edgar Cayce's writings, U.S. Patriot conspiracy theories, Black Freemasonry... . A far better sense of Dr. York may be gained from watching the man in action; by viewing DVDs of his Savior's Day appearances in Georgia during the late 1990s, or of his sermons

---

[1] The bookstores were called the *Original Tents of Kedar* before 1993.

in the Brooklyn mosque during the Ansaaru Allah days in the 1980s.[2] On film he appears as a robust middle-aged man, handsome, confident, and thoroughly enjoying himself.

His discourse is riveting—but not what one might expect from a conventional religious leader. He does not formulate doctrines, relate moral parables or explain ideas in a coherent fashion. Rather, he shakes the very foundations of belief. He mocks mainstream religions and attacks orthodox doctrines, Christian, Muslim and Jewish. He plays his audience. They roar with laughter and shout out responses to his questions as he relentlessly punctures their preconceptions, challenges their social conventions, and assaults their deepest conceptions of "Reality." "Don't believe me! Do your own research! Check it out for yourself!" is the *leitmotiv* running through all his discourses.

His rhetorical style brings to mind some of the more controversial and sophisticated mystics of our age—Georg Gurdjieff, Krishnamurti, Bhagwan Shree Rajneesh, Chogyam Trungpa Rinpoche, Franklin Jones, E.J. Gold, John de Ruiters, to name a few.[3] Highly original and playful in their approaches to religious language, they all point to the ineffable, mysterious nature of direct spiritual experience. They tell their audience to "wake up!" to seize the moment, to "become your own guru." Like these better-known spiritual teachers, Dr. York's discourse is self-consciously metaphorical and filled with paradox and humor.

Unlike them, however, Dr. York is a black man who speaks to African-Americans. His rhetoric is steeped in Black nationalist ideas and concepts borrowed from Marcus Garvey, Noble Drew Ali, Elijah Muhammad, Stokely Carmichael and the other inspirational mentors within the American school of Blackosophy. His peculiar brand of racialism does not correspond to the religious "fundamentalism" of the Nation of Islam, or to the radical political philosophy of the Black Panthers. Rather, it belongs to the ancient, esoteric schools of Gnosticism. Dr. York's ideas are not meant to build a church or to bring about a social revolution, but rather to function as a *pedagogical device* to awaken his disciples from "sleep." In one of his more succinct statements, he declares his mission as follows: "I have devoted my visit to this planet to the resurrection of the mentally dead, which I affectionately refer to as mummies."[4]

For future historians studying the "alternative altars"[5] of Black History, Dwight York will occupy an important place in its gallery of messiahs, prophets, mystics

---

[2]   Some of these speeches are available on DVD at the bookstore in Brooklyn, and several are currently on *youtube*.

[3]   Herff Applewhite and Bonny Nettles, known as "Ti and Do" of the Heaven's Gate "suicide cult" also exhibited this quality in their speeches.

[4]   *Is there Eternal Life after Death?* (Inscribed by the Grand Al Mufti Divan Noble: Rev. Dr. Malachi Z. York—El 33*/720*, n.d.)

[5]   I borrowed this evocative term from the title of Robert S. Ellwood's book, *Alternative Altars: Unconventional and Eastern Spirituality in America* (University of Chicago Press, 1979).

and philosophers. These men or women proposed creative practical solutions to the socio-economic problems of their people. Many forged his/her own theodicy, trying to make sense of a people's 400-odd years of suffering since the slave trade came to the Americas. The result has been to imbue the African-American experience with an uplifting moral and spiritual significance.

Dwight York is acutely conscious of his place in this gallery—and he recreates the ongoing narrative of the Black Jeremiad in America in such a way as to reinforce his own charismatic claims. In *The Holy Tablets* (the Nuwaubian bible) this becomes quite apparent:

> But they all knew a savior was coming. Some thought it was Marcus Garvey who wanted to go back to Africa. Others thought Noble Drew Ali, others thought it was Elijah Muhammad or his teacher, W.F.D. Muhammad. Others thought it was Clarence 13X, even others thought it was Martin Luther King, some said it was Rap Brown or Stokely Carmichael from the 60s. Or Eldridge Cleaver or Bobby Seale, some thought it was Ron Karenga or Leroi Jones. Some think it's Warith D. Fard, son of Elijah Muhammad; Others think it is Minister Louis Farrakhan or Yahweh ben Yahweh or Ben Ammi Carter. And even others think it is themselves and the list of saviors goes on… . From the early 1900s all the way up to 1970 A.D. when something new started happening [sic]. A teaching unlike any other started spreading.[6]

York relies on his mentors, he adopts their vocabulary, extrapolates on their messages—and even reproduces their texts. Some he will later denounce as his competitors.

Dr. York firmly plants his message within the American social context of the 1960s: the race riots, the rise of the Black Panthers, and the struggle for social justice and the beginnings of Black Pride. As he explains, "this made way for the first part of our liberation…what I have to give would liberate the mind of the Nubian Nation and the physical will follow."[7] He portrays himself as a young spiritual seeker during the tumultuous period of Black nationalism in the 1960s, in Harlem and New York, and his writings show a keen interest in the "spiritual politics" of the era, particularly in the internecine struggles and problems of the succession occurring within the Nation of Islam—a situation he was quick to capitalize on. Dr. York was keenly awareness of new fashions as they appeared on the Black spirituality scene, and he was quick to incorporate them into his movement.

---

[6] *The Holy Tablets* (Eatonton, n.d.), 1640-41.

[7] *The Holy Tablets*, 1641.

The Origins of the Nuwaubian Movement

Like many prophets in Blackosophy, Dwight York's birth and origins remains shrouded in mystery.[8] York claims he was born in the Sudan on 26 June 1945. The FBI report supplies the same date, but states that he was born in the state of Maryland. Bilal Phillips claims that York is ten years older, born in 1935, and that he revised his birth date in order to bolster his claim to be the great-grandson of the Sudanese Mahdi, whose rebirth was prophesied to occur in the West exactly one hundred years later. Phillips bases his argument on a 1974 edition of *The Muslim Prayer Book* (Edition 12), published by the AAC. In this book, he claims, York's birth date is featured as "1935," but from 1975 on the date "1945" was pasted on, obscuring the old date. In 1977, after York changed his title to "Al Mahdi," a large picture of York was featured on the inside cover with his new signature and birth date ("and this was quite obviously pasted on")—Phillips' point being that York wanted to fit the *hadith* that proclaims a reformer or *mujeddid* will be sent every 100 years.[9]

Little is known of Dwight York's father. Even York's son, Jacob, admits he knows very little about his grandfather: "My dad's father was a topic that was *hush hush* in the family. There was a rumor going around that he was a gangster, a pimp…spent time in jail—not a good role model for his son."[10] York announced in 1973 that his true biological father was Al Haadi Abdur Rahman al Mahdi, the grandson of the famous Mahdi Muhammad Ahmad (1845-85) who led an uprising against the British in Sudan.[11]

The young Dwight York worked as an assistant to an antique shop owner, and married her daughter, Dorothy Mae Johnson, when they were both 18-years-old. She bore him five children. Dr. York's son, Jacob, described Ms. Johnson as, "the only woman he was ever actually legally married to."[12]

---

[8]   There is ample information on Dr. Malachi Z. York as a god, but very little data on the man. An investigation into his life reveals an enigmatic and complex personality, to say the least. For biographical data I have relied on four sources: the 1993 FBI report, Bilal Phillip (a Muslim heresiologist), interviews with members, ex-members and relatives, and hagiographies of York, the "Master Teacher" that are found in his books or "scrolls."

[9]   Bilal Phillips, *The Ansar Cult in America* (Riyadh, Saudi Arabia: Tawheed Publications,1988), 1.

[10]   Interview with Jacob York in Atlanta, Georgia, 19 August 2003.

[11]   Al Mahdi As Sayyid Isa al Haadi, *The Ansar Cult. The Truth about the Ansaruallah Community in America. Rebuttal to the Slanderers* (Brooklyn: the Original Tents of Kedar, 1989). See also, Al Mahdi As Sayyid Isa al Haadi. *The Call of the Mahdi in America* (Brooklyn: the Original Tents of Kedar, 1987). See also Ahmed Gurbi Mahdi, "Muslim Organizations in the United States." In The Muslims of America. Haddad, Yvonne, ed. (New York: Oxford University Press, 1991).

[12]   Interview with Jacob York, Atlanta, Georgia, 19 August 2003.

York confesses in his 1989 book, *Rebuttal to the Slanderers*, that he was involved in a New York youth gang in his teens, and became a "youthful offender." According to the 1993 FBI report, York has a criminal record. It states that, in June 1964 he was charged with statutory rape; in October 1964 with possession of a dangerous weapon and resisting a police officer. York received a three-year prison sentence on 6 January 1965. He spent some time in prison at the Elmira Reception Center but was paroled on 20 October 1967.[13]

The Nation of Islam has a strong missionary outreach in the U.S. prison system. Like Malcolm X, York may have encountered Muslim missionaries during his stay in prison and converted to Islam.[14] On his release in 1967, he began to attend the Islamic Mission of America, Inc. Mosque on State Street, founded by a West Indian, Sheikh Daoud Faisal, who became his only living spiritual teacher. Sheikh Daoud (1891-1980) had set up two temples attracting African-Americans in Philadelphia and in Harlem, and was reported in the newspapers as having 100,000 followers. His mission was to establish a peaceful Muslim community, a theocracy under the laws of Allah. To this end, he purchased the Talbot Estate in East Fishkill, Duchess County, N.Y. This became a famous spiritual retreat for Black Muslims, called "Medina Salaam." Sheikh Daoud condemned the Nation of Islam for their unorthodox recognition of W.D. Fard as divine, and embraced a more orthodox Sunni Islam. In 1967 he insisted that members of his mosque carry "Sunni identification cards" to prove that they were not affiliated with the Nation of Islam.

Dr. York maintained a warm relationship with his mentor, even after starting his own (heretical) Islamic organization. *The Nuwaubian Village Bulletin* features photographs of Sheikh Daoud and his wife Khadijah seated beside Dr. York at festivals held in the Ansaaru Allah Community mosque on Bushwick Avenue. One caption states, "Sheikh Daoud offers wise words of advice to Our Master." Dr York remained loyal to his old mentor after his death in 1980, and still carries a State Street Mosque identity card in his wallet along with his Moorish Science Temple of America card.[15]

The young Dwight York was an energetic and intrepid spiritual seeker who explored many of the innovative religious movements and mystical circles percolating in the New York area in the 1960s and '70s, These fall into three categories: 1) the orthodox Sunni Islam groups with *tabligh* (missionary outreach) to African-Americans; 2) the politically-oriented Black Nationalist movements working towards their people's emancipation from "slave mentality" and general

---

[13]   FBI Report: "The Ansaru Allah Community, also known as The Nubian Islamic Hebrews, The Tents of Kedar." The United States Department of Justice, Federal Bureau of Investigation, Domestic Security/Terrorism, 1993. (File number deleted.)

[14]   There are conflicting reports as to whether York was converted to the Nation of Islam or to mainstream Sunni Islam while in prison.

[15]   Personal communication from a source who wishes to remain anonymous. One finds reprints of these cards in many of his books and scrolls.

socio-economic "uplift"; 3) the new esoteric spiritual movements found in Harlem and other black ghettoes whose primary concern was to discover the hidden spiritual identity of the Black Man. This third type of group became a major source of York's material.

After his release from prison, York supported himself by peddling incense, African perfumes and body oils on the streets of Harlem and Brooklyn, where he engaged passers-by in philosophical discussions. He assimilated a wide range of esoteric teachings, through conversations on the street, through reading, and by attending the local mosques and temples. He himself provides a glimpse into how he launched his charismatic career:

> I began publishing the pamphlets of peace. I wrote, typed, illustrated, reproduced and distributed them almost single handedly. I diligently treaded the streets of New York and the surrounding areas as I propagated Sufi Islaam. I was blessed with the "gift of gab" and combined with a sense of humor and charisma that draws people of all walks of life to me. People began to wonder who this man that spoke so profoundly and so persistently on many subjects which were previously considered unmentionable.

Around this time, York began to formulate and preach his own, original theory about the nature of the Black man. His theory rejects the revelations of Noble Drew Ali and Elijah Muhammad concerning the true identity of African-Americans as "Asiatics."[16] York argues that that his people originated from the Sudan region of Africa. His followers therefore define themselves as "Nuwaubians." "Nuwaubu" appears to be an Arabicized spelling of "Nubia," but the Nuwaubians explained that the term "Nuwaubu" (sometimes spelled "Nuwaupu') is Arabic for "prophet" or "prophecy." York's disciples are "Nuwaubian," as opposed to "Nubian." "Nubians" are the masses of African-Americans still sleeping under the spell of "Kingu," not yet awakened to "Right Knowledge."

From the ancient Nubian kingdom in Sudan, York traces the lineage of his people back to the Sumerian and Egyptian civilizations, and even beyond that—to the stars. He finally expounds the "ancient astronaut" theory of the "Annunaki"— the angelic extraterrestrial astronauts who arrived from the planet Rizq, colonized our planet, and built the first great civilizations of Sumeria and Egypt.[17]

In 1967 Dwight York enlisted his friends to join his very first spiritual circle, "Ansaar Pure Sufi." He adopted the title "Isa Abdullah" and set up a center at 25 Bedford Avenue in New York City. He and his friends wore black and green

---

[16]   Michael A. Gomez, *Black Crescent, The Experience and Legacy of African Muslims in the Americas* (New York: Cambridge University Press, 2005), 218-19.

[17]   His debt to Zecharia Sitchen is discussed below.

tunics and adopted the symbol of the Crescent, the Star of David and the Ankh, all intertwined.[18]

In 1968 York changed the name to "Nubian Islaamic Hebrews" and the dress code was switched to African robes (*dashiki*) and black fezes. His "Nubians" were identified by a small bone in their ears and a nose ring. At that point, York assumed the new title of "Imam Isa" ("Imam Jesus") and began expounded his racialist myth of the "Canaanites" whose pale skin was the consequence of the Curse of Ham. Between 1973 and 1992, he claimed to be the "Mahdi" and presided over a large Islamic community in Brooklyn known as the Ansaaru Allah Community.

In 1992, Dr. York suddenly repudiated Islam and disbanded the AAC. He reverted to the earlier "Hebrew" or "Jewish" themes, discarded the title of "Mahdi," and revealed he was "The Lamb," addressed as "Rabboni." He set up the "Holy Tabernacle Ministries" (HTM), and his disciples dressed up as ancient Babylonians and performed morality plays on the streets of New York, bellowing their lines through megaphones. The HTM represents a secularizing phase of the Nuwaubian movement, as it placed a strong emphasis on "Science" and on independent investigation. "Check it out" and "Do your research" were the new slogans. The theology was presented as a "study of the facts," or "factology." Around this time, York also revealed himself to be "Yaanuwn," an extraterrestrial from the planet Illyuwn in the galaxy of Rizq, who was a font of advanced scientific knowledge from a technologically superior civilization.

In 1993 York's movement adopted the overarching title, the "United Nuwaubian Nation of Moors" (later simplified to the "United Nuwaubian Nation").They sold all their properties in Brooklyn and purchased 475 acres of farmland in Georgia. Dr. York and his executive leaders relocated to Georgia and began constructing an "Egiptian" [sic] village, advertised as "the Mecca in the West."[19] They began to call themselves the "Yamassee Native American Moors of the Creek Nation" and claimed their sacred territory was a "Sovereign Nation." Dr. York once again redefined his charismatic *persona*. He claimed he was a descendent of Pocahontas through his mother, and that his followers were "red" Amerindians who belonged to the Yamassee tribe of the Creek Nation. On arriving in Georgia, the Nuwaubians discarded their exotic HTM gear and donned cowboy hats, boots, belts, fringed shirts and jeans. They now referred to their Master Teacher as "Maku" or as "Chief Black Eagle."

A retrospective look at the last 40 years shows us that Dr. Malachi Z. York has not just led one NRM, but he that he has founded, renamed, and debriefed an exotic *series* of Black spirituality movements. His groups often imitate and even replicate some of the better known Black NRMs, such as the Nation of Islam, the Moorish Science Temple of America, and Ben Ammi's Black Hebrews.

---

[18]   Bilal Philips, *The Ansar Cult in America* (Riyadh, Saudi Arabia: Tawheed Publications, 1988), 1-6.

[19]   When I asked the Nuwaubians why "Egypt" was spelled with an "i," I was told that "i" had a special mystical significance in the Nubic language.

York appropriates—and mutates—their symbols, costumes, rituals and rhetoric freely.[20] York's followers have experienced corresponding shifts in their racial and religious identity. They have defined themselves as black Jews or Muslims, as "brown" Moors, as "red" Indians—and even as the "green" descendants of extraterrestrials whose skin turned rusty as they entered our atmosphere. York's spiritual groups have appeared, disappeared, and reappeared on the streets of New York, Brooklyn and other major U.S. cities under the following, often overlapping, titles:

> 1967 Ansaar Pure Sufi
> 1968 the Nubian Islamic Hebrew Mission
> 1969 the Nubian Islamic Hebrews
> 1973-92 the Ansaaru Allah Community
> 1992 the Holy Tabernacle Ministries
> 1993 the United Nuwaubian Nations of Moors
> 1993 the Yamassee Native American Moors of the Creek Nation

The Significance of the Changes

It is not so unusual to find rapid, startling transformations in new religious movements. Many scholars in new religious studies have documented what the brilliant late Irish scholar, Roy Wallis, referred to as the "remarkable divagations" in NRMs. He found these divagations to be particularly striking in the Children of God, but they are quite as evident in the Rajneesh Foundation/Osho Commune, in the Holy Order of MANS, and in the Church of Scientology. Indeed, one of the defining characteristics of a new religious movement is its mercurial nature. As "baby religions," NRMs pass through developmental stages of rapid growth. Charismatic prophet-founders are in the process of defining their own roles and *personae*, and their revelations are still in the primitive oral phase, hence fluid. Myths, doctrines and rituals begin to unfurl as the prophet and his/her core group set in place the building blocks of a future religion. Millenarian expectations mutate and will change course. Dress codes, dietary habits, work patterns, and even sexual mores, will be tried on, tried out, experimented with—and then discarded. In the Nuwaubian movement, however, these divagations are even more rapid and extreme than in other NRMs. York's critics and supporters have given four reasons to account for these radical changes; as marketing strategies; as signs of a fake religion; as pedagogical devices; as tests of loyalty.

Hostile ex-members tend to interpret Dr. York's eclecticism and experiments as a *marketing strategy* aimed at Black youth. A former Ansaar, Abdul-Muta'aal,

---

[20]   See Susan J. Palmer and Stephen Luxton, "The Ansaaru Allah Community: Postmodernist Narration and the Black Jeremiad," in *New Trends and Developments in the World of Islam*, ed. Peter B. Clarke (London: Luzac Oriental, 1998), 353-70.

explained the group's change of name to "Nubian Islamic Hebrews" as a "psychological ploy":

> [Its purpose was] to attract people, black people, anyone seeking Islamic knowledge, also to attract black Jews. The title of the organization has changed and will keep changing as a psychological ploy to attract people and replenish those who leave. There was a time when the...African drum was a symbol... and when the steel drum became the...symbol to accommodate people coming from the Caribbean. He took on titles like the Lion of Judah because a lot of these people were Rastafarians formerly. He packaged himself wisely. He just reorganized his presentation.[21]

York's critics pounce on the changes as proof of the essential phoniness and illegitimate status of York's spiritual system. Journalist William Osinski portrays York as a salesman who, in order to "sell his utopia," needed to "find a new way to dress up." "Packaging is everything," Osinski writes. "Like any successful businessman launching a new venture, York test-marketed."[22] An FBI agent goes even further, claiming that, "York was a criminal who was simply trying to use race as a smokescreen for his plan to make Tama Re the base for expansion of his criminal empire."[23] Phillip Arnn, a researcher with the Watchman Fellowship (a Christian fundamentalist organization) called the United Nuwaubian Nation "almost a caricature of a cult."[24]

York's disciples, however, suggest a more sophisticated interpretation—that the radical transitions in their movement are a *pedagogical device*. They claim their Master Teacher has intentionally guided them through the world's great religious traditions in order to educate them, to help them cultivate an "overstanding" of all the world's religions. This notion is expressed in a 1992 publication right after the group transformed from a Muslim organization to a Hebrew one, as the Holy Tabernacle Ministries:

> We, the Nubian people, went through a religious metamorphosis. In the 1960s to the 1970s our spiritual guide Rabboni...took us through the religion of Christianity.... Also in the 1970s he taught us about African, 5%, Hebrews and Islamic doctrines which was the time of knowledge. During the 1980s he educated us about Egyptology and Islam, which gave us wisdom. Now in the 1980s there is no faith in any foolishness, only truth and wisdom you couldn't possibly overstand! He has taught us that he took us through all these phases in

---

[21]   Phillips, 165-6.

[22]   Bill Osinski. *Ungodly:The Story of Unprecedented Evil* (Macon, G.A.: Indigo Publishing Group, 2007), 105.

[23]   Osinski, 215.

[24]   Osinski, 177.

order to create an immunity from all the garbage that we have been taught all of our lives by the evil one. We had to live through it to make it.[25]

The disciples claim this teaching method encourages independent inquiry and skepticism. As one disciple put it, "when I talk to a Jew or a Christian, I can really talk, because I have lived through their experience. So I can't be fooled."[26]

Dr. York himself offers a fourth explanation of the transformations—as *tests of loyalty*. He elaborates on this point in *The Holy Tablets:*

> At first, many people joined the mission because it was the style: to be "black" and cultural. I drew many hypocrites—phonies who just wanted to "play Muslim." They didn't want to work to build a nation. They just wanted to dress in African clothing, play drums and listen to me speak. I called them the "first fruits." In nineteen seventy and two A. D., after returning from Sudan I drew a literal line in the masjid floor, and said: those who wanted their "culture," but did not want to sacrifice to build for the future were excluded. The mission was then carried on by those who were willing to work for perfection.

In 1993, after York relocated the group to Georgia, his disciples explained the new "cowboy" theme as a test of loyalty:

> ...in order to get everybody away from doing their own thing; those that truly followed the Lamb wherever he may lead them, trusted in him and wore western clothes and even listen to country western music, simply because he asked them to.[27]

A fifth explanation for York's eclectic, mercurial tendencies may be found in the micro-sociology of NRMs. If we look closely at York's formative years, if we scrutinize the ecological niche that sustains his movement, we come face to face with the "cultic milieu."

The "Cultic Milieu"

The British sociologist Colin Campbell (1972) coined the term, "cultic milieu," to describe the spiritual underground of esoteric teachings, pseudo-scientific theories, and "forgotten knowledge" found in most post-industrial societies. He argues that it is in this fertile milieu that "cults" take root, sprout up, and begin to grow:

---

[25]   *The Making of the Disciples*, 1992.

[26]   Conversation with a Propagator on 14th Street, July 1990.

[27]   *The Making of the Disciples*, 1992.

> The cultic milieu can be regarded as the cultural underground of society…it includes all deviant belief systems and their associated practices…. . Unorthodox science, alien and heretical religion, deviant medicine…the world of the occult, and the magical, spiritualism and psychic phenomena, of mysticism and new thought, of alien intelligences and lost civilizations…these heterogeneous assortment of cultural items can be regarded as one entity—the cultic milieu.[28]

Throughout the history of Western civilization, historians have discovered small, dedicated undergrounds of spiritual seekers after "Truth," who dabble in esoteric, countercultural forgotten or forbidden knowledge, from the Middle Ages to the 1960s counter culture.[29] The "cultic milieu" tends to thrive during periods of revolution and social ferment, and it is oppositional by nature. It is a zone where proscribed, forbidden knowledge can be accessed; a place where countercultural ideas, theories, speculations can be presented, discussed, mutated and exchanged by spiritual seekers and leaders of *ad hoc* groups that come and go. But the cultic milieu is not a "cult" *per se,* but rather a "society of seekers."[30] The sole thread that unites these denizens of the cultic milieu is a shared rejection of the paradigms, the orthodoxies, of their societies. Their ideas are considered "unscientific," hence unacceptable to the social, cultural and political mainstream—although some ideas (like reincarnation) may eventually become fashionable in the mainstream.[31]

The "white" cultic milieu is quite well known to scholars of Western esotericism. It is accessible to the public through New Age fairs and bookstores, and is even advertised by movie stars like Madonna and Shirley MaLaine.[32] Its practices (Tarot, channeling, psychic readings, etc.) may be sampled by contacting its practitioners *via* their workshops and websites. The "Black cultic milieu," on the other hand, is barely visible to "white" New Agers, or to the general population— and it has been virtually ignored by "cult-awareness" groups.[33] Historians of Black History recognize this milieu, and have described it in considerable detail (without referring to Campbell's model or terminology).

---

[28]   Colin Campbell, "The Cult, the Cultic Milieu and Secularization," in *A Sociological Yearbook of Religion in Britain* 5, n1972, pp. 119-36.

[29]   Jeffrey Kaplan and Helen Lööw. *The Cultic Milieu: Oppositional Subcultures in an Age of Globalization* (Boston: Altamira Press, 2002).

[30]   Kaplan and Lööw, 18.

[31]   Kaplan, Jeffrey and Helen Lööw, *The Cultic Milieu: Oppositional Subcultures in an Age of Globalization* (Boston: Altamira Press, 2002).

[32]   Madonna's enthusiastic participation in the Neo-Kabbalah movement is well-known, and Shirley MacLaine's book, *Out on a Limb*, which explores the doctrine of reincarnation, was a best seller.

[33]   These include anticult groups, such as the Citizen's Freedom Foundation, the Cult Awareness Network, the American Family Foundation, and the International Cultic Studies Association.

George Eaton Simpson[34] and Essien-Udom[35] each describe the rich matrix of Black occultism in Harlem that contributed to the education of its leading prophets, notably Noble Drew Ali, founder of the Moorish Science Temple of America. Michael A. Gomez describes how Timothy Noble Drew was nurtured in the cultural environment of Harlem in the early 1900s:

> The black diasporic experience had become an ontological question of the first order, such that religion, ideology, political discourse, and cultural production were all called upon…to achieve some degree of over-arching, perhaps totalizing, resolution…it was into such a tempestuous swirl of intense self-examination and energetic reconfiguration that Noble Drew Ali entered.[36]

The eclectic nature of the "Black cultic milieu" has been aptly described by Jeremiah Wilson Moses, as "the ideological proximity of Christian, Islamic, Hebraic, and atheistic black nationalism…and the messianic rhetoric characteristic of these movements."[37]

Dwight York's Mentors

The Moorish Science Temple of America was established in 1913 in New York by Timothy Noble Drew (1886-1929), who called himself "Prophet Noble Drew Ali" and claimed to be the last in a line of prophets stretching from Buddha, Confucius and Zoroaster. Noble Drew said he was commissioned by the king of Morocco to awaken American Blacks to their true identity, and offered them his own translation of the *Holy Koran*, also known as *Circle Seven*—which, on closer examination, turned out to be the plagiarized text of *The Aquarian Gospel of Jesus*, authored by Levi H. Dowling (1844-1911).

Dwight York had been a member of the MSTA in his youth and carried a Moorish Science Temple of America "passport" in his wallet.[38] Many of Noble Drew Ali's doctrinal and ritual innovations found their way into the Nuwaubian movement. In their earliest stages, York and his friends defined themselves as "Moors" and wore the fez. York reprinted (or, as he claims, "translated") Noble Drew's already plagiarized text, *The Holy Koran: Circle 7* to be sold in the

---

[34]   George Eaton Simpson, *Black Religions in the New World* (New York: Columbia University Press, 1978).

[35]   U. Essien-Udom, *Black Nationalism* (Chigago: University of Chicago Press, 1962).

[36]   Gomez, 214.

[37]   Wilson Jeremiah Moses, *The Golden Age of Black Nationalism* (New York: Oxford University Press, 1988), 1850-1925.

[38]   Photographs of his Moorish passport appear in several of his books.

Nuwaubian bookstores.[39] His preface notes that "Prophet Noble Drew Ali prepared these lessons through the guidance of Allah" and recommends they be read as "a great source of inspiration." Photographs of Noble Drew are featured, but Dr. York's photograph appears on the front and last page of the book.

A similar claim was made by these two prophets. Drew claimed his mother was a Cherokee, while York claimed to be a direct descendant of Pocahontas through his mother.[40] Gomez has suggested that Noble Drew's association with the Cherokees "could…be read as a device by which [his] personal heritage is made to be both different from, and superior to, that of the average African-American." This analysis might also be applied to York.[41]

Dr. York also drew on the traditions of the Black Hebrew prophets in America. Prophet F.S. Cherry was the founder of a Black Hebrew association that lasted between 1919 and 1931, and after him at least eight Black Hebrew NRMs arose in Harlem. The Black Jews claim to be the Ethiopian Jews, the *Falashi*, whose names were taken away during slavery, who are the true descendents of some of the original tribes of the ancient Hebrews of the Torah.[42] Arnold Black from Barbados was one of the most successful of these prophets during the Marcus Garvey era. According to Bilal Phillips, "these groups were given to splintering, disappearing and reorganizing."[43] Dr. York founded his Nubian Islamic Hebrew Mission in 1968, and photographs of Ben Ammi Carter and Yahweh Ben Yahweh, leaders of two successful Black Hebrew movements in the late twentieth century, soon appeared in York's scrolls.

The young Dwight York received his first teachings in Islam under Sheikh Daoud at the Stateside Mosque in New York City. The largest Sunni Islamic group in America in the 1960s was composed overwhelmingly of African-American converts, and was led by Yahya Abdul-Kareem until the late 1970s, when the leadership was taken over by a Pakistani Sufi, Ahaikh Sayyid Mubarak Ali Jilani (whom Bilal Phillips describes as an "extremist"). Those who did not accept Jilani's leadership re-organized under Jamil al-Amin (Rap Brown) who was based in Atlanta.[44] Dr York alienated all these Imams and Sheikhs when he assumed the titles of the "Prophet Isa" (Jesus) and "Al Mahdi" and began to teach his own "heretical" version of Islam.

York also borrowed ideas from the Nation of Islam. He quotes from the writings of Elijah Muhammad, and appropriates his creation myth of the evil

---

[39]   *The Holy Koran of the Moorish Holy Temple of Science: Circle Seven* (clothbound, no date, no publisher, no city).

[40]   He made this claim after his group moved to Georgia and defined themselves as an Indian tribe, the Yammassee.

[41]   Gomez, 204.

[42]   George Eaton Simpson, *Black Religions in the New World* (New York: Columbia University Press, 1978), 268-9.

[43]   Phillips, 2-3.

[44]   Phillips, 140.

scientist Yacoub, who bred the first white babies through a laboratory experiment on the Island of Patmos. But York does not denounce Elijah Muhammad. Rather, he acknowledges the Messenger as "the third Elijah sent to prepare the way for myself, Malachi...the Elijah for this day and time" (the second Elijah being St. John the Baptist).[45] Thus, he is suggesting that he, Dwight York, is in the role of Jesus Christ in relation to the Messenger, who stands in the place of John the Baptist.

York elaborates on this claim in *Malachi: I Will Send you Elijah*, a scroll that reprints many of Elijah Muhammad's sayings.[46] York begins by apologizing to the NOI for a statement he made in a previous scroll that offended them, and explains he was merely talking about "Do for Self." Then he claims to have discovered, through listening to old tapes of Elijah Muhammad's sermons from the Savior's Day Gatherings of the 1950s and 60s, that the Messenger had prophesied the Second Coming of Elijah—who could be none other than himself, Dr. Malachi Z. York.

Dr. York also draws on the lessons of Clarence 13X of the Five Percent Nation. He actually reprinted the latter's teachings and sold them in the Tents of Kedar bookstores, entitled "*The Book of the 5%ers*." This book contrasts the Five Percenters' "distorted lessons" with the original NOI version and then abrogates both with York's "Real Meaning by the Reformer."[47] York's stated goal was to merge the Gods and the Ansaars under his own leadership: "We are establishing the greatest black nation on the planet earth...guide by ALLAH Himself...by way of me...Let's work together. United we are an undefeatable force."[48]

York may have based his three pillars of "Right Knowledge, Right Wisdom and Right Overstanding" on Afrika Bambaataa's "fifth element" of the Zulu Nation—or vice versa. It is often difficult to know who borrowed from whom. Certainly, Afrika Bambaataa's anti-doctrine of "Sound Right Reasoning," meaning "factology" (as opposed to blind beliefs) is quoted in both the Zulu Nation's and the Nuwaubian Nation's publications.[49] It is also possible that Dr. York "grafted" his three "Rights R's" from Clarence 13X's "Supreme Mathematics." The Ansaars, in turn, have influenced the Nation of Gods and Earths. Michael M. Knight, in his study of the Five Percenters, finds "a massive amount of [Ansaar] literature has

---

[45]   *The Holy Tablets*, 1642.

[46]   The Grand Master Dr. Malachi Z. York of the Ancient Mystic Order of Melchizedek. Malachi, *I Will Send You Elijah, by the Honourable Elijah Muhammad* (The Holy Tabernacle Ministries P.O. Box 4490 Eatonton, GA., n.d., circa 1993).

[47]   Michael Muhammad Knight, *The Five Percenters: Islam, Hip Hop and the Gods of New York* (Oxford, England: Oneworld Publications, 2007), 202.

[48]   Al Mahdi, As Sayyid Issa Al Haadi, *Book of the Five Percenters*: 625.

[49]   See the biography of Afrika Bambaataa in Jeff Chang's *Can't Stop, Won't Stop: A History of the Hip-Hop Generation* (New York: Picador, 2005), 90.

smuggled ideas and motifs into the NGE."[50] Many of York's linguistic breakdowns resonate with Five Percenters, such as "gospel" as "ghost spell"; "understanding" as "overstanding" (originally a Rastafarian innovation), and the prayer for "undertakings" as "overtakings."

Traces of Sun Ra's legacy can be found in the Nuwaubian movement. This was pointed out by Ian Simmons, writing for the *Fortean Times.*[51] Sun Ra, a great jazz musician and mystic who founded and toured with his jazz band, Arkestra, preached an original Gnostic philosophy (Sun Ra's "equation") that combines Kabbala, Rosicrucianism, channeled revelations, Freemasonry and Black Nationalism. Sun Ra's "equation" inspired many eminent jazz musicians to join his commune in Philadelphia. Much of the Afrofuturism and Egyptian imagery of Sun Ra can be seen in Dr. York's scrolls. Even the apocalyptic image of the "Mothership" can be traced back to Sun Ra.[52]

Influences in York's Racialist Mythology

Race is the consistent *leitmotiv* running through York's 400-odd scrolls. His most important works on this theme are *The Paleman, He's a Disease, What Race was Jesus?* and *Sons of Noah*. In these works we find at least four conflicting etiologies.

The notion of white skin as resulting from the biblical "curse" of leprosy may have been appropriated from two obscure Black Hebrew prophets who wrote in the 1920s; Clarke Jenkins and Father Hurley. Clarke Jenkins was a self-educated theologian from Detroit who wrote a book called *The Black Hebrews*. In this he claims that since Genesis tells us that Adam was created by God out of Black earth, only dark-skinned people are truly human. He proposes that white skin is a symptom of the disease of leprosy, according to his reading of Leviticus 13. His other ideas, that African-Americans trace their ancestry to the ancient Hebrew tribes, Levi, Benjamin and Judah, and that Jesus was not Caucasian, but a man with reddish eyes, copper skin and lamb's wool hair, are ideas that reverberate through the writings of Dr. York, Yahweh Ben Yahweh and other Black Hebrew teachers. Father George W. Hurley (b. 1884) who founded the Universal Hagar's Spiritual Church, also taught that blacks were the original people, the real Hebrews of the Bible, whereas whites were the "gentile" descendants of Cain whose pale skin was a symptom of leprosy.

In *What Race Was Jesus?* and *The Paleman*, York expounds a theory that is a fascinating reversal of the 'white supremacy" myth of the "curse of Ham." This is

---

[50]   Michael Muhammad Knight, *The Five Percenters: Islam, Hip Hop and the Gods of New York* (Oxford, England: Oneworld Publications, 2007), 203.

[51]   Ian Simmons, "Mothership Connection," *Fortean Times*, London: Dennis Publishing, February 2009, 30-35.

[52]   See Chapter 5 for an explanation of the Mothership.

based on the cryptic Bible story of Noah's son, Ham, who beheld his father naked and drunk:

> Noah predicted the physical manifestation of the pale race of Jinn after his son Ham looked at him with the thought of Sodomy. This curse was manifested through Ham's fourth son Canaan and mentally manifested through Jacob... . Thus the Canaanites (meaning cave-dweller) were born and lived in caves for 600 years "until Moses and Aaron were sent to civilize the lepers."[53]

York claims the white man is descended from the "Amorites" (Hebrew for "mountain dweller") since the children of Canaan sought refuge in the mountains where the colder climate alleviated their painful leprous condition. York predicted in 1990 that the "Paleman" will continue to suffer from sun blisters, asthma, eczema, AIDS and other symptoms of leprosy as our sun grows hotter and the ozone layer thinner, until the year 2000, by which time Shaytan's reign will have ended. Then the Paleman will be forced to abandon the earth's surface and retreat into cool underground caves, leaving the noble Nuwaubians to rule the planet.

The "two seed" theory of race originates from the Christian Identity movement.[54] In *The Curse and Mark of Cain*, York reverses the symbol of evil from black to white, and argues that all Caucasians are descendants of Cain:

> Adam and Eve were sent to the Aegean Islands between Asia and Europe, where they started having children, and each couple's first born child was an Albino and those Albinos are called Cain in the Bible, "Cain" being short for "Caucasian."

York managed to extract an etiology of race from the "ancient astronaut" hypothesis of the Jewish paleolinguist, Zechariah Sitchin, who wrote the famous 1976 book, *The Twelfth Planet*. In his 1996 scroll, *Extraterrestrials Amongst Us*, York accounts for racial differences as the legacy of a "Star Wars" between rival colonizing extraterrestrials. Caucasians are descended from lizard-like "reptoids," whereas fat people are the children of the elephant-nosed Deros. Mongoloids are descendants of the 48-chromosomed Teros, who "mingle among us daily."[55] The Nuwaubians, however, are the "children of beautiful angelic beings from the planet Rizq." He claims the brown-skinned Nubians were originally green-hued extraterrestrials (due to the presence of chlorophyll in their skin), but when the "Ether 9 beings" entered Earth's atmosphere, their skin rusted because the magnesium in their melanin was replaced by iron.[56]

Since the different races on our planet descend from rival, warring alien invaders, York insists that interracial marriage is treachery to one's race. In *Is God*

---

[53]   *The Paleman*, 1990: 256.

[54]   Michael Barkun, *Religion and the Rascist Right*.

[55]   *Extraterrestrials Amongst Us* (1996).

[56]   See the *Spell Of Leviathan 666: The Spell Of Kingu*.

An Extraterrestrial? York claims that a new race is emerging, the "Neutranoids." These people bear no discernable racial traits, and are the puppets of the sinister forces that oppose "right racism" and humanity's natural, divinely-ordained diversity.

York also appropriates Elijah Muhammad's myth of John of Patmos, who is recast as the villain of Revelations, the evil scientist "Yacoub." In this well-known NOI narrative, Yacoub concocts the first white men in a laboratory through an experiment involving genetic manipulation that requires the mass slaughter of black babies. York appropriates this myth, but "arabicizes" the spelling of Yacoub's name in his scroll, *I Am Your Chance: I Have Warned You!*:

> When the rebellious angel, Ibliys, refused to bow to Adam who was created from dry clay of black mud formed into human shape, as Allah commanded, he was cast out of heaven. Ibliys (Satan) then vowed revenge—to tempt mankind to sin. He vowed that he would make a devil, graft him from his own people and that he would teach them how to rule his people for six thousand years. Yakuwb set up a genetic experiment on the Island of Patmos (Rev. Ch. 1, v. 9) then proceeded to create a nation based on "tricknowledge" (deception) to rule the Nubian race for 6000 years. The "so-called jew" has grafted Al Islaam to form their own so-called Judaic nation by which they rule the world [57]

Besides these competing racial theories, one also finds some startling revisions in his hierarchy of race. The spiritual status of the red, yellow and brown races will rise and plummet. *The Paleman* (1990) asserts that Native Americans and Asians suffer from Downs syndrome, one of the side-effects of leprosy. We are told that "mongoloid, "mongrel" and "mongolism" have the same etymological root, meaning "mental deficiency" or "a disorder of the chromosomes." Two years later, however, this opinion is revised, and they become heroes:

> Native Americans…were robbed of their land and went through much abuse even unto this day. We will see how Yahuwa Eloh will shower his blessing and protection on the Native American Indian…. Indians are the descendants of the Midyanly from Midyan, one of the dominant sons of the Prophet Abraham.[58]

York's most startling revision of all occurred in 1992. After proclaiming the beauty and sacredness of "blackness" for almost two decades, suddenly he announced a brand new revelation—that the real humanity is *brown*.[59] Adam is no longer fashioned of BLACK MUD (as every previous publication emphatically and repeatedly stated), but of BROWN DUST: "So, then what color would you say

---

[57] *I Am Your Chance: I Have Warned You!* 1985, 2.

[58] *The Nubian Bulletin: The Truth*, 1992, Vol.I: 9.

[59] *Nubian Village Bulletin*, Edition 9, 25.

the Prophet Adam was? However you look at it, he was a brown man, no doubt about it!"[60]

Once Nubians were redefined as *brown*, black people were perceived as potentially demonic. Thus in the booklet, *Are there Black Devils?*, York warns that there may be "black brothers and sisters among us who are demons." In *The Paleman*, he writes, "The Pale race are a race of Jinns, Devils. But Nubians can also become instruments of the Devil, and have the mentality of the devil."[61] Black people, we are told, are the children of Shaytan's army ("Fallen Angelic beings") who mated with the wicked women of Nod.

York's stance on white people as "the devil" is also nuanced and shifting. In a recorded lecture (*Egipt and the Mask of God*) York states unequivocally: "White people are the devil. They say the Nuwaubians are not racist—bullcrap! I am. He might not be; that's his prerogative. I am. White people are devils, and always was, always will be." But paradoxically, York will periodically *denounce* racism and insist that his movement is open to all races. Officially, the UNN disclaims "racist" attitudes, and posts this disclaimer on its website: "We accept as fact that no one race of people is better than the other. In fact no one wins the race in racism."[62] York will denounce other groups as "racists" and urges his followers to overcome their "prejudice complex":

> And you people who have the prejudice complex, when you see a person, whether his skin is black, white, purple, green, or aquamarine, and that person tells you, "I believe in Allah…and I believe in his prophet"…embrace that person and squeeze him into yourself. Hold him close…and call him brother. I say this unto you because I know there is a race problem in America, everyone seems to hate each other.[63]

Another mitigating factor is the notion of "white angels." I was told, for example, that not all white people are demons, that a few of them might even possess—not an entire soul, but a *remnant* of a soul. These people are known as "white angels" and have been placed on earth to help Nubians in their struggle, notably the "white angels" who ran the underground railway to assist black slaves fleeing North during the Civil War. Through their virtuous acts they may eventually grow a soul, and their skin will darken accordingly.[64]

---

[60]   *Nubian Village Bulletin: An Inside Look at Mount Zion*, 1992, Ed. 3, 17.

[61]   *The Paleman*, 1990, 258.

[62]   http://www.nuwaubians.org/arenuwaubiansracist.html.

[63]   *An'nisfu Min Sha'baan: The Night of the 100 Raka'aat*, n.d., 46.

[64]   I was informed of this doctrine by a Nuwaubian who told me he had accepted my request for an interview because he believed I might be a "White Angel."

Black Freemasonry

Black Freemasonry is a major source of esoteric symbols and rituals in Black nationalist movements. Many outstanding Black nationalist philosophers in America were Freemasons, including Marcus Garvey Jr. and Sr., who were Prince Hall masons. According to Scheiderer, "the UNIA was organized along Masonic lines."[65] Garvey's potentate helmet closely resembled the ceremonial hat worn by Prince Hall masons in their parades. Noble Drew Ali was a "Black Shriner" and adopted the red fez and colorful breeches or doublet of the Shriners for his movement. Wallace Fard may have been a member in the Moorish Science Temple of America. Elijah Muhammad, Fard's disciple, was a both a Freemason and a Black Shriner in the Detroit area before he founded the Nation of Islam, and one of his speeches is called "A True Mason."[66] Clarence 13X was a mason. Yahweh Ben Yahweh's connections to Freemasonry are not known, but a NOY 1999 publication (*The Crucifixion of the Messiah*) displays the following caption under his photograph: "I am the Grand Master of the Celestial Lodge, Architect of the Universe."[67]

The impact of Black Freemasonry on Dr. York's movement is profound.[68] Dr. York reveals that he came into contact with Freemasonry through a W.M. Charles Tinsley, a 33 degree mason, "who forced my eyes open to Freemasonry."[69] As Michael R. Scheiderer notes in *The Crescent and the Craft*, "almost every picture you see of York he is wearing some sort of Masonic regalia."[70] Dr. York has assumed many Masonic titles, such as "Imperial Grand Potentate of the Mahdi Temple #19"; "33 degree Mason in the Ancient Egyptian Order of the

---

[65]   Michael R. Scheiderer, *The Crescent and the Craft*, n.d. (circa 1995): 26 www.mastermason.com/millennium382/thecraftandthecrescent.pdf, 8.

[66]   Scheiderer, 10.

[67]   It is relevant to note that many "white" founders of new spiritual groups have also been trained in Freemasonry; and have appropriated its rituals and symbols, using them as building blocks to construct new, emergent religions (see Henrik Bogdan, *Western Esotericism and Rituals of Initiation*, forthcoming with SUNY Press). According to J. Gordon Melton, Helena Blavatsky's famous Theosophical treatise, *Isis Unveiled* relies heavily on ideas from Speculative Freemasonry. Joseph Smith became a Mason after founding the Church of Jesus Christ the Latter Day Saints, and incorporated Masonic handshakes into Mormon ritual. Masonic symbols appear in his writings, in Temple architecture and on Mormon Temple undergarments (Michael Homer, CESNUR 2005). Joseph Di Mambro of the infamous Ordre du Temple Solaire was a former Freemason and Rosicrucian grandmaster. Auguste Bougenec, founder-prophet of Phare-Ouest in France was also a former Mason and grandmaster.

[68]   E.U. Essien-Udom, *Black Nationalism* (Chigago: University of Chicago Press, 1962), 33. Eric Lincoln, *Black Muslims in America* (Boston: Beacon Press, 1961), 52.

[69]   Is there Eternal Life After Death? n.d.

[70]   Michael R. Scheiderer, *The Crescent and the Craft*, n.d. (circa 1995): 26 www.mastermason.com/millennium382/thecraftandthecrescent.pdf

Noble Mystic Shrine," and "The Grand Master of the Nuwaubian Grand Lodge of the Ancient Free and Accepted Masons." He himself explains that he first entered The Order of the Acacia at King Solomon's Lodge No. 4, then joined The Grand Enoch Lodge (Prince Hall Affiliated) in Brooklyn, N.Y., and finally, the Scottish Rite Freemasons of Amos Grand Lodge of Macon, GA.

Scheiderer (a freemason) questions York's credentials, objecting that "the Lodges that he claims to have been raised in are not recognized by either the Philadelphia Grand Lodge or by the Grand Lodges of the various states."[71] The same author complains that "[York's] followers wear Shrine fezes which causes some confusion for the people of Georgia because they associate this group with the A.E.O.N.S.."

In 1992, Dr. York founded his own, clandestine obedience within the bosom of the Nuwaubian movement: Lodge 19 of the "Ancient Mystical Order of Melchizedek." Many of York's male disciples are in this obedience, but under an oath of secrecy, thus unable to talk about it.[72] Dr. York has written at least six books on Freemasonry and his latest one contains a special revelation for women.[73]

A woman disciple I spoke to at the *All Eyes on Egipt* Bookshop in Brooklyn, explained: "today's Masonic Orders only have 33 degrees, but the original Order was in Egypt, and it had 720 degrees…it was originally known as the Order of Ma'at."[74] She indicated a four-foot gilded statue of an Egyptian goddess, her head adorned by a large feather. "Ma'at represents the wisdom of the heart, of intuition. Dr York has restored the true roots of Freemasonry, offering us all the degrees." To my surprise, she mentioned that she would be attending a chanting meeting of the A.E.O. that evening. In 2003 I had watched a parade of Nuwaubian women in the Eastern Star. Since then, Dr. York had merged the male and female Orders. When I asked why women, traditionally, had been excluded from the Lodges, she explained, "men created the Eastern Star so that women would not ask questions and would stay away from their Lodges."[75] She showed me Dr. York's most recent book on display in the bookstore, *The Original Handbook for the Order of the Eastern Star As Never Before*. In another startling innovation, Dr, York has opened the Ancient Egiptian Order to accept women, and "feminized" Freemasonry by claiming its wisdom originated from a goddess. He has also enveloped the whole

---

[71]   Scheiderer, 26.

[72]   Personal communications in interviews.

[73]   His six books dealing with Freemasonry are: *Prayers of the Sons of Light: A Masonic Prayerbook*; *The Universal Lesson of the Masonic Lodge*; *The Nuwaupian Masonic Quiz Book*; *Hidden Symbolism of Freemasonry*; *Shriners and Freemasons Family Guide*; *The Original Handbook for the Order of the Eastern Star As Never Before* (n.d.).

[74]   This idea can be found in the teachings of Claence 13X of the Five Percent Nation also.

[75]   Conversation with a Nuwaubian disciple in the *All Eyes on Egipt* bookstore in Brooklyn on Saturday, September 13, 2008.

Masonic tradition under his own mantle by claiming to offer a more ancient and complete version.

The authenticity of these claims cannot be assessed by this researcher. I concur with Gomez, who writes: "to be sure, one can only enter the obscure waters of Freemasonry with considerable trepidation and with the caveat that, given the clandestine nature of the phenomenon, arguments are contingent and interpretations open to ongoing debate."[76]

Prince Hall and the History of Racial Segregation in America

But Black Freemasonry is more than just a repository of symbols. Its history is a grim record of the forces of racial segregation in America—a racism that has been imposed and, at times, consciously chosen. This history demonstrates the wisdom of "Do for Self" for African-Americans interested in Black Nationalism. A study of "Negro Masonry"—from the first African lodge, No.459 founded in Boston by Prince Hall in May 1787 to the present—offers many dramatic examples of racial intolerance and discrimination on the part of white American businessman confronting the prospect of a racially integrated Masonic brotherhood.[77]

Prince Hall, born in 1748 in Barbados, was the son of an English father and free Franco-Caribbean mother. He was a leather tanner by trade who moved to Boston in 1765 where he became a freeholder exercising the franchise. He was also an ordained Methodist minister and social activist who opposed slavery. In 1775 a traveling Lodge of a British regiment conferred the symbolic degrees upon Prince Hall and fourteen of his friends, "other free colored citizens of Boston." They applied to England for a charter which they received in 1787, and under its legitimate authority the first Negro Masonic Lodge was instituted, with Prince Hall as its master.[78] Two other Lodges were later established, in Philadelphia and in Providence. These three lodges formed a Grand Lodge which, in 1827, declared itself independent from the Grand Lodge in England. By 1949 there were 30 Grand Lodges, all sprung from Prince Hall's original African Lodge.[79]

---

[76]   Gomez, 2005, 238.

[77]   I relied on the following books, available in the Concordia University rare books collection at Loyola campus: *Negro Masonry in the United States* by Harold Van Buren Voorhis, P.M. (New York: Henry Emmerson, 1940); *Negro Masonry: Being a Critical Examination of Objections to the Legitimacy of Masonry Existing* by William H. Upton (New York: AMS Press, 1975); *Prince Hall and His Followers: Being a Mongraph on the Legitimacy of Negro Masonry* by George W. Crawford, 33° (New York: The Crisis, 1949).

[78]   *A History of Freemasonry among Negroes in America* by Harry E. Davis, 33° (published under the auspices of the United Supreme Council, Ancient and Accepted Scottish Rite of Freemasonry, Northern Jurisdiction USA, Prince Hall Affiliation, 1949), 205.

[79]   See Davis.

The African Lodge soon came under attack from the "Caucasian lodges." In a revised edition of Gould's 1936 *History of Freemasonry in America*, it states that the African Lodge was formed in 1791 "without any authority…nor permission from the Grand lodge of England." Davis (a Prince Hall Mason) points out that a double standard was being applied here, for "practically *all* Grand Lodges were erected without authority or permission."[80] He also complains that when Prince Hall and his fellow masons submitted a petition for recognition to the Caucasian jurisdiction of Massachusetts in 1779, and again in 1868, their petition was never "properly answered."[81] When African-Americans petitioned the Caucasian Grand lodge of Massachusetts for the privilege of conferring the degrees in its lodges, the Grand Secretary "arose in a session and denounced the petition of those Negroes as a 'firebrand'."[82]

This was quite a contrast to the European example, where the lodges upheld the highest ideals of universal brotherhood. The French lodges fostered social change and allowed exceptions to the class system, as is illustrated by the life of the *Duc d'Orleans* during the onset of the French Revolution. The Masonic lodges in Germany during the 1940s were venues where Jews could forge social and business relationships with gentiles—and were consequently being disbanded by the Nazis. Jacob Katz points out that Jews joined the Lodges in Europe as a way of becoming integrated into gentile society and expanding their business networks and that Freemasonry was a major instrument for the creation of our modern "neutral" society. Aristocrats in the eighteenth and nineteenth century were willing to associate with members of the rising middle class, as well as with upwardly-mobile adventurers, so that freemasonry served to undermine feudal society and bind the new classes together.

In the United States, in contrast, one can observe a strong tendency towards a mutual rejection of the prospect of friendship, intimacy and brotherhood between white and black masons. Despite the enlightened arguments of William Upton and George Crawford, who advocated racial integration in American Freemasonry, one finds powerful, insulting, inflammatory counter-arguments posed by grandmasters from the lodges of the Deep South.[83]

---

[80]   Davis, 205.

[81]   Harry A. Williamson Ezra A. Cook, *The Prince Hall Primer* (Publisher Inc., McCoy Publishing and Masonic Supply Co. 1925, 1946, 1949), 9.

[82]   Cook, 9.

[83]   See the following books for a discussion of this issue, available in the Rare Book Room of Loyola campus of Concordia University: *Middle Class Blacks in a White Society: Price Hall Freemasonry in America* by William A. Muraskin (Berkeley: University of California Press, 1975); *The Prince Hall Primer* by Harry A. Williamson Ezra A. Cook (Publisher Inc., McCoy Publishing and Masonic Supply Co. 1925, 1946, 1949); *Negro Masonry in the United States* by Harold Van Buren Voorhis, P.M. (New York City: Henry Emmerson, 1940); *Negro Masonry: Being a Critical Examination of Objections to the Legitimacy of Masonry Existing* by William H. Upton (New York: AMS Press, 1975); *Prince*

Cook notes that the printed proceedings of almost all the Caucasian jurisdiction of the United States, and the articles in numerous Masonic magazines, such as *The American Tyler* and *The Southland* were "unfavorable towards Negro Freemasonry."[84]

Many local grand bodies discussed the question of admitting "Negroes" into the degrees of freemasonry, and the Grand Masters of certain states have clearly demonstrated racist attitudes. Cook writes, "the Caucasian jurisdiction of New York adopted two resolutions concerning…the American Indian and the American Negro…and declared that Freemasonry was for Caucasians only."[85] In Kentucky, the 1919 Constitution (5th edition, page 38) stated that a candidate for the degrees "must be a free-born white man." The 1914 proceedings of the Kentucky Grand Lodge stated that a person with "one-eighth to one-sixteenth of Negro blood" cannot be initiated into a Lodge. In Louisiana, a Grand Master was recorded in the 1924 proceedings as saying, "I ruled that a mixture of white and black blood made a man ineligible for the degrees of Masonry."[86]

In Texas and Mississippi the Grandmasters went on record saying "Negroes would not be initiated into the lodges." Several eminent Freemasons have made harsh, outspoken statements on this issue. General Albert Pike, a distinguished Scottish rites scholar declared, "I took my obligations to white men, not Negroes. When I have to accept Negroes as brethren or leave Masonry, I shall leave it."[87] Frederick Speed, the Grand Secretary of Mississippi, was quoted in a local newspaper as follows:

> But *Scipio Africanus* is simply a brute, with no revenge or resentments and no regard for the truth or the purity of women. Whiskey and cocaine and miscegenation are his bane and until some remedy is found for these great evils, the poor fellow will continue to go down lower and lower in the social scale until finally the time will come when he and the white man must part company.[88]

The African Grand Lodge was erased from the English Registry in 1813 after an argument concerning its payment of membership fees. But today, after a long, controversial struggle to regain its charter, it is finally recognized as a legitimate

---

Hall and His Followers: Being a Monograph on the Legitimacy of Negro Masonry by George W. Crawford, 32nd (New York: The Crisis); *A History of Freemasonry among Negroes in America* by Harry E. Davis, 33 (published under the auspices of the United Supreme Council, Ancient and Accepted Scottish Rite of Freemasonry, Northern Jurisdiction USA, Prince Hall Affiliation, 1949).

[84]   *The Prince Hall Primer* by Harry A. Williamson Ezra A. Cook (Publisher Inc., McCoy Publishing and Masonic Supply Co. 1925, 1946, 1949).

[85]   Cook, 40-41.

[86]   See Cook, 42-3.

[87]   Cook, 43.

[88]   *The Southland*, April 24 1909 Vicksburg, Miss., quoted in Cook, 44.

and equal body in American Freemasonry. But since then, even after the Civil Rights movement of the 1970s, it has remained oddly segregated from the Caucasian lodges—apparently by choice.

William Muraskin has argued that the success of the Prince Hall lodges was due to the support they provided for men seeking to escape the "alternative" lifestyle of the lower middle and working class blacks and to achieve a middle-class status without having to compete in, or compromise with, white society.[89] Gomez explains the importance of Black Freemasonry as a positive influence for training in business and social skills: "Black Freemasonry, an interlocking nexus of social obligations and economic cooperative ventures, succeeded in forging a sense of expansive community while restricting admission into its inner workings to the circle of those possessing secret knowledge."[90] He also notes its pervasive influence on Black nationalist new religious and social movements, describing it as a "master template" that provided a "cultural *lingua franca* and common point of reference."[91]

Today, in our post-Civil Rights world, North American Freemasonry appears to be an anachronism in its mutual segregation of White and Black Lodges, a segregation which is no longer ideologically based, but is *de facto*. It appears reasonable to assume that the history of Black Freemasonry in the African-American experience might have exerted a powerful influence on the formation of racialist and sectarian policies in the Moorish Science Temple, the Nation of Islam and other "Black" NRMs—particularly since the biographers of these leaders have discovered that they, and their fathers before them, happened to be Prince Hall Masons.

The Question of Plagiarism

Dr. York has been accused of plagiarism by many, including journalist William Osinski, and the Muslim heresiologist, Bilal Phillips. Even York's own son, Jacob, said in our interview. "My Dad was *reader*. In the early days he wrote for days at a time—but he used to plagiarize a lot." Jacob then related a fascinating anecdote that proved his point:

> He was given Zecharia Sitchen's *The Twelfth Planet* by a brother who came in and said, "You've got to read this book!" So, he stayed up all night reading it. The next day, he sent the brother and his whole family off on a mission to the Trinidad mosque to get him out of the way so he could steal the book. He gave it to his secretary and told her to incorporate it into the philosophy. He would

---

[89]   William A. Muraskin, *Middle Class Blacks in a White Society: Prince Hall Freemasonry in America* (Los Angeles: University of California Press, 1972).

[90]   Gomez, 244.

[91]   Gomez, 244.

give books and ideas to his all-girl research team, and they would cobble it all together. He would then look it over, edit it—and it would come out in the next publication.

In new religious movements the line between inspirational influences and plagiarism can often be quite tenuous. It appears reasonable to assume that many mystics and prophets undergo a period of apprenticeship while they peruse esoteric writings and attend the discourses of spiritual masters—and that these influences may be evident in their theology. Moreover, inspired prophets do not consider themselves subject to the mundane rules of copyright that govern the material plane. Dr. York complains that the "Holy Books" have been adulterated and "plagiarized," and that his mission is to *restore* the revelations of the Eloheem to their original form. In *The Bible Mastery Series* he complains:

> Both of these so-called holy books [Bible and Koran] that you hold in your hand today, were plagiarized and taken from ancient tablets such as the Enuma Elish (which can be found in *The Holy Tablets*), as a guide for you by Tammuz, one of the Eloheem (Elo-Heem, Aramic/Hebrew—*these beings*) assigned to you.

York reveals that each "copy" of the "ancient tablets"—first the Torah, then the New Testament, and then the Koran—"was getting further away from the original written truth," and that the true versions of these original "tablets" can be found only in *The Holy Tablets*.

Gomez offers a sensitive analysis of plagiarism in his discussion of Noble Drew's process of "innovation, reciprocation and appropriation": "Noble Drew certainly initiated some ideas, but he just as certainly borrowed other concepts and was influenced by the whirl of events around him. The line of demarcation [that separates] original from recycled ideas...are not always evident." In his broader discussion of mutual influences among Black social movements in the early nineteenth century, Gomez observes, "the congruency of perspective among the various movements allowed for the absorption of multiple influences without necessarily compromising the integrity of the core beliefs and practices."[92]

Gomez' insights would apply to Dr. York's use of source material. Dr. York clearly pays homage to his gifted predecessors, but he cannot be dismissed as a mere copyist, for he has developed his own synthesis of earlier doctrines. On occasion he uses these disparate influences in the most inspired ways. While his sources are recognizable, his evocations are not dry or stale. He rewrites the past in order to revitalize it for the present.

---

[92] Gomez, 215.

The Nuwaubians *Niche* in the "Black Cultic Milieu"

Over the 40-odd years of its existence, the Nuwaubian movement has established its own ecological niche within the Black cultic milieu. It began with the formation of small, experimental "cult-like" groups, such as Ansar Pure Sufi and the Nubian Hebrews. These groups were highly eclectic, syncretic—and short-lived. Next, the fluid boundaries of his movement commenced to harden into a sect-like formation during the Ansaaru Allah Community phase.[93] For Campbell, a *sect* is distinct from a *cult*, because "their belief in a revealed truth leads to a believer-nonbeliever distinction, rather than the notion of degrees of seekership prevailing in the cultic milieu in general." Dr. York began to reshape his movement into a "sect" when he began to attack the credentials of his rival prophets. One of his scrolls (*The Truth: Who do People Say I Am?*)[94] features photographs of 20 Black spiritual teachers, interspersed with disclaimers like: "We need the whole truth, not half truths or opinions or spookism or myth or the paleman's religion." Photographs of Clarence 13X, Marcus Garvey, Ben Ammi, Yahweh Ben Yahweh and Minister Farrakhan are displayed with the caption, "These people can't save us. They don't know the way. They speak well, but they get nothing done. They complain, but that's all. No more lies, no more games!" Once York revealed himself to be Al Mahdi, he offered the one, exclusive path to salvation, as is typical of a "sect."

Sometimes the forces of external pressure or persecution may act upon the flexible boundaries of a "cult" to mould it into the harder "sect-like" formation. Roy Wallis, for example, has argued that, while Scientology originally emerged from the cultic milieu, it rapidly transformed into a *sect*—partly in response to persecution, and partly in response to an escalation in L. Ron Hubbard's charismatic claim as the Maitreya, offering the *one way* to salvation.[95]

In the late 1970s, various orthodox Sunni Muslim imams and missions in the Americas began to attack Dr. York's credentials, and to declare the AAC a Muslim heresy. York responded with a counter attack. In his 1989 scroll, *A Rebuttal to the Slanderers*, he denounced all previous translations of the Qur'an, claiming only his "19th translation" offered the "Supreme Code of the Qur'an." He condemned mainstream Muslims for hiding the fact that Muhammad was black. He dismissed the first three Khalifs in Islamic history as "usurpers," and rejected Abu Bakr as Muhammad's successor, claiming he was a white man. He traced the true line of succession back to his great-grandfather, the Sudanese Mahdi, a situation which

---

[93]   See Roy Wallis' discussion of the differences between a "cult" and a "sect," and how the first may transform into the second, as in the case of Scientology (Roy Wallis, *The Road to Total Freedom*, Belfast: The Queens University, 1978).

[94]   *The Truth: Who do People Say I Am?* (Brooklyn: The Original Tents of Kedar, 1992).

[95]   Wallis, *The Road to Total Freedom*, 1978.

proved that he, Isa al Mahdi, was the only legitimate successor to the Prophet of Allah.[96]

But in 1992 York suddenly debriefed the AAC, and rejected Islam. He dissolved the sectarian boundaries of his movement, and it quickly subsided back into the Black cultic milieu. The Holy Tabernacles Ministry then surfaced, drawing on the wide range of materials available in this rich, fermenting compost heap of forgotten knowledge. The HTM was characterized by a rampant eclecticism and syncretism, embracing Hebrew motifs blended with ancient Egyptian, Babylonian symbols, ufology and masonic lore.

But the result of all this borrowing did not of necessity herald a transformation into a *cult*. The HTM was not opening up to other study groups or movements in the Black nationalist milieu. Rather, it was withdrawing inward, away from his rivals. As its boundaries expanded, they also began to crystallize, so that by 1993 the United Nuwaubian Nation of Moors had become a self-contained "spiritual supermarket" offering access to a wide range of doctrines, myths, theories and rituals that had been appropriated from other groups.

If one compares the Nuwaubian movement to other "Black" NRMs, like the NOI, we find a tendency in the maturation process to purify and solidify their own religious tradition. One can see this process in The Commandment Keepers, founded by Wentworth Matthew in the 1920s in Harlem. This NRM started out as an eclectic Jewish-Christian synthesis, but Matthew applied twice to be a member of the New York Board of Rabbis, and after his death his scrupulously Jewish orientation toward black Judaism was carried forward by the current rabbi of the Beth Shalom B'nai Zaken Ethiopian Congregation in Chicago. A similar process can be noted after Warith Muhammad assumed the leadership of the NOI upon the death of his father, Elijah Muhammad in 1975, for Warith proceeded to purge the movement of Christian apocalyptic rhetoric, of UFO lore and of anti-white sentiments—and then he led his congregation back into mainstream Sunni Islam.[97]

As Campbell explains, "the continuing pressure to syncretization is a unifying force, counteracting the fragmentary tendencies caused by enormous diversity in cultural items."

But the Nuwaubian movement has behaved quite differently. If I might be permitted to use an agricultural metaphor, most of the Black nationalist religions take root in the matrix of the Black cultic milieu, but then they tend to grow like saplings, and sprout up vertically towards a self-contained maturity. York's ephemeral groups, in contrast, behave more like rhizones (i.e. potatoes or strawberries). Lacking firm stems or "trunks," they reach out their tentacles

[96] Isa al Mahdi 1986 *The True Story of Noah [PHUH]* Part One (Brooklyn, AAC, 1989); Isa Al Mahdi. *A Rebuttal to the Slanderers* (Brooklyn: The Original Tents of Kedar, 1989).

[97] Martha Lee, *The Nation of Islam: An American Millenarian Movement* (Syracuse, N.Y.: Syracuse University Press, 1996).

or tubers, pulling up their shallow roots so as to drift horizontally, sprouting up as new plants, nurtured in the rich soil of the Black cultic milieu. For over 40 years, York has continued to borrow from many sources and his movement waxes ever more eclectic as it matures. To facilitate this nomadic process, York must periodically fold up his tenets and his tents, debrief his schools, and contradict his own (exoteric) teachings—behavior that might appear to be counter-productive to an outsider.

I would argue that this erratic behavior does not necessarily "prove" the insincerity of Dr. York's vision, as his critics insist. Rather, it points to a new and unusual survival strategy for a NRM is dependent on the Black cultic milieu for its nourishment

York has created for his followers a self-contained spiritual supermarket, offering a wide range of Black nationalist products. Spiritual seekers who join his movement can sample a wide selection of esoteric lore and ritual practices. They may "try on" different charismatic racial identities. They study the teachings of Elijah Muhammad or Clarence 13X through Dr. York's reprints—without ever having to venture outside the boundaries of the United Nuwaubian Nation.

York's critics will explain this phenomenon as a clever marketing strategy—which indeed it is. But it is also something deeper and more complex, as the next chapter will reveal.

Figure 1   Dr. York arrives for his court hearing

Chapter 2
Holy Madness, Crazy Wisdom

Over the years, Dr. York has led his disciples along a convoluted route that is full of surprises. While defining themselves as Nuwaubians, they have tried on and discarded the masks of Hebrews, Egyptians, Moors, Muslims, Yamassee Indians, Freemasons and Shriners. York's critics have argued that the instability and experimentation that characterize his short-lived "cults" prove that he is a con artist, a fake, a madman. But I would argue that the external forms of York's movement (and his cryptic style of teaching) are quite consistent with his underlying message. This message is a Gnostic revelation of the mystical Self—the Self that has been obscured by racial stereotyping, self-hatred and self-forgetfulness—a miasma which engulfs and confuses the so-called "black man" in America.

Kurt Rudolph begins his famous book, *Gnosis: the Nature and History of Gnosticism*, by observing that this ancient religion "was known almost exclusively through the work of its opponents."[1] These opponents were Christian apologists and orthodox theologians, and by reading their heresiological writings, "we receive but a weak and distorted reflection" of the ancient religion of the "so-called Gnostics."

Rudolph might be describing the current situation regarding the Nuwaubians. To date, the public has received information through stigmatizing news reports about the "Nuwaubian nightmare"; the "quasi-religious sect" founded by a "child molester" and "black militant." The only two book-length studies of Dr. York, one by a Muslim heresiologist, and the other by a journalist, feature the words "cult" and "evil" in their titles.

The journalist, Bill Osinski, summed up Dr. York's religious mission in one sentence: "York was a young ex-con who figured out a great way to get all the sex and money he wanted; it was to declare himself a god, all this religion stuff was a façade!"[2]

This is a blatantly reductionist statement that ignores a fascinating and complex issue introduced into sociology of religion by Max Weber—the issue of charisma. A longitudinal study of York's movement reveals that Malachi Z. York's charismatic claims escalate, de-escalate and mutate at various stages. While York certainly claims to be divine, there are certain subtle qualifications to his claim. As one finds in the leadership of other contemporary prophets (such as Reverend

---

[1] Kurt Rudolph, *Gnosis: the Nature and History of Gnosticism* (New York: Harper Collins Publisher, 1987), 9.

[2] Interviewed on the Montel Williams Show, "Cult Survivors Speak Out," aired on 10 February 2007.

Sun Myung Moon, Da Free John, Bhagwan Shree Rajneesh, John de Ruiters) the notion of the godman is a mystery, to be referred to obliquely by the devotees, and not to be stated in a crass, bold fashion. Sometimes it is asserted outright, but more often it is hinted at—and at times it may be coyly disclaimed by the leader himself. Like Reverend Moon and other messianic leaders, York displays the paradoxical attributes of hubris and humility:

> Now there are many people that have tried to attribute titles to him. He has been called Christ, a Prophet, an Apostle, the Mahdi and many other things, all of which he denies.[3]

Roy Wallis argues that charisma is never imposed from above, but operates "from the bottom up" as a dynamic, "give-and-take" relationship between master and disciple.[4] We find on the alternative altars of American Black History a veritable host of Messiahs whose divine status points to the inherent divinity of the Black man. For their devotees, to recognize their leader's divine nature is to acknowledge a corresponding divinity within the self. This is an important doctrine shared by Nuwaubians, Rastafarians, Five-Percenters, Black Muslims, Moors and Black Hebrews. Prince A Cuba notes in his brilliant article ("Black Gods of the Inner City") that the Nation of Islam's "Lost-Found Muslim lessons" contain "the basic elements of an ancient mystery school," and that "central to these teachings were the knowledge of self and the Black man's godhood."[5] The Five Percenters actually greet each other as "gods," thereby acknowledging a state of perfection and absolute power.

Mattias Gardell makes a similar point in his analysis of Dr. York's messianic claims during the Ansaaru Allah Community phase:

> Observe that York claims to be *a* Messiah, not *the* Messiah. The Ansaar teach that the foretold return of Jesus Christ, the Messiah (Isa al Masih) will be in the spirit of all devout believers or Ansaars ("helpers of God"). The AAC thereby adopt the idea of the Body Christ.... . Isa's claim that Isa al Masih will return as the *Mujeddid*, however, indicates that he himself has an additional messianic spark, making him a Messiah, head of the Body Christ.[6]

One Nuwaubian, when asked if he considered Dr. York to be divine, responded, "we are all deities incarnate. He doesn't say he's God! In the Bible Psalms it says,

---

[3]   *I Don't Claim to Be Who I Am* (Nuwaubian flyer, n.d.).

[4]   Roy Wallis, *The Elementary Forms of the New Religious Life* (London: Routledge and Kegan Paul, 1984).

[5]   Prince-A-Cuba, "Black Gods of the Inner City," *Gnosis Magazine*: (San Francisco, Fall 1992), 7-14.

[6]   Mattias Gardell, *In the Name of Elijah Muhammad: Louis Farrakhan and the Nation of Islam* (Durham and New York: Duke University Press, 1996), 342.

'ye are all Gods and all of you are children of the most high!' In Job 10:34 it says, 'It is not within your law, I say ye are Gods!'"[7] In this way, by encouraging his disciples to meditate on the mystery and the paradox of a god who is also a wholly human, a man of black flesh, Dr. York invites them to turn inward and find particles of godhood within their own human nature.[8]

While the theory of charisma offers an explanatory framework for Dr. York's unusual *modus operandi* (his changing honorific titles, changing costumes, and doctrinal revisions), a deeper examination would suggest it fits the model of a relatively rare and radical style of spiritual teaching called "crazy wisdom" or "holy madness."

Georg Feuerstein, in his book, *Holy Madness:The Shock Tactics and Radical Teachings of Crazy-Wise Adepts, Holy Fools and Rascal Gurus*, describes a type of spiritual teacher who deliberately resorts to paradoxical, humorous, even obscene behavior—all for a noble end.[9] The purpose is to shock his disciples out of their social conditioning, and to assault their egos as the first step towards preparing them to receive direct spiritual experiences and enlightenment. Feuerstein argues that "holy madness" is a universal category of religious life, found in religious traditions around the world—although it has been virtually ignored by historians of religion. In order to teach spiritual truths, Feuerstein notes, these masters often adopt quite unconventional means—certainly means that are not ordinarily associated with "holy folk." They may resort to alcohol and other drugs, or they may use sexuality for instructional purposes. They are equally indifferent to filth and to luxury, and "their generally outrageous behavior does not at all conform to our cherished ideas of religiosity, morality and sanctity."[10]

The Trickster's "Tricknology"

One common strategy of a "Crazy Wisdom" teacher is to assume the *persona* of the trickster. As Feuerstein explains, the trickster's aim is to startle and shock.[11] He is a master of inversion, a breaker of taboos, and a lover of surprises. The tricksters found in tribal mythology delight in irrational, malicious deeds and display a voracious sexual appetite. The trickster is a juxtaposition of carnality and spirituality, who celebrates material existence. He embodies the anti-cultural forces that surround society are kept at bay by the countless institutions of his

---

[7]   Interview with Yusuf at the Savior's Day Festival at Tama Re, June 20, 2003.

[8]   The notion of the divinity of Black women is more complex, however, and fluctuates wildly over the course of the Nuwaubian movement.

[9]   Georg Feuerstein, *Holy Madness: The Shock Tactics and Radical Teachings of Crazy-Wise Adepts, Holy Fools and Rascal Gurus* (New York: Penguin Books, 1990).

[10]   Feuerstein, xx.

[11]   I apologize for the sexist language here, but Feuerstein does not include one single example of a female "crazy wisdom" teacher.

culture. But his task is to tear off all our cultural blinders and rational pretensions so that we may see "Reality" unmasked.[12] Finally, the trickster is neither good nor evil, but utterly amoral. He operates outside the conventional sphere of morality.

Within the American Blackosophical tradition, we often find the Trickster appearing as a mythic hero or, alternatively, as an evil god. In Elijah Muhammad's creation myth, Yakub is the evil god who creates the first white men artificially in a laboratory.[13] Theophus H. Smith explores the meaning of this evil godlike figure whose attributes are mischief and deceit. Yakub created the first white "devils" who have inherited Yakub's power of *tricknology*. This enables the white man to rule over the black man, by creating a false reality founded on illusion, lies and treachery.

Dr. York's charismatic attributes must be considered within this potent concept. As Michael Lieb explains, *tricknology* "implies all that is fallacious and delusive in Yakub as the Father of Lies whose descendants now practice what has been disseminated through their very genes."[14] If white man's culture is the product of a *Demiurge*—an evil god who ensnared the godlike spirits of the original human beings in a miasma of falsehood and lies; if every white man is an Archon equipped with the magical power of tricknology, then what is needed is a hero, a magician, a savior who can turn the tables on the enemy by wielding his own weapons against him. And this is where Dr. York comes in.

Dr. York's ability to trick, to deceive, to escape, is described proudly by his loyal disciples—and less positively by his critics. An ex-member, Abdul Mut'aal, notes, "I remember on one occasion he ordered some eggs and bacon and he didn't like how they looked, so he shoved the plate to me and I ate them. They brought him some more eggs but he did not like the way they looked so he shoved them over to me too. He was playing games."[15]

Another ex-member, Abdul Halim, reports: "People believe he does magical things. They...wanted to give him a party, so they locked him in a closet. And, when they went downstairs, he was there laughing. Like he dematerialized or something. ... They also say he can move heavy objects without touching them."[16]

One Ansaar booklet ("or scroll"), *The Man of Miracles*, features photographs of Dr. York performing feats of magic.[17] His own son, Jacob York, reports that he grew up watching his father practice different magician's tricks from books and

[12]   Feuerstein, 4-6.

[13]   Theophus H. Smith. *Conjuring Culture:Biblical Formations of Black America* (New York: Oxford University Press, 1996), 248.

[14]   Michael Lieb, *Children of Ezekiel* (Durham and New York: Duke University Press, 1998).

[15]   Bilal Phillips, *The Ansar Cult in America* (Riyadh, Saudi Arabia: Tawheed Publications, 1988), 169.

[16]   Phillips, 177.

[17]   *The Man of Miracles in This Day of Time*, Edition 138 (New York: Nubian Islaamic Hebrews, 1985).

gadgets he had purchased from a magic store: "He was a conjuror. He had all these trick gadgets, he would put white powder in his ring, and sprinkle it around, it would fall on people's heads. 'Oh! It's angel dust!' they'd say."[18]

One disciple described Dr. York as a "great escape artist."[19] A member of the Triad, Khunsu Hotep, gave a speech on the same occasion, in which he claimed that the Master Teacher would shortly be released from prison and returned to Liberia, since his true identity as a Liberian diplomat had just been revealed to the U.S. authorities: "They can't hold him, he's got them fooled, he's got them confused and runnin' in circles. Just when they think they got him figured out—boom! He vanishes. Where did he go? [He ran in circles blinking, mimicking clumsy white officials.] Over there? How did he get over there?"[20]

As these examples illustrate, Dr. York's leadership qualities include deception, trickery and identity shifts that make it quite easy for white anti-cultists to portray him as a charlatan, a snake oil salesman, a con artist—all attributes of the stereotypical "cult leader." But York's disciples see him as their hero, their warrior, their revered Savior, who is come to "break the spell of Kingu," to set free the souls of Nubians in Amerikah by outsmarting the evil white slave-masters. And how does he do this?—by employing good tricknology to subvert the evil tricknology of Yakub and his deceitful Creature, the "Paleman."

Dr. York, the Clown

Feuerstein describes the humorous or clownish aspects of his Crazy Wisdom masters: "clowns wear masks and strange outfits…assuming different *personae* so that their disciples can never be sure of who is confronting them." Ritual clowns can be looked upon as institutionalized agents of antinomianism. They are safety valves for pent-up personal and societal energies, as in the mediaeval "Feast of Fools." York's "politically incorrect" jokes about white people appear to function as sort of catharsis—as a safe, nonviolent expression of his peoples' collective resentment of the pervasive racial discrimination and injustice in the surrounding society.

Many of York's disciples describe him as a great comedian who makes them laugh ("He's *bad*, man!"). Even his enemies admit he can be funny. The journalist, William Osinski, after listening to an audiotape where York insults whites as "diseased lepers" who "belong back in caves" notes, "this white author has to admit that York can be quite funny. He delivers his message of hate with a comic flair and timing reminiscent of an early Richard Pryor or a Dick Gregory."[21]

---

[18]   Interview with Jacob York in Atlanta, August 2003.

[19]   Conversation with a Nuwaubian at the Savior's Day Zed Festival, 26 June 2003.

[20]   Behavior observed at the Savior's Day Zed Festival, 25 June 2003.

[21]   Bill Osinski, *Ungodly: The True Story of Unprecedented Evil* (Eatonton: Indigo Press, 2007), 46.

Sheriff Howard Sills, who became York's main cultural opponent after the group moved to Georgia, expressed astonishment at York's comic routines. He explained how, while he was conducting surveillance on the compound just before the 2002 raid, "we could hear York's speeches because they were coming over the loudspeakers," and offered an interesting comment.

> I don't understand the appeal York has for his followers! We were expecting a holy man, a dynamic speaker, charisma or brainwashing (actually, same thing). But what we heard were...jokes! York gave a stand up comedy act, just like Richard Prior—jokes based on racism, anti-white insults. There were sprinklings of theology, but it was basically a comedy act. And his followers loved it. They would sit there for forty minutes, an hour...and laugh their heads off and give him a standing ovation. This is not what I expected of a religious leader![22]

Sills also made an insightful comment that just so happens to fit Feuerstein's portrait of the "Crazy Wisdom" teacher:

> Did you ever see *Little Big Man*? Well, I see Dwight York as a "*contraire*." In the Sioux culture, a *contraire* is a medicine man who does everything backwards. He rides a horse backwards, he'll answer "yes" when he means "no." He washes his hands in the dirt....

York is often quoted saying, "Do as I say, not as I do." Crazy Wisdom teachers are typically antinomian, they are moral anarchists. Rajneesh says, "even sin is beautiful, because sin gives depth to your saintliness."[23] Feuerstein describes the ritual obscenities of Love Da Ananda who presided over Tantra-style encounters called "sexual theatre"—where he even seduced Feuerstein's own wife.[24] In a manner similar to Love Da Ananda, York tested the loyalty of his disciples by using their wives as his concubines:

> If a sister...was good-looking, he would approach her...Isa loved women. Sometimes it would happen there would be 4 or 5 sisters pregnant from him at a time and he not married them. They were all concubines, some of them wives of the older brothers, and some of the brothers went for it because they were sort of hypnotized by Isa.[25]

Phillips notes that, on one occasion, York told a follower's wife to come around to his house "as he had some special work for her. We did not see her all day or night

---

[22] Interview with Sheriff Howard Sills, August 12, 2003 in his office in Eatonton, Georgia.

[23] Feuerstein, 66.

[24] Feuerstein, 90-91.

[25] Quoted from an interview in Phillips, 152.

and we teased Adel that he was laying his wife. Plenty of sisters went in there…in his bedroom… . If he wanted a woman he had her!"[26]

Dr. York even goes so far as to flout moral boundaries in his formal teachings. As Phillips points out disapprovingly, "Isa reveals the more seamy side of his teachings in which he promotes immoral and perverted sexual practices, ranging from the despicable to the prohibited.[27] In *Sex Life of a Muslim* York actually recommends oral and anal sex and sperm drinking, claiming it is *halaal* in Islam.[28] This, of course, would shock conservative Sunni Muslims.

In the transcript of a lecture, "Does God Exist According To Our Time?" (n.d.) York defends incest, as an ancient Egyptian practice among the Pharoahs:

> I do not live under your law, I am not a student enrolled under Earth principles, I don't have the morals you have, your idea of morals is different. Go back in ancient times, you'll find out that Anu was married to his sister…and Ishtar was married to her son back then that existed. …I come from a world where we don't have your laws, and the way we go about things is different. I come from the Pharaoh's world and in the Pharaoh's world the Pharaoh saw Sarah, he saw her with himself so he took her. In Abraham's world that was the wrong thing to do, but the Pharaoh didn't care about Abraham's world because he was living in his world and his ritual.

York also makes an inflammatory statement that apparently justifies sex with underage girls. It was later used by the prosecution during his trial to support the allegations against him of child molestation. In his letter to "Najwa and Davina, Kirsten" (n.d.) York wrote: "Negroids living under the laws of Caucasoids have learned their ways, follow their laws, love their women, and her image and skills. If you travel outside of European lands you find in Africa women marry and have children very young. They live in incest. …We *are Africans*. We have our own laws, morality, customs, rules, regulations. No, not set up by me, but set up for both you and me."

This is the only passage, to my knowledge, in Dr. York's writings that might be interpreted as condoning sex between adults and teenagers.[29]

---

[26]   Phillips, 171.

[27]   Phillips, 107.

[28]   *Sex Life of a Muslim, Vol. II.* (Brooklyn: The Original Tents of Kedar, 1980).

[29]   Other charismatic prophets of NRMs who have been accused of this particular form of social deviance (e.g. David Brandt Berg, David Koresh, Little Pebble, and Daniel Cormier) have all produced theological arguments that justify the sexual awakening of minors or that offer an apocalyptic rationale for child brides.

A Teacher of Gnosis?

Dr. York's breaches of taboo and violation of social norms conform to a pattern we find in some Gnostic schools. Hans Jonas points out that many of the ancient Gnostics were libertines who displayed antinomian tendencies and contempt for the illusory, fallen world. Freedom from conventional morality was considered a sign of self-realization, of godhood. Jonas writes:

> In this life the.... possessors of gnosis...are set apart from the great mass of mankind. The immediate illumination not only makes the individual sovereign in the sphere of knowledge, but also determines the sphere of action. Contempt for all mundane ties could lead to asceticism or libertinism. The pneumatic is free from the yoke of moral law...all things are permitted since the *pneuma* is saved in its nature and can neither be sullied by actions nor frightened by... retribution.[30]

Dr. York's cryptic style of teaching points to an underlying message that corresponds to the Gnostic revelation of the mystical Self—a Self that, for African-Americans, has been long suppressed by slavery, racial stereotyping, self-hatred and prevailing ignorance.

Kurt Rudolph has identified a number of ideas which occur repeatedly and form their basic framework in most of the Gnostic traditions. He lays forth the definition and main tenets of Gnosticism as follows: "Gnosis is Greek for `knowledge' but for the Gnostics it was not an intellectual, or theoretical knowledge they sought, but rather a direct, experiential knowledge...which has a liberating and redeeming effect. The man who possesses gnosis is a redeemed man."

Rudolph quotes from *The Gospel of Phillip*: "He who has the knowledge of the truth (gnosis) is free. Ignorance is a slave."[31] The Nuwaubians possess a similar concept to Gnosis, that of "Right Knowledge." This "Right Knowledge" is also referred to as "Nuwaubu," "Nuwaupu," and sometimes, "Wu-Nuwaubu."

For the aspiring Gnostic this experiential knowledge may be accessed through the ascetic ordeals of fasting, celibacy, meditation, chanting; and through mystical communion with a spiritual master who can impart the Gnosis by gazing into their eyes, touching the forehead, uttering a mantra (or by other means). Gnostic traditions thus emphasize the need for a redeemer. Rudolph writes, "Man can only become aware of his calamitous situation...by means of revelation. The Gnostic view of the world demands a revelation which comes from outside the cosmos and displays the possibility of deliverance, for of himself man cannot escape from his prison."[32]

---

[30]   Hans Jonas, *The Gnostic Religion* (Boston: Beacon Press, 1958), 46.
[31]   Quoted in Rudolph, 56.
[32]   Rudolph, 119.

Gnosticism reveals that Man is profoundly alienated, exiled from his true home, distant from, ignorant of, and perhaps unknown to, his heavenly Creator. Man is "asleep," "drunken," a slave to the senses. The redeemer's mission is to awaken the "sleeping soul," the "seed of light"; or to "awaken the dead." [33] York awakens his disciples to their true identity. As one disciple claimed, "he lifted me out of my sarcophagus!" Nuwaubians see themselves as trapped in the "false prison" of racism in America, held captive by evil wardens, the "Palemen" or "Amorites" (the equivalent of the "Archons" of Gnosticism). Nuwaubians believe that the Spell of Leviathan ("The Spell Of Kingu") is cast over the Nubians of America through the Christian Church, the U.S. government, the media and popular culture. Dr. Malachi York has come as the "Prepared Savior," the "Messiah" to awaken the Nubian people to their true glorious spiritual identity as Divine Beings, as gods.

Gardell writes, "as does the Nation of Islam, the Ansaar teach a specific black Gnosis combined with white demonology and the necessity for racial solidarity and separation from evil." But he notes that York's Gnostic anthropology is quite different from the Nation of Islam, in that is derived from "esoteric Sufi speculation."[34] He points to a creation myth, borrowed from mystical Islam, in *Rebuttals to the Slanderers*. In this myth, the universe is divided into seven planes, each with their own musical tones or vibrations, the lower tones comprising the material realm. Man was originally created as a soul (*Ruhw*), but as his vibrations lost speed, he took on an etheric form as a spirit. As his speed kept decreasing, Man assumed his physical body. Gardell notes that this tripartite model of Man is consistent with Gnostic anthropology, where man is made up of the flesh (*sarx*), soul (*psyche*) and spirit (*pneuma*). The *pneuma* still lingers in and belongs to the heavenly realm from whence it fell, but can be contacted by ascetic practices and redeemed through Gnosis.[35]

> Both women and men…contain a spark of Allah in their soul, and by praising Allah will gain an inner Light that will illuminate their heart and inner senses. The seven "seats" or chakras of man, energy points in the body, are correlated to the seven planes, and Man ascend up towards his origin through activating his chakras, until he reaches union with Allah.[36]

Rudolph observes that "dualism dominates the whole of Gnostic cosmology." In most Gnostic traditions this dualism imagines a radical body/spirit dichotomy.

---

[33] Rudolph, 119-20.

[34] Gardell, 192.

[35] In this myth, York refers only to the black *man*, for women were created on the physical plane, he claims, and given souls from men, and this places them below men in the ontological hierarchy. It is interesting to note, however, that after York announced himself as "the liberator of women," new creation myths explaining the differences between the sexes were concocted. One myth actually places women above men ontologically.

[36] Gardell, 192.

The devaluation of the flesh and the material realm is often mentioned as one of the defining characteristic of Gnosticism. But this particular type of dualism is not found in Nuwaubian philosophy. On the contrary, Nuwaubians embrace a radical materialism; they consider black flesh as divine, and reject the transcendental realm as the "pie in the sky" offered by white Christianity to keep the slaves and oppressed workers docile. In York's message of the divinity of the Black man, the Spirit resides in the blood and in the genes.[37]

This materialistic dualism is found in York's creation myth of the "Paleman." The white devil is the offspring of Fallen Angels who mated with the wicked women of Nod when they fell to earth. The White man was neither soul nor spark of Allah, but only the spirit of the Jinn. Since the soul is the seat of emotions whereby morality and laws are controlled, the white man lacks these elements and is therefore incapable of surrendering to Allah. Soulless, like cold-blooded reptiles, the white devil can feel no emotion or compassion and he is driven by instinct: "As reptiles shed their skin, the Paleman has sensitive skin which peels easily under the rays of the sun."[38]

Paradoxically, the Nuwaubians reject the spiritual realm and espouse a radical materialist philosophy. Like the Nation of Islam, the Rastafari, and the Nation of Yahweh, the Nuwaubians do not perceive their gods as inhabiting any transcendent, spiritual realm. Rather, their gods are material beings, walking on earth like Warith Fard, or travelling in UFOs ("Ezekial's Wheel"). Dr. York de-spiritualizes Jesus by insisting that His father was the Archangel Gabriel "who came down in the form of a well-made man to go into Mary to give her a pious lad,"[39] In a similar vein, Mary was not a virgin, and "Jesus was not created from little angel babies floating down from the sky."[40] In his 1980 book (*Was Christ Really Crucified?*) York claims that Jesus escaped the crucifixion and traveled around esoteric schools in Africa and the Middle East. Here he is clearly relying on the *Aquarian Gospel of Jesus*, authored by Levi H. Dowling, which he may have encountered by reading Noble Drew Ali's *Holy Koran (Circle Seven)* or the teachings of Father Hurley.

For a Gnostic to believe in material gods appears to be a paradox. This paradox might be resolved through a new paradigm of the struggle between Good and Evil, Light and Darkness. The old Body/Spirit dichotomy of the Gnostics is replaced by a new racialist dichotomy: the evil White Man *versus* the good Black Man.

---

[37] The Grand Al Mufti "Divan" Noble: Rev. Malachi Z. York-El 33 degrees/720 degrees. *Is There Life After Death?* (Macon G.A.: The International Supreme Council of Shriners Inc., n.d.).

[38] *The Paleman* (Brooklyn: The Original Tents of Kedar, 1989), 214-25.

[39] *Who was Jesus Father?* (Brooklyn: The Original Tents of Kedar, 1988), 43.

[40] *Who was Jesus Father?*, 42.

A Gnostic Approach to Language

If one recognizes Dr. York as a Gnostic teacher, many of the puzzling aspects of his movement might be analyzed as hermeneutical devices peculiar to the Gnostic tradition. Gnostic teachers, past and present, have exhibited a certain detachment from external forms, and a sophisticated use of paradoxical symbols. Dr. York exhibits the same self-consciously metaphorical approach to religious language. He borrows ideas from many seemingly incompatible sources: Theosophy, Rosicrucianism, Freemasonry, the Shriners, the Christian-Islam of Mirza Ghulam Ahmad, and the alien crypto-zoology of David Icke. At times, he has even flirted with Christian Patriot anti-government ideologies, urban legends, and conspiracy theories.

As William James explains in his famous *Varieties of the Religious Experience*, one characteristic of the mystical experience is its "ineffability"; the notion that it is impossible to express the noetic quality or secret knowledge, derived only from direct experience, in mere words.[41] Several contemporary mystics have dramatized this notion by using terms that are deliberately silly and playful. Herff Applewhite and Bonnie Nettles of Heaven's Gate adopted deliberately silly names like "Guinea and Pig," "Bo and Peep," "Ti and Do" that pointed to the ineffable mystery of their charismatic duo.[42] One of Dr. York's most famous axioms is, "I came giving you what you would want so that you could learn to want what I have to give." This seems to imply that he uses language as bait. It is the "milk" offered to "babes" to prepare them for the "meat" of the real lesson. In a passage in *The Holy Tablets* he reveals his metaphorical approach to religious language:

> I began my mission as…Amunnnubi Rooakhptah, an unknown writer of the Science of Nuwaubu, but knowing the Nubians weren't ready for that level of information as of yet, I started teaching under the name Imaam Isa, for Muslims seem to be the most influential movements of that time and didn't dare question each other.[43]

If one considers York's spiritual groups as theatrical performances that point to a hidden, ineffable "Truth," they begin to make more sense. He draws attention to the meaning underlying the words, a mysterious, fluid "truth" that can never be adequately expressed in any language. This maintains an aura of mystery and prevents the group from developing into a "church" with rules and stock axioms. York's series of "schools," disguised as Hebrew, Muslim or Moorish traditions

---

[41]   William James, *Varieties of the Religious Experience* (Gifford Lectures, University of Edinburgh, 1902).

[42]   Robert Balch, "Bo and Peep: A Case of the Messianic Origins of Leadership." In *Millennialism and Charisma*, edited by Roy Wallis (Belfast: The Queen's University), 13-71.

[43]   *The Holy Tablets* (Eatonton, G.A.:The Holy Tabernacle Ministries, n.d.), 1643-4.

are mere masks, soon to be discarded once a new group of loyal disciples are awakened and inducted into the hidden, esoteric school of *Nu-waupu*, or "Right Knowledge."

York's ever-evolving mythology of race might also be analyzed as a Gnostic pedagogical device. Nuwaubian creation myths evoke a sense of mystery and wonder in his disciples. These myths offer a charismatic discourse for exploring the meaning of dark skin: "Is our skin black because Ah-dam means "black mud" in Hebrew (which tells us how Adam was created by Allah)?"; "Or is it made of brown dust?"; "Was our skin originally green, because our green ancestors, the Annunaqi, colonized earth and the oxygen in the atmosphere caused them to turn brown?"

Many Black nationalist groups, as part of their goal of "uplift" and self-improvement, have deconstructed the English language so as to purify it of its racist elements (i.e., "black" denoting "evil"). As in the Nation of Islam, Nuwaubians are involved in expanding their vocabulary, in deconstructing the English language, and in exploring the roots of words. Aware that in the time of slavery their ancestors were discouraged by law from learning how to read, Black nationalists have promoted literacy and encouraged their people to expand their vocabulary so as to make their minority voices heard. Since words have power, a mastery over language is a means to seize status in society and to control destiny. The Nation of Islam advocates a daily study of the Webster's Dictionary. The Nation of Yahweh actually requires that members bring a dictionary to the four annual Feasts, where members will read out definitions of words as an integral part of their liturgy, as they "Praise Yahweh!" The Five Percenters have developed the Supreme Alphabet as is a system of interpreting sacred texts and lessons of Elijah Muhammad by assigning symbolic meanings to the letters of the alphabet. Their Hip Hop artists ("jive percenters") disseminate sacred knowledge through Hip Hop performances on the streets. They use street jargon, create neologisms, and dissect words in order to convey their faith to their audience.[44]

Like these groups, the Nuwaubians use words as a means of empowerment, but they focus on the *sound* of words, and rhythm of syllables.[45] The standard scientific methods in philology and linguistics are discarded in favor of poetry, phonetics and musical logogenics.[46] Spiritual ideas are not taken literally, but are played

---

[44]   Michael Muhammad Knight, *The Five Percenters: Islam, Hip Hop and the Gods of New York* (Oxford, U.K.: Oneworld Publications, 2007), 53-4.

[45]   In trying to "figure out" their theology, I would make notes during the meetings, but when I left and reviewed my notes, I would wonder, "what was that all about?" I began to realize the ministers were there to raise the questions and encourage debate, not necessarily to provide coherent answers.

[46]   I once brought a blonde scientist to the Question&Answer meeting in Brooklyn, and he found the Nuwaubians' phonetic approach to language so aggravating that he kept raising his hand and correcting them in a pedantic fashion, pointing out the Latin and Greek roots. They just laughed and ignored him.

with, extrapolated upon, recited as poetry, and discussed in a speculative mood. The Question&Answer functions as a laboratory where spiritual seekers cultivate their own experimental study methods in the quest for "Right Knowledge." It occurred to me that one of the attractions of the "Question-Answer" sessions for African-Americans was it helped them to cultivate an inner distance from the stereotypes of "race" that still persist in U.S. mainstream culture. Paradoxically, the Gnostic sense of alienation and elitism cultivated in these meetings seemed to have the effect of actually improving the adepts' ability to integrate into and succeed in the larger white-dominated society.[47] Underprivileged youth gain self-confidence as they pick up skills in reading, in public speaking, in administration and fundraising. They may then go out into society, having mastered a range of guerilla tactics to break the "Spell of Leviathan" and to subvert the Paleman's campaign to destroy, disinherit and dilute the Nubian people.

---

[47] This would be described by the anti-cult movement as the "us and them mentality" typically found in "the cults."

Figure 2   Ansaar propagating Right Knowledge in the 1970s in New York

Chapter 3
The Ansaaru Allah Community

When the Ansaaru Allah Community first moved into Brooklyn in 1973, it was perceived by the local authorities as a new variant of the Nation of Islam; a group that provided a healthy alternative to the crime-ridden, drug-infested subculture in the inner city. By the 1970s, the public authorities of New York City had already received a lesson in racial tolerance from the Nation of Islam. Despite Elijah Muhammad's heavy-handed myth of "the white man" as a genetic mutant and "devil," the NOI demanded—and eventually earned—public respect as a congregation of self-disciplined, peaceful and law-abiding citizens.

The Ansaar moved into the run-down area around Bushwick Avenue, York set up a security force modeled on the Nation of Islam's "Fruit of Islam" called the "Swords of Islam" (*mujahim*) and they quickly established order. The Swords of Islam was a vigilante force that protected the neighbourhood from shoplifters and armed robberies, and rid Brooklyn's Flatbush section of drug dealers and crime.

Mayor John V. Lindsay had founded the Urban League in the 1970s, which supported the Five-Percent Nation as an effective tool for fighting poverty and crime. Concerned about the racial tension between blacks and Jews, the Mayor had sent his aide to speak to Clarence 13X in 1967. Clarence wanted bus trips to the parks and to Long Beach for his people, and Mayor Lindsay had acceded to his requests. The Five-Percent Nation received funding for their school, and Mayor Lindsay was photographed with their leader, Clarence 13X, at the opening of the school for the inner city youth on 2122, 7th Avenue. When Martin Luther King was assassinated on April 4, 1968, the Five Percenters launched a peacemaking mission in Harlem, thereby diverting a potential riot. They received a commendation from Mayor Lindsay for their good work in keeping the peace and providing education and vocational training programs for youth.[1]

The Ansaaru Allah Community coasted along in the wake of the good reputation of these groups. News reports in the 1980s featured interviews with Mayor Ed Koch and the Brooklyn police praising the Ansaars for the good work they were doing in the Bushwick community. But, as the communal structure of the AAC developed, its unconventional economic patterns, missionary strategies and sexual mores led to the same kind of conflicts with secular authorities that we find in many other utopian ventures in American history.[2]

---

[1]   Michael Muhammad Knight, *The Five Percenters: Islam, Hip Hop and the Gods of New York* (Oxford, U.K.: Oneworld, 2007).

[2]   Notable examples of this are the Oneida Perfectionists, the Shakers, the Mormons, the Church Universal and Triumphant, Shiloh, the Rajneesh, and the Branch Davidians.

The Origins and Development of the AAC

The Ansaaru Allah Community lasted for 19 years, from 1973 to 1992. It was a highly visible African-American ghetto that took up a whole neighborhood on Brooklyn's Bushwick Avenue. Ansaaru Allah means "helper of Allah," and the daily life of the Ansaars was centered on religious activities performed in the mosque (*masjid*). The men wore long white robes and turbans, the women wore face veils, and the children were raised to speak only Hebrew, Arabic and "Nubic" (a language invented by Dr. York) and could be seen daily in the mosque, sitting in rows and chanting the Qur'an. The Ansaars' publishing office produced a newsletter called *The Nubian Village Bulletin*, as well as hundreds of booklets ("scrolls") to spread their prophet's message to the sleeping Nubians of America.

The AAC evolved out of the Nubian Islaamic Hebrews, gradually transforming into a Muslim group as it discarded its Hebrew themes. The members began to live communally after York announced a new revelation. On June 26, 1970 (his twenty-fifth birthday) he spoke of "the victorious opening of the seventh seal" that would usher in the Aquarian Age, sometime between 2000 and 2030.[3]

In 1970 the Nubians moved into a house on Neptune Avenue and opened the Pure Sufi Bookstore on 720 Flatbush Avenue, with an adjacent printing and layout shop. York (then known as "Imam Isa") did not live with them, but moved to 2813 W. 29th St. on Coney Island where he held his meetings and lectures. Then the group moved to 22 Utica Avenue where they opened their *Masjid* (mosque). In 1972 they relocated to 450 Rockaway Avenue where classes were held in the "Upper Room." The same year they re-opened their *Masjid* with a bookstore attached at 833 St. John's.[4]

The movement embraced Mahdism after York returned from his summer vacation of 1973. York had traveled to the Sudan and to Egypt in order to perform the minor pilgrimage of *Umrah*. There he sought out the descendants of the famous Mahdi, Muhammad Ahmad (1845-85) in the Sudan. Like many African Americans pilgrims from the Nation of Islam, York had his photograph taken standing before the Mahdi's tomb at Kartoum University.[5] He met several members of the Mahdi's family and had photographs taken in their company.[6] They gave him some family photographs and he also took pictures of historical artefacts in the museums, which appeared in his scrolls. He writes about his meeting with As Sayyid Mahmuwd, who initiated him into the Order of Al Khidr, and he joined a Sufi Order of Khalwatiyya which prepared him for his role as the *Mujeddid* (Reformer). York reports that

---

[3]   Mattias Gardell, *Countdown to Armageddon: Louis Farrakhan and the Nation of Islam in the Latter Days* (Chicago: C. Hurst & Co., 1996), 191.

[4]   *The Holy Tablets* (Eatonton, G.A.: The Holy Tabernacle Ministries, n.d.), 1643-8.

[5]   Mark Sedgewick, the famous Islamic scholar, told me during a conversation at the 2006 CESNUR conference in Sicily, that the Mahdi's tomb at Khartoum was a main attraction for NOI members who liked to have their photographs taken in front of it.

[6]   *The Final Link* (Brooklyn, N.Y.: The Original Tents of Kedar, 1978), 3-4.

when he was standing at the junction of the White Nile and the Blue Nile in Egypt, he experienced a mystical visitation. The Archangel, Al-Khidr appeared to him. Al-Khidr is the Muslim version of the Archangel Michael who had guided Moses and is held to be still walking the earth as an immortal man in folk Islam. York described Al-Khidr as the "Highest of all Angels."[7] On the same occasion, York beheld the 24 Elders of St. John's Revelations.[8]

Upon his return to New York, York announced that he was the grandson of the Sudanese Mahdi, and that he had acquired a degree in Islamic law during his stay in Sudan. He added the title "Mahdi" to his honorific name ("al Imam Isa Adbullah Muhammad *al Mahdi*") and in 1976 published a new book, *Muhammad Ahmad the Only True Mahdi*, laying forth his claim to be the direct descendant of al Mahdi, born in June exactly one hundred years after his grandfather.[9] York then discarded the name as well as the Jewish features of the Nubian Islaamic Hebrews, and renamed his movement the "Ansaaru Allah Community." He rationalized this development as follows:

> I opened the seal in 1970, as prophesied. I founded this community exactly one hundred years after the foundation of the Ansaru ALLAH Community… in Sudan by Muhammad Ahmad Al Mahdi, my great grandfather. There is no co-incidence!"[10]

His disciples then abandoned their "Hebrew" dress, and began to wear the long white robes and turbans of the Sudan. The women put on modest gowns and face veils, and the Ansaar literature projected an image of a rigorous, conservative Islam. York even tried to legitimate his new title by applying for a new passport on 7 October 1987 under the name, "Isa Al Haadi Al Mahdi." He was immediately arrested for passport violation, but released on probation.

The AAC built a Mosque, and quickly acquired 30 buildings, including a large communal residence with a home school, apartment buildings, a bookstore, two recording studios, restaurants, a grocery store, and a laundromat. The FBI launched an investigation and estimated that around 500 people were living in the Ansaar commune during its heyday in Brooklyn. One ex-member who became the FBI's informant claimed York had as many as 2000 to 3000 followers across North America during the 1970s.

In 1973 York traveled to Trinidad. There, the local blacks complained of being ostracized by the Indian Muslims who monopolized the mosques. When

---

[7]   See *Prehistoric Man and Animals—Did They Exist?* (Brooklyn N.Y.: The Original Tents of Kedar, 1980), 11-12.

[8]   *The True Story of Noah, Part One* (Brooklyn N.Y.: The Original Tents of Kedar, 1986).

[9]   *Al Mahdi Muhammad Ahmad the Only True Mahdi* (Brooklyn, N.Y.: The Original Tents of Kedar, 1976), 21.

[10]   *The True Story of Noah*, Part Two, 79.

the handsome African-American from New York who called himself the "Mahdi" arrived in Port of Spain, he struck a chord. He preached a message of Nubians as the true Muslims, and helped them set up their own *Masjid*, leaving his trusted friend, Imaam Yahya Abdullah Muhammad, in charge. While he was in Trinidad he took on a new wife in an Islamic marriage and fathered a daughter with her. He defends this action in *Rebuttal to the Slanderers*:

> We were not officially a church or a Mosque and we weren't going to the white man's system…to get married under Christian laws. That's how we did it. We didn't have our contracts because didn't have printing facilities, we were poor. …Therefore, when I arrived in Trinidad I met a woman that I wanted to make my wife. We did it by our consummation, become husband and wife. Now if you have a problem with that, go back to the Bible and read the story of the Prophet Abraham and see how Hagar and he got married.[11]

The AAC sent out missionaries to Baltimore, Cleveland, Atlanta, Newport, Virginia, Washington D.C. and Philadelphia. They established teaching centers in their chain of bookstores, known as the *Tents of Kedar*[12] where classes in esoteric philosophy and Black nationalist theology were held, called "Question&Answer meetings." Sister communities sprouted up in Montreal, Toronto, in the London suburb of Brixton, in Port of Spain, and in the Jamaican Islands.

In 1983 York purchased a lodge on 80 acres of woodlands in the Catskills for $145,000. He called it Camp Jazzir Abba and it became a summer retreat for AAC families. It featured a large common room carpeted with a thick white rug, decorated with plastic palm trees and trophies of deer heads and a rhinoceros. In 1988 York retired from his role as Imam at the Brooklyn mosque, delegating a new Imam, and in 1989 he began to spend most of his time at Camp Jazzir.

A Son's Perspective

A useful historical perspective on the AAC was provided by Jacob York, York's third son by his first and only legal wife. In our interview Jacob offered fascinating (if somewhat unflattering) glimpses into his father's life and leadership, and insisted that the success of the AAC, in terms of membership growth and financial stability, was due to his mother's hard work and skill as an administrator. Jacob left the movement with his mother when he was 16, and he has since become one of his father's sternest critics.

Our interview took place in three stages—at his boutique in Atlanta, at his loft and recording studio, and in his car while he was driving to pick up his girlfriend

---

[11] *Rebuttal to the Slanderers* (Brooklyn, N.Y.: The Original Tents of Kedar, 1989), 501-2.

[12] Later the name was changed to *All Eyes on Egipt*.

at the airport. I have reproduced sections of the interview in first person format, using our first names.

Susan: "Tell me about your parents."

Jacob: "My mom was the only woman he [Dwight York] was ever actually legally married to. My dad married my mother when they were both 18. He met her working at her mother's antique store. He was attending the Stateside mosque at the time. His father (my grandfather) was a topic that was *hush hush*. There was a rumour going around that he was a gangster, a pimp, spent time in jail—not a good role model for his son. My Dad had six kids with my mother. I have two older brothers (not in the movement). We all left with my mother when I was 16. My Dad has had 198 children by many women, according to the FBI. Personally, I know around 60 of my half-brothers and sisters."

Susan: "What was your father's religious background?"

Jacob: "He wasn't a religious man. Their first daughter died at the age of eight. That's when he rejected God and decided there was no justice in the universe, because the drug dealer who lived in the apartment next door had a daughter who was just going off to college, and his own daughter had just died."

Susan: "What was your father like as a person?"

Jacob: "He was a charming, well-spoken guy, extremely funny! He wore blue jeans, cowboy hats and high-heeled cowboy boots. Dad always wore high heels to disguise the fact he was a little man. He was very juvenile, insecure, very emotional. But my mother would never let us speak against my Dad in her presence. She would always say, 'I have known your father since I was 18! He is a good man!'"

Susan: "Was he very extravagant? Did he take drugs?"

Jacob: "Dad loved fancy cars and drove a Cadillac…and he would often add a new accessory. He was never into drugs…he occasionally drank some wine. *Fame* was his drug. He wanted to be famous—like a rock star."

(Jacob spoke of his father's burning desire to become a famous singer. York had two record companies—*Passion* and *York Records*).

Jacob: "Many artists came through his Passion studio and he helped promote their careers. But as soon as they became more successful than he was, he dumped them and would turn to someone else. He was a crappy singer, he had terrible taste. I told him, 'Look, Dad, this stuff you're singing is *shit*. Nobody wants to hear that shit.' I remember the time he was all worked up, excited about arranging a tour to Japan—but anybody can get a tour in Japan! He would dress up in a white suit, part his hair in the middle and sing these sappy-assed 1940s ballads in nightclubs. And his record was a hit in Britain! Even his flunkeys are embarrassed about his CDs. But he had good taste in choosing new artists. Many famous singers recorded at his studio. But he realized he had failed as a singer, so he turned to religion."

Susan: "What was your mother's role in the Ansaaru Allah Community?"

Jacob: "The AAC was a good thing for the neighbourhood. He did make Brooklyn clean and safe and drug-free, that part is true. But, the only reason it was a success was because of my mother. She ran the business side, she dealt with people. My Mom would give him 25, 50 grand a week for allowance—that's all he cared about."

Susan: "What was your parents' relationship like?"

Jacob: "He was always surrounded by women. In Brooklyn he had seven wives. She would say, `Good! Now I don't have to sleep with him, she can do it.' She would make friends with his mistresses and they would work together running things. One of my Dad's other wives worked closely with my mom—but then she betrayed her."

(I asked him to explain.)

Jacob: "My Mom oversaw the whole operation in Brooklyn. We used to have a bookstore, a Laundromat, a restaurant, grocery store, and apartment buildings. She was in charge of finances for the AAC and had been saving up to send the kids to college. She had been very careful to keep it a secret from him, just how much money was coming in. But one of his other wives wanted to get in his good graces, so she told him about all the money that was in a fund especially for the children. My Dad came to my Mom with two of his bodyguards and ordered her to hand it over. She was upset because he had always preached that the kids from the Ansaaru Allah Community were special—that they would all go to college and they would be the great doctors, lawyers and politicians of the next generation. Then, in the late eighties, 30 to 40 kids suddenly came of age, ready to go to college. They had the credentials to get in, they were motivated. But instead, my Dad took the first two girls as soon as they turned 18 and made them his own concubines. There was a lot of talk behind his back about that! Then, in 1988, he took the next two and married them off to two gentlemen from the Middle East—you could buy the tapes of the wedding in the bookstores. He made a big deal of it, a lavish wedding to compensate for his own decision to not to send these girls to college. Then, more kids kept coming of age—and it turned out to be a huge problem. The next year there were eight more who turned 18... .

"Then, in 1989, he blew all the money on a house in the Catskills—Camp Jazzir Abba. He had bought a camp, a few years before, worth 5 to 6 million...It was a monstrosity that needed a lot of repair. My Mom was very upset at that. Then he took the children's food money and bought two vans. At that point, once he got control of the money, my mother decided she had had it. She left with me and my brothers and sisters."[13]

The Disciples

Interviews with current disciples and with defectors provide insights into the Ansaaru Allah Community's appeal for its members. These interviews were conducted by myself, by a Dawson College student, and by Bilal Phillips and his

---

[13]   Interview with Jacob York on August 19, 2003 in his Boutique near the Roxy Theatre in Buckhead district of Atlanta, GA.

assistant. Phillips' book features six interviews with ex-members in the Appendix. Phillips' sole purpose in conducting these interviews was to discredit the AAC and prove it was not orthodox Islam, but rather a deviant "cult." Thus, he asks leading questions like, "Can he [York] be put upon the same level as Jim Jones?" and his informants are railroaded into denouncing York and his *Deen* as false Islam, and encouraged to conclude each interview with testimonials to the "real Islam."

In spite of Phillips' flawed methodology, these interviews contain vivid little anecdotes that yield valuable data and glimpses into the daily life of the commune. Phillip's informants describe typical "commitment mechanisms" designed to enhance the individual's commitment to the whole community, as identified by Rosabeth Moss Kanter in her 1972 book, *Commitment and Community: Utopias in Sociological Perspective*.[14] These patterns include the renunciation of family ties, the discouragement of "dyadic withdrawal," the investment of assets upon joining and voluntary labor, the "mortification" of dissident members through ritual humiliation or punishment, and the "surrender" to Dr. York as to a divine being.

On joining the community, new brothers and sisters would fill out a form and have their photographs taken. The form encouraged them to renounce their biological families. One questions was: "How do you feel about entrusting your child to other people?" Husband, wives and unmarried couples were all sent to live in same-sex quarters. The sisters slept three to six in a bedroom, each with their own mat and bag of belongings, sharing one bathroom. The brothers slept on shelves or on the floor in "barracks." New members would turn their money and furniture over to the community. Clothing brought in was shared also. Contact with outsiders, with former friends or blood kin, was forbidden, for outsiders were regarded as *Kaafirs* (unbelievers), and secular society was *Dunyaa*. York's family, his male executives and bodyguards, lived in their own apartments with their biological families near the mosque on Bushwick Avenue.

There were two levels of membership in the AAC, as in all York's groups. The majority of York's disciples might be called the "revolving door" variety— youth who were attracted initially to York's exoteric group, advertising itself as "Hebrew," Moorish, "egiptian" [sic], or "Muslim." These youth would embrace a new racial/religious identity, imbued with romance and glamor. These short-term members wore the appropriate costumes and symbols, read the scrolls, and participated in the Sunday afternoon Question&Answer meetings. A few of them would move into the commune, housed above, or next door to, the bookstore and participate in the esoteric level of the movement. But the great majority of these self-styled "Muslims," "Hebrews," or "Moors" defected during the group's next convulsion, as it went through its next metamorphosis. Many of them moved on to the more mainstream branches of African-American Islam.

---

[14] Rosabeth Moss Kanter, *Commitment and Community: Utopias in Sociological Perspective* (Boston: Harvard Univerity Press, 1972).

The fewer, more loyal and committed members of the inner circle were composed of York's ministers, his chief propagators, his *mujahid* (bodyguards and security force), and his "wives" or concubines.[15]

The Ministers preached, taught and presided over the Question&Answer meetings that were held on Sunday afternoons at bookstores located in the crowded black ghetto areas of the major cities in America and the West Indies. These bookstores were called *The Tents of Kedar* during the AAC period, but they were renamed *All Eyes on Egipt* [SIC] after the group transformed into the Holy Tabernacle Ministries in 1992 and relocated from Brooklyn to Middle Georgia in 1993.

The Propagators were the fundraisers and missionaries who went out every day to work on the street as peddlers and "propagators" of "Right Knowledge." They sold exotic-scented oils and incense on the street. Beside *tableeghing* (missionary work) they sold Dr. York's "scrolls" and passed out flyers to spiritual seekers and pedestrians of African descent, seeking to engage them in philosophical discussions about "Right Knowledge." These men were given a certain quota to bring in, from $35 to $45 a day (sometimes $55). The Propagators who returned in the evening with less than the daily quota were chastised. Phillips' informants claim they were beaten up by the *Mujahid* (body guards) if they failed to bring enough cash home. One of Phillips' informants reports: "whoever was in charge would go on the radio (within the community) and announce: 'Brother so-and-so did not turn in the quota this morning.' Then they would send sisters out as spies on the brothers and see what they were doing and come back and report what they saw."[16]

A woman named Raisa, who was a fringe member of the AAC, relates an amusing story of how she fell in love with an Ansaar brother in 1979, and whenever she wanted to spend time with her "mate," she would invite him to spend the day at her house and she give him the necessary amount of money, so he could take a day off from propagating and meet his quota.[17]

Ansaar literature advocates polygamy, but in reality, only the top male leaders had more than one wife. A Propagator I spoke to on the street explained that a man had to be in the community at least ten years before he was eligible for a second

---

[15]   I suspect that the "glue" that keeps these long-term disciples adhering to the movement is their initiation into the secret Masonic orders that operate inside the more ephemeral series of groups. The men belong to the Order of Melchesidek, and the women to the Eastern Star. I became aware that York's masonry was more than just a series of fancy titles when I sat beside a brother on the bus to Georgia, and noticed he was reading a book illustrated with Egyptian symbols. When I asked to look at it, he snatched it away and said, "This is secret!" I also watched a parade at Tama Re where several Masonic brotherhoods marched past me, sporting Masonic symbols, aprons, Egyptian headdresses and military coats.

[16]   Bilal Phillips, *The Ansar Cult in America* (Riyadh, Saudi Arabia: Tawheed Publications, 1988), 156.

[17]   Phillips, 154-61.

wife ("otherwise the whole thing would degenerate into a sex trip"). Imam Isa explains in *Hadrat Fatimah, Part Two* that, ideally, a man should have four wives, one of each type: the Domestic Wife, the Companion Wife, the Educated Wife and the Cultured Wife, each wife specializing in certain tasks and possessing desirable qualities. The Domestic Wife does cooking and laundry, the Companion Wife listens to her husband's problems and offers friendship, the Educated Wife's job is "to be an encyclopedia of facts for her husband" and to educate the children, and the Cultured Wife creates money-making schemes for her husband, has knowledge of the arts and culture, and "is naturally talented at pleasing him sexually."[18]

A photograph of Dr. York with his four veiled wives is featured in *Hadrat Fatimah, Part Two*. The number four was traditionally allotted by Muhammad, but an ex-member and former wife I spoke to declared: "That was just to make us look more organized! He had a whole *bunch* of wives—at least 50. He just wrote that to appear more orthodox to the Muslims."

York's harem of women lived with him, or in adjoining apartments. During the AAC phase, they worked in the publishing office or in Passion, the recording studio. They spent their days researching material, typing, editing, printing and publishing the scrolls and handling mail orders and deliveries. Some of them presided over the children's boarding school as teachers or administers. They led a secluded life, apparently relegated to the domestic role. But York's wives and concubines actually ran the movement behind their veils. They controlled the finances, handled the publishing and the administration.

This work was described by Wafia, a former member, who was assigned to correspondence and filling book orders. She was told to answer each letter "as if we knew the person, using the scriptures." She was later relegated to packaging, mailing, supervising and eventually moved on to the kitchen where she "cooked food on a large scale for everyone who lived in the building."[19]

Mothers and pregnant women would apply for public assistance and turn their welfare checks over to the whole community. One of Phillips' informants described a woman who "was complaining that she had to turn over her whole check to the community, and sometimes she needed personal money to do things. So, she took some out secretly because it was hers. That's how they had to do it."[20] An interesting rationale for going on welfare was offered: "Isa justified this dependency on welfare by saying that during the time of slavery all black people got a certain amount of mules and after slavery it stopped, so this is a way of the white people paying black people back."[21]

Two lavish weddings were held in the AAC to celebrate the marriage of two second generation girls to men from the Middle East—one of them being York's

---

[18]   *Hadrat Fatimah, Part Two* (Brooklyn, N.Y.: The Original Tents of Kedar, 1988), 23-4.

[19]   Phillips, 136.

[20]   Phillips, 135.

[21]   Phillips, 151.

18-year-old daughter. She married As Sayyid Kamal Ahmad Hassib, the Arabic teacher in the community, in a ceremony in the mosque that blended Islamic and Jewish symbols and featured a procession under held canopies.[22] After that there were no weddings. Members simply chose their own "mates" in an informal fashion. York sometimes assigned "mates" for his men. On occasion, he would choose people who were completely inappropriate and match them together as a joke.[23]

Ansaar Women behind the Veil

The interviews offer glimpses into the appeal this way of life held for women.

Maryam was 22 when she joined the Montreal, Quebec community in 1983.[24] She was impressed by the spiritual prestige awarded to wives and mothers in the AAC, in contrast to "white society" where, she claimed, women are judged solely by their success in their careers:

> "Mother"…it's the greatest title that one could ever have. You're supposed to be educated, not just make being a wife and mother the last resort. In the western society, it's a sort of last resort. If you don't have brains, then you could be a wife and mother and let a man take care of you. But in Islam, a woman is different. A woman is very educated, because if she is not, her children won't be educated. She has to be educated. If you are educated and know how to run a home and take care of your husband and he takes care of you, then this is the best thing that can happen. He is a happy part of you, and you are a happy part of him, and both a happy part of the children.

Maryam explained why women are dependent upon the man in "Islam":

> The man is seen as the head. The woman can't get to paradise without the man… because the man was created in the heavens. Adam was up there with the angels while Eve was created on earth and in order for the woman to get back to heaven

---

[22]   Bill Osinski, *Ungodly: A True Story of Unprecedented Evil* (Eatonton, G.A.: Indigo Publishing Group, 2007), 60-61.

[23]   Interview with Jacob York on August 19, 2003 in his Boutique near the Roxy Theatre in Buckhead district of Atlanta, GA.

[24]   This interview was conducted by one of my Dawson students who attended the AAC meetings in Montreal in 1980, but then became a Rastafarian. He interviewed Maryam, a 22-year-old Dawson student who was involved in the AAC in Montreal from 1983 to 1984. At the time of this interview, in 1991, she was living with her Rastafarian husband and her small daughter, Fatimah. When asked why she joined the Ansaars, Maryam explained how she came to Montreal at the age of seven to live with her aunt, who worked as a housekeeper for a wealthy white family.

she has to be part of the man. …In other words, woman is nothing without the man.

Maryam claimed that the more labour pains a woman has, the more her sins will be washed away through her suffering, and the more children she has, "the more eligible she will be to enter paradise." She also defended wife beating ("but only as a last resort and not in front of family or friends, only in private and not on the face…to show marks…but on the soles of the feet").

When asked how she liked living communally with the Ansaars, she replied:

> I think it is perfectly fulfilling, because you do need someone to encourage you, someone to say, "OK, it's time to pray." I think you do need a communal life; the community finance where all the money is put into one, seeing about each other, taking care of your brother and sister's needs. It's a good way. It makes you very strong, but it takes a lot of washing on the inside. People come in with egos which need checking, because they don't want to be told to come and go at certain times. Communal life has regulations, just like society has regulations, but only, there's a broader expansion in society, where in a commune everybody has to check.

Maryam found traditional domestic chores less onerous because of collective cooperation:

> It's just like in a house where there is one woman, but, only thing, here is a number of people participating in all the household chores. Some take care of the children, cooking, sewing, teaching, washing, and if one is a dancer, she gives dance classes and things like that.

When asked how she felt about wearing the veil, Maryam described it as an empowering experience:

> I felt superior wearing the veil, because it was not easy. There were many women who liked everything about the movement except the veil. I liked fashion, but at that time I put away western ideas of beauty when I became a Muslim. I had to be strong to make such a move, knowing that when you walked down the streets. It made me feel like Eve when I learned that Eve dressed this way after the world got populated—also Sarah, Abraham's wife and all the other righteous women in the Bible. Personally, I felt I got more respect from men, especially men who knew themselves, who had an idea about who they are.[25]

Maryam was married briefly to a brother in the Montreal community. When it did not work out, she left and returned to her former husband who is a Rastafarian. Thus, it would seem, her views on women's role and marriage in the AAC reflect

[25] Interview with "Maryam."

the ideals of Islam set forth in the scrolls, rather than the lived experience. One lasting effect of Maryam's involvement in the AAC is that she continues to attends the mosque, if not regularly, she observes Ramadan. She follows the dietary taboos of Islam (eating pork and drinking wine) and the daily ablutions, and she avoid contact with dogs, and transmits these practices to her daughter.

Elizabeth joined the AAC in 1986.[26] She had lived in Puerto Rico as part of the AAC mission from 1997 to 2002 with her husband. She had met him in Brooklyn when she was going to Monroe College. He was a propagator selling oils and incense on the street. She stopped to talk to him, and eventually asked permission to move into the community. For her, the appealing aspect of this life was the fellowship she enjoyed with other women:

> I felt safer in the Community. I would babysit the administration's kids. We [the woman] all lived together, we would call each other "sister" and we grew very close. I missed my sisters when I moved to Puerto Rico. There were only three guys, and although my husband was wonderful with me, I missed the girl talk. I was so close to my sisters in Brooklyn.

The Role of Children

Children played a central role in the apocalyptic expectations of the AAC, for the salvation of their parents depended upon them. There were over 100 children living in the AAC, according to Fatimah, one of Phillips' informants, who were "the children of the sisters who worked at Passion, children of the other sisters who were in the community, and children of a lot of sisters who had left."[27] Ansaar children were raised communally, and separated from their parents. One woman described how she decided not to join the ACC because she disagreed with the way they restricted the members' contact with their own parents outside the AAC, and with the way they separated children from their parents inside the community:

> I didn't like being told I couldn't visit my children except at certain times of the day. That I could not just walk in and do what I wanted to with my child. I was told that we do this because our children are not ours, they only come through us. And we have bad habits from the *Dunyaa* and we would inflict these habits on our children so it is best that they stay pure and stay separate from us.[28]

Dr. York (whose title was "Imam Isa" at the time) expounds upon the notion of "genetic breeding" as part of his millenarian plan in the *Nubian Bulletin, Ed. 9:12*.

---

[26]   This informal interview took place while we were waiting outside the Brooklyn mosque for the bus to arrive, that would take us to Tama Re.

[27]   Phillips, 152.

[28]   Phillips, 159.

He exhorts Ansaar parents to make haste in giving birth to the 144,000 "Nubian" children who will "rapture" their parents when the reign of Shaytan winds down to an end around the year 2000. Imam Isa warns his Nuwaubians that, because they are "subliminally taught that light skin is more attractive," they will tend to choose a light-complexioned mate, and produce children who, in four generations, will have straight hair.[29] He warns them that the Paleman is "trying to break the code in order to break the Nubian race and repair his own decaying race… . He will try to pick apart our genes and take what is beneficial to him…and incorporate it into himself." This is why the Paleman is resorting to "sperm banks, fertilized egg banks and DNA banks," he explains.

Imam Isa outlines his principles of eugenics as follows: "If a man has sex after his three-month period of perfection and a woman before, then they will produce a perfect child." But, he warns, "if the man has sex before the three month period of perfection, whereas the woman abstains for three months, then her genes will dominate the male genes and the child will come out looking like her. The sex of the child can be determined by diet, for foods with zinc will help produce a male child."[30]

This passage might be interpreted as offering a rationale for York's practice of sleeping with his disciples' wives and mates. Since the women were all living with York, or in same-sex quarters nearby, if they were to have sex outside the three-month period, the only man available to them would, in fact, be Dr. Malachi Z. York. One of Phillips' female informants noted that whenever a good-looking sister joined the community, she would be assigned to work in *Passion*, Isa's recording studio, located at 716 Bushwick Avenue.[31] Isa's living quarters were attached to the studio, and the woman would soon join the ranks of his concubines.

Phillips' informants report that men were denied access to their wives or "mates" until they brought in sufficient funds. Then they would be rewarded by an overnight assignation in the "Green Room, also known as "Eden"—a room decorated with murals of a tropical plants and jungle scenes. Many of Phillips' informants complained of how their sex life was controlled by Imam Isa. There appears to be some truth in this complaint, for the Nuwaubian "factology" website offers an apologetics for the Green Room:

> Resurfacing is the history of one of our schools (Islam). Green rooms were lodgings for couples who achieved a certain criterion, to spend a night therein. We lived communally and genders were separated. A few faultfinding former fellows feel, "oh, the embarrassment…they wanted to control our sex lives!" Followers joined the Ansaaruallah community to grow spiritually, advance the cause and were always free to leave.[32]

---

[29]   *Nubian Bulletin* (Brooklyn, N.Y.: Holy Tabernacle Ministries, 1992), 12.

[30]   *Nubian Bulletin*, 1992, 17.

[31]   Phillips, 152.

[32]   "Green Room Blues" (www://factology.com/20020921.htm#york). Downloaded 28/01/2008.

Some reminiscences of the children's life in the boarding school were provided by two men who had spent their childhood inside the AAC. They both described a happy, privileged childhood.

Yusuf's parents joined the AAC when he was a child, and they left with him when he was in his teens. He described an idyllic childhood in the children's commune: of visits to the theatre, the zoo, museums, of eating good food and living in pleasant quarters. He mentioned that he did not miss his mother, like some of the other children, because she made a point of being a teacher in the school so that she could spend the days with him. When I interviewed him, he had just completed his Masters thesis at Cornell University in History, and was starting his first job as a High School teacher.[33]

Jacob (cited above) defected from the AAC at the age of 16 with his mother. Paradoxically (since he is a hostile apostate) he described his childhood in the AAC as a positive experience:[34]

> At first we [the York Family] lived in the top floor of the building in Brooklyn. We were the Royal Family. We [my brothers and sisters] would get up at six, and by seven we were in school. I played with the other kids. Then I went to the AAC boarding school from the age of 10-16. I liked it. We were highly privileged children. Babah (it means "Father" in Arabic—that's what we called him then) would take us on trips by plane to the Middle East, and we would all go out to museums, to the zoo, to the theatre. We would all dress in white, we had good food, good teachers, a great education. There would be a lot of parties—it was fun. Sometimes my brother and I wore gold crowns for special occasions. I felt uncomfortable at home because of how everyone was always kissing my Dad's ass. "Can you bless my baby?" these women were always asking me, shoving their babies in my face. It was weird!

When I asked him about the children's curriculum, he replied:

> The kids in the community all spoke Arabic and some Hebrew. We also studied Nubic…it's a combination of Ebonics and bad Arabic, mispronounced. He [York] made it up himself. I didn't learn to speak English until I was ten. In 1984 the truancy officer came and found that none of the children who grew up in the community could speak a word of English, so the Board of Education insisted that all the children have private tutoring in English. So, we had a crash course in English and then we were sent to out to regular schools. The tutor would come every evening and help us.

---

[33]   Yusuf's M.A. thesis is called "The Ansaaru Allah Community" and is available in the Africana collection at Cornell University Library.

[34]   Interview with Jacob York, August 19, 2003.

Three Conversion Motives

The disciples' motivation for conversion to this radical new religion appears to fall into three categories: a) the appeal of Black Nationalism; b) the quest for the "true Islam"; c) the need for moral reform.

The theme of Black Nationalism surfaced in many of these interviews. Maryam noted, "my whole childhood I spent with white people and it was not until I was in High School that I found a group of black friends. I was into black awareness… black history, anything black attracted me."

Maryam's girlfriend lent her one of Dr. York's books. "Being raised in a white family, and knowing everything about white superiority, it made me feel good to know Jesus is black. The first man Adam was black. I intended to go the full length, to get involved strongly."

When asked if her experience in the AAC had had any lasting impact on her life, she answered that her view of white people changed:

> I always see them as devils, but I had white friends growing up. My first seven years were with white people. But when I got to high school and I found out about Black Power, I realized they were the reason for a lot of black people's problems. Before joining Ansaar I see them as the reasons to why we are the way we are. After joining Ansaar, I saw their *nature*. Ansaar taught me about the nature of the white man, which is a devilish nature. I saw their nature as human devil. They are like the Devil's seed… . But all of them are not evil…I think the Maker chooses who He wants to be good and He makes them good, but in such a way that they will help black people. They are used in this way. The black man has a natural instinct to be good…the white man, it's easier for him to be bad and harder to be good. The difference between us is the physical heart.[35]

Raisa Muhammad is another informant who spoke of the appeal of York's racialist message. She joined at 21 through one of the brothers *tableeghing* on the street in New York:

> I was interested in Black awareness, and a lot of the Ansar doctrine has to do with being Black, your roots, etc., the oppression of the Black man and Black woman and so on… . It also attracted me because I had dealt with the Nation of Islam at one point.[36]

---

[35] It is interesting to note that Maryam was quite frank in revealing her negative feelings concerning white people in this interview conducted by a young Trinidadian Rastafarian, and I suspect she might have been less forthcoming had I interviewed her myself.

[36] Phillips, 173.

A minister at the Atlanta bookstore and one of the Triad, described how his black awareness began as a child:

> Growing up as a child in North Carolina, I would get beaten up for going to a "whites only" bathroom. One day when I was six I was playing in the park, and I needed to go to the bathroom. I had just learned how to read, so I looked at the sign. There were two bathrooms. One said "White," and one said "Colored"…so I thought, "Hmmm, well, I know sinks are white, so that must be the cleaner one!" So I went in, and there were some white men in there and they said, "what are you doing here, kid!"—and they beat me up! And then, when I got older, I still couldn't understand. I told them my name was Evans, so how come they call me names like "nigger," "coon," "jigaboo?" So, I decided to devote my life to solving the problem. And in the Nuwaubians we know we are not what they call us. We know we have a culture, an identity. So I decided to spend my life helping my family. Always remember your family and never forsake them!

Abdul-Hakim, an ex-member interviewed by Bilal Phillips, noted: "They also come at you with this "Blackism" thing and black people in our country don't have an identity, so he comes in with this Black Sudanese thing to give you identity. You feel bad about yourself as a person and he comes with this philosophy, it kind of bowls you over."[37]

Rodney, a Propagator in his late 20s, expressed a post-9/11 disillusionment with the American Empire, and forged a racialist interpretation of these cataclysmic events. He was raised as a Jehovah's Witness and spent his childhood going door-to-door as a missionary ("I stopped at 18 because I realized it was false. Right Knowledge is more reasonable, because it deal with facts"). After he left the Jehovah's Witnesses, he studied witchcraft, telepathy, spiritualism, levitation, and the "flip side of things." He described his dramatic conversion experience to "Nuwaupu" as follows:

> I had a job on Wall Street working with a company that provided security in computers. When 9/11 came, I was right there! I was already aware that America is responsible for most of the suffering and famine in the world, but after the terrorist attack, I was shocked! People were saying "why is this happening?" I looked on it as an attack of reprisals. So I joined [the Nuwaubians] after September 2001. I thought, 'How could they do this? We must never forget!' You need to have a cold heart to survive in this system, and it is made up of mostly Caucasions. 'OK, I thought, these people are really evil!' So I decided to find out more about my own culture, where I came from. I was able to accept the ways we do things to stay on top. At first, I wanted to be a 5% er or a Muslim, so I went to a brother selling oils and books. I needed to find out about me! I went to *All Eyes on Egipt* [the bookstore]. Some things [about the UNNM] are

---

[37]   Phillips, 174.

far fetched, but life changes things. I became more positive. I became happier. I know who I am. Being around Truth—then you go in what direction you want to go. Instead of having a job, I propagate the Truth. If I ever go back to computers, I want to work for myself. Last year, at the Zed festival, I saw a UFO behind the pillar of the Pharoah!

The "Real Islam." After the death of Elijah Muhammad in 1975, his son and successor, Warith Deen Muhammad, led his flock back into mainstream Sunni Islam, discarding his father's racialist rhetoric and apocalyptic expectations.[38] York was quick to exploit this situation and attacked the spiritual credentials of both Elijah Muhammad and his son Warith in his scrolls. Several interviewees noted that they were dissatisfied with other available forms of Islam in America, finding them overly accommodating towards white society. The Ansaars appeared on the surface to be more "orthodox" than the Nation of Islam, simply because of their strict dress code and communal way of life. Phillips cites three informants who are searching for the "real Islam":

Siddiq Muhammad who joined in 1968 and was one of York's five initial followers, states: "I was totally fed up with the Darul-Islam Movement, may Allah reward them for their efforts, but what they taught was not good enough for me."

Wafia 'AbdAllaah, a Trinidadian woman, who joined at 19, notes, "the first time I encountered the group, I was just introduced to Islaam and I was looking for someone to give me more Islaam. [My husband and I] thought their teachings were more militant than the World Community [of Warith Deen Muhammad]. They seemed to be more definite about what they were doing."[39]

Abdul-Mutta'aal, who joined in 1974, states, "the most important thing that attracted me was their Imaam. He writes his books by using the Bible. He sort of appealed to both sides by accepting the Bible (the Christians used to say the Qur'aan was wrong, and the Muslims said the Bible is wrong)."

Muhammad, a man in his sixties, was in the Nation of Islam for five years (1963-68) before he encountered the AAC. He explained in our interview why he changed his allegiance:

> I was a Muslim prison chaplain on Long Island, connected with Malcolm [X] in the Harlem Temple No. 7, on Seventh Avenue. I first saw Malcolm when he gave a talk on vice—on smoking cigarettes, drinking and eating pork. I felt he was talking to me. He proved in his talk that cigarettes were shit. He said, `Take green weed, store it in a silo, you see, turns brown. Wrap it up in toilet paper, what is it called—BUTTS? Tramps pick them up, you see... .' I never smoked again after that. He also told us not to eat pork because the pig is part dog.

---

[38] Martha Lee, *The Nation of Islam: An American Millenarian Movement* (Syracuse, N.Y.: Syracuse University Press, 1996), 19.

[39] Phillips, 133.

At the time I was hustler, a card sharp, I used to gamble in bars. I used tricks, fraud, to rip off people at Long Island. I started out when I met a guy from Brooklyn who taught me to be a card sharp—we were partners for a while....

Then Farrakhan became the leader after Malcolm left, and replaced him as the national spokesman. He was assigned to New York, and I was a minister under him. For seven years I worked in a prison program at the Suffolk county correctional facility. I was a Muslim chaplain in a Long Island prison. We had a service for Muslims, we provided gowns for their service, and made sure they had a pork-free diet while in prison. I saw myself as a Muslim chaplain. I was one of the few ministers who was there when Warith [Muhammad] came in transformed the Temple into a Mosque. The Ansaar Community offered to teach us *Salaat* of traditional Islam, and help train Imams how to lead *Salaat*. We had unity meetings. All the Ansaar members came to our mosque on Sunday, then we would go to their meeting. We exchanged scrolls for information. It was very progressive. It wasn't necessary to join the [Ansaar] Community [to participate].

Then I joined the Islaamic Hebrews in 1968. I dressed in white and start to sell oils.... . It had its own atmosphere, the same goals [as the NOI]. I read the scrolls—at first only to prove them incorrect—but I am still here today!

[Later] I joined the Holy Tabernacle Ministries...where I could be ordained, get credentials, for my work in the prison. This was an effort by Malachi to bring all the religions together—the Jubilee every 50,000 years. I had read the Scrolls, studied the dates, checked all the references. Maku [York] wants me to write a book on how I went from NOI to Ansaar.[40]

Sayid, a second-generation member of the Nation of Islam, also switched allegiances:

My parents were in the NOI, but I joined the Ansaars in 1982. I was staying at the army base and a friend invited me to a meeting for Muslims. A lot of NOI stood up and introduced themselves, then one man said "I'm an Ansaar." "What's that?" I asked him later. He gave me books when I met him in Brooklyn. I checked it out. I read Dr. Malachi York on prayer. "That's deep" I thought— then I discovered there was a whole neighbourhood of Ansaars. So I started to go to the meetings to hear what Dad [York] had to say on Islam. He gave you a deconstruction, he told what it really means, and would end up with, "Muhammad did it! So now you do it!" After several years, the brothers would say, "Hey man! Why don't you join us?" So, I finally put in my application—but then I discovered they'd all moved to the mountains—everyone had left. That was in 1988, when everything suddenly changed. Suddenly, no more Islam, it

---

[40]   I interviewed this man sitting on a bench outside the Museum of Black History at Tama Re. I had seen him often at the Brooklyn bookstore, and he told me he had been in the (Masonic) Ancient Egiptian Order since 2000.

was all about "Right Knowledge" "Factology"—a lot of people left then. Those that stayed on would listen to him attack religion—tell them to check it out, do their own research—just stick to the facts… . I went to a meeting with some other Muslim brothers. Dad attacked Islam—he picked up the Qur'an and threw it on the floor—and stepped on it! Wooah! He said, "you might think I am crazy, but check it out for yourself!" So we left saying he is crazy—that was too much. (We were heavily into the Islam trip.)

Then, a few years later, I went to a Muslim meeting and a brother from the Holy Tabernacle Ministries was there and showed me the latest books. I told him I used to be in the Ansaars and left, and he said, "Hey man, why did you leave?" So, we started to talk and stayed up all night in a hotel lobby and he showed me the books and I thought, "this stuff is deep"! So, I came back. I joined the Ancient Order of Melchesideck.

(I asked Sayid what he thought of Dr. York):

Dad? He's *bad*, man![41] Someone would be giving the class and Dad would be sitting quietly in the audience, we wouldn't notice him, and someone would ask a question—and suddenly, he'd stand up and say, "No, this is the way it goes!" He was *bad*, man![42]

Moral Reform

Like the Nation of Islam and the Nation of Yahweh, the Nuwaubian Nation offers a new way of life and new hope for repentant criminals and "sinners." Several disciples I interviewed described how they were converted while in prison. Others were former street hustlers or con artists who repented their immoral ways and seized the chance to live a clean, upright way life. The Ansaars have an extensive prison outreach. Sheriff Sills (the Nuwaubians' main cultural opponent in Georgia) told me about this program:

We get a lot of calls from prisons because of the Nuwaubian outreach. They have their literature in prison libraries, they have missionaries go in. They had a lot of the questions about the nomenclature—the specialized words; the Arabic, their made-up "Nubic" language, the way the group keeps changing its name. We get calls from all over the U.S.—and I notice there seems to be a *lag*—the literature in the prisons is not the current ideology—they tend to be out of touch with the

---

[41] I was puzzled by this expression until I realized it actually meant "good."

[42] I interviewed this disciple during the bus ride from Brooklyn to Tama Re. He was home on leave from the U.S. army in Iraq because he had injured his hand lifting weights. He was hoping to cure himself before his wedding, to be held next summer.

latest changes. For example, there are some prisons in the Caribbean or some states where they are still known as the Ansaaru Allah![43]

Bilal. I interviewed "Bilal" at Tama Re, after watching him win a few rounds of Speed Chess. He was 46, and a self-confessed former 3-cup monty swindler, who had lived for many years by his wits on the street. He told me he would earn up to $400 a day, but then would go out and spend it all on bars, women, booze, crack, cocaine.

> I would see the Ansaar brothers peddling on the street and felt sorry for them. So I would buy the books. I thought maybe they have a wife and kids, and I would just spend it all anyway. So, I had all these [AAC] books stacked up in my apartment. One day it was raining and I decided to just stay home. I got tired of earning money and blowing it the same day with drink and drugs. I realized I was stuck in a cycle—the same thing over and over. So, I picked up *The Making of a Disciple*. I read it right through, then picked up the rest of Pop's books. When I finished, I threw my hands in the air! 'This is it man! This is me! I've found the answer!' I felt he was talking right to me.
>
> So, I started going to the mosque. It changed my life. Pops [York] helped me to give up drugs. I discovered the power of prayer. For example, recently I prayed that I would have my kids come and live with me (I am no longer with their mother). Then, suddenly she got sick (I did not pray for that!)—and now they live with me.[44]

Mounting Conflict

In the late 1970s tensions between the AAC and secular authorities escalated. The first police investigation concerned the murder of Horace Green, a local daycare worker. Green had been lobbying to halt what he feared as the AAC's "takeover" of his neighborhood in Brooklyn, and had refused an offer on his building. On the morning of 19 April 1979 he was shot dead as he went to open the daycare center that he managed on Hart St., near the AAC mosque. Suspicion fell upon Roy Savage, known as "Hasim the Warrior" who (according to FBI informants T-5 and T-4) was part of the *Mujahim*. Savage's guilt was never proven and the murder remains unsolved to this day.

A criminal investigation into possible arson was launched after a series of five fires broke out near the AAC mosque on Bushwick Avenue between 1976 and

---

[43]   Interview with Sheriff Sills on 14 August 2003 in the Sheriff's office in Eatonton, GA.

[44]   I found out later that Bilal used to live in the AAC and had worked as a propagator, but left because he found the life too restricting. He continues to attend the Sunday meetings and has many friends in the movement.

1991—fires that facilitated the AAC's expansion into the area, at least according to the FBI Report:

> It is common knowledge that many buildings in the areas in Brooklyn…had mysteriously burned [and] York would subsequently purchase these properties at city auction.

In 1983 York purchased an 81-acre camp near the town of Liberty in Sullivan County, N.Y. for Camp Jazzir Abba. The AAC constructed six bungalows and a huge house built around a double-wide trailer and proceeded to hold summer camps for AAC families.[45] Armed guards and dogs manned the gate of Camp Jazzir Abba. Inspectors were sent in to check on building codes and land use violations.

An AAC newsletter from that period advertises workshops in survival skills, in preparation for impending disasters. It features a photograph of military training exercises with rifles. In October 1983 the NYSP received complaints of gunfire coming from Camp Jazzir Abba in Sullivan County, New York. The informant T-2 claimed he had seen many guns and thousands of rounds of ammunition at the Camp Abba Jazzir. In May 1989 the BATF began to investigate the guns purchased at various guns shops on Long Island by two of York's disciples, who gave the AAC address and were accompanied and driven away by Dr. York. The BATF reported that 19 assault rifles, one M1 and over 4000 rounds of ammunition were purchased in May to June 1989. The FBI Report features a list of the guns purchased in the New York area: seven Ruger mini-14's, four 12-gage shotguns and one .22 calibre rifle—all purchased within a four-month period.

A network of interest groups representing quite different concerns began to form, and to share information concerning the AAC. These groups included orthodox Muslim missions, the NYPD, the Welfare Office, the IRS, the INS, the FBI, the ATF, and disgruntled ex-members, who were beginning to form their own, informal networks. The 1993 FBI report records the various complaints received from the different interest groups. The report cites fifteen confidential informants and calls for a "full domestic terrorism investigation" of the AAC. The criminal connections of the AAC are mentioned, and it notes that many of York's disciples are ex-convicts or parole violators. The view expressed in the FBI Report is that the AAC was not a real religious community, but rather a criminal enterprise disguised as a religious community that harboured thieves, murderers and escaped convicts. But, like many religious movements that appealed to the underclass, like the Nation of Islam and early Christianity, the aim of the AAC's prison outreach was to *rehabilitate* criminals and to inspire a moral regeneration among the poor and oppressed black people of America.

---

[45]   Jacob York said in our interview that the camp was hardly the paramilitary training camp described in the FBI report. Rather it was used for recreation, and kids' summer holidays.

A few of York's disciples who had held high positions in the AAC defected and became his most vociferous critics. Two of his former wives filed child support actions against him: Pauline Rogers, who had three children by York, and Sakinah Parham, who had one son, filed their legal actions through the State Department of Human Resources' child support recovery office. These suits were later dropped, but the two women went on to testify against York and their stories of abusive treatment appear in Osinski's book.[46]

Another 38-year-old defector, Robert Rohan, claimed he was writing a book about his experiences in the Nuwaubian movement, called *Holding York Responsible*. Rohan joined the AAC in his early teens in 1980, and spent 16 years working as a Propagator, preaching and peddling on the streets of New York. He dropped out shortly after Dr. York abandoned Islam, when the group moved to Georgia and "claimed to be in affiliation with Masons and with the Jewish, Christian and Egyptian faiths." He explained to a journalist that "once [York] started changing religious ideas, the older followers became skeptical and left the group. That was what happened to me." Rohan's book portrays Dr. York as a charismatic con artist.[47]

Several of the male defectors became FBI informants. Saadik Redd joined in 1970 and worked for eight years as York's driver, accompanying him to Trinidad in 1978 to open a branch of the AAC. He also helped him establish the AAC in Baltimore and in Washington D.C. After serving York for eleven years, Redd left in 1981, claiming the AAC was not "true Islam." Saadik Redd's name appears in the 1993 FBI Report, where he describes the harsh living conditions inside the AAC. He claims he shared barracks with other men in an abandoned house with no heat or hot water or beds. He notes that the conditions in York's house were "totally opposite from how the people lived." He described York as an irresponsible womanizer: "He would meet a person and their wife and sleep with their wife just to show he had control over you."[48]

The FBI Report presents the vigilante peacekeeping activities of the AAC's *mujahim* as a "protection racket." The FBI's informant "T-C" claimed that in the summer of 1990 the AAC "muscled their way into a security contract with a number of local businesses and used force against the security company already under contract. On apprehending a shoplifter, the AAC guards would not call the police, but beat up the culprit themselves." Informant T-3 also claimed that the AAC raked in $5000 to $6000 a week in protection payment from intimidated storeowners.

---

[46]   Pauline and Sakinah appeared on the Montel Williams television show in 2007 to tell their stories.

[47]   Robert Rohan was interviewed by Sharon E. Crawford ("Former Nuwaubian writes book, tells how York duped followers," *Macon Telegraph*, 14 March 2005). This book he claimed to be writing has never been published, to my knowledge.

[48]   FBI Report, "The Ansaru Allah Community," 1993, 10.

The AAC received congratulations from Ed Koch, New York's mayor in the 1980s, for purging the Brooklyn streets of crime and drugs.[49] But at the same time the AAC was under investigation by the New York Police Department for suspected arson. The Federal Bureau of Investigation suspected the AAC of harbouring criminal fugitives and men who broke their parole, and the Bureau of Alcohol, Tobacco and Firearms launched an investigation into the AAC's alleged purchase of and stockpiling of illegal weapons.[50] Welfare officials were investigating the possibility of welfare fraud. The FBI's informant T-9 said that all the women in the AAC commune were on public assistance. As soon as one woman would become pregnant, T-9 claimed, all the other women would take a specimen of her urine to the women's center in Manhattan to obtain a letter verifying their pregnancy. By this means, every single woman was able to apply for welfare as an unwed mother, each using a different, fake address. These checks would be cashed and handed over to the AAC to support the commune.

The Muslim Counter-Cult Opposition

Meanwhile, various orthodox Sunni Muslim imams and missions in the area were denouncing Imam Isa as a heretic. Dr. York had condemned all previous translation of the Qur'an, claiming only his own "19th translation" was "the supreme Code of the Qur'an." He blasted mainstream Muslims for "hiding the fact" that Muhammad was black. He dismissed the first three Khalifs as usurpers, and rejected the "Caucasian" Abu Bakr as Muhammad's successor, implying that the lineage of Islam was compromised right at the beginning.[51] York then traced the "true line of succession" back to his great-grandfather, the Sudanese Mahdi, which made him, "Isa al Mahdi," the only legitimate successor to the Apostle of Allah. Finally, he antagonized the Nation of Islam by insisting that the Ansaaru Allah Community offered the one, exclusive path to salvation, and that he, Al Mahdi, was the One whom Elijah Muhammad of the Nation of Islam had come to herald.

In 1979 Dwight York formed a music group called *Doctor York and the Passion*, and began to perform in the nightclubs and dance halls of New York—an activity explained in his writings as a "sacrificial ministry."[52] The notion of an imam working as an entertainer was offensive to orthodox Muslim leaders, as was the early AAC custom of soliciting funds on trains.

Soon a counter-cult movement formed among the orthodox Muslim groups in the Brooklyn area to oppose the AAC, and local imams began to denounce

---

[49]   Conversation with Paul Greenwood, documentary filmmaker in Brooklyn, N.Y., July 2003.

[50]   FBI Report, "The Ansaru Allah Community," 1993: 6-12.

[51]   Phillips, 181-2.

[52]   Phillips, 13.

York's community as "a dangerous anti-Islamic cult operating in America." In 1988, Abu Ammeenah Bilal Philips wrote *The Ansaar Cult in America*, dedicated to "exposing the falsehood of heretical movements disguised under the cloak of Islam."

Initially, York weathered the criticism with aplomb. He denounced Bilal Phillips and other orthodox Sunni leaders in his scrolls, while freely appropriating passages from their sacred literature. Then, suddenly, he abandoned Islam altogether. An explanation of this abrupt transition was provided by his son, Jacob York:

> Then Dad wrote *360 Questions to Ask a Muslim*. This got a negative reaction from the Muslim community. He already had a lot of New York mosques opposing him. This was after the assassination of a Jewish journalist by a Muslim. The same man came to see Dad the day before and asked him to come downstairs and talk to him. But Dad never went, because he was changing his clothes and kept getting delayed. There were always a lot of people waiting to talk to him. Then, the next day he heard this guy had murdered a Jew. He concluded that someone had taken out a contract on him as a heretic, that if he'd gone downstairs, it would have been him who was killed. He was anti-Muslim after that.[53]

Jacob was referring to the 1992 assassination of Meir Kahane, the founder of the Jewish Defense League, by a Muslim terrorist, Sayid Nosair. Nosair was acquitted of Kahane's murder, but was later tried and convicted for his role in the 1993 World Trade Center bombing.

After this close encounter with an assassin, Dr. York wrote a book attacking Islam (*360 Questions to ask a Muslim*), and announced he was now "The Lamb, Liberator of Women." Women were instructed to take off their veils and modest robes. They were now permitted to wear shorts, drive cars and preach in the mosque—now referred to as a "Tabernacle."

The Nuwaubian movement transformed rapidly throughout the early 1990s. York debriefed the Ansaaru Allah Community, and called his movement The Holy Tabernacle Ministries, reverting to earlier Hebrew motifs. He adopted the Star of David as the main symbol, discarded the titles "Imam" and "Mahdi" in favour of "Rabboni" and "The Lamb." The movement adopted the umbrella name of United Nuwaubian Nation of Moors (UNNM) and sold all their properties in Brooklyn and relocated to Georgia, and began constructing an Egyptian village to be the Mecca in the West. They began to call themselves the "Yamassee Native American Moors of the Creek Nation" and they claimed their sacred territory in the state of Georgia ("The Land") was a "Sovereign Nation."

Once they moved to Georgia, the Nuwaubians were met with an overwhelming level of opposition that was impossible to evade, no matter how often Dr. York changed their costumes, religious affiliation, or revised his title.

---

53   Interview with Jacob York, August 19, 2003.

Figure 3   Sheriff Howard Sills at the gates of Tama Re

Chapter 4
Tama Re: The FBI Raid on a "Sovereign Nation"

In 1993 the HTM sold all its property in Brooklyn, headed south, and relocated in the Bible Belt of Middle Georgia. In making this migration they were reversing the narrative of the northward direction of alternative African-American spirituality, for Father Divine, Noble Drew Ali, Wallace Fard, and other great founders of Black nationalistic NRMs had all established their communities in the northern urban centers after the Great Migration in the first half of the twentieth century.[1]

Dr. York, accompanied by around 100 disciples, arrived in Eatonton, GA, and purchased 475 acres of land on 404 Shady Dale Road in Putnam County for $975,000. On this land, they proceeded to construct their communal residence, an "egiptian"-style village that was also designed as a theme park called "Tama Re."

The Nuwaubians were hoping to make a fresh start, to leave behind all the conflicts generated in Brooklyn during their "Muslim" phase. But, as it turned out, the opposition they had encountered in New York State was mild compared to what they were about to experience in Georgia.

Upon arriving, the group claimed to be a Native American tribe—the "Yamassee of the Creek Nation." Dr. York revealed that he was directly descended from Pocahontas and Ben York, a member of the Lewis and Clark expedition, through his mother's lineage.[2] He was now called by his tribal names, "Maku," or "Chief Black Eagle." The disciples changed their Middle Eastern garb to Western gear. They dressed in jeans, cowboy hats and boots—more practical for the construction work required for the building of Tama Re.

Tama Re was dominated by a black pyramid 40-feet in height, echoed by a smaller gold pyramid. Its winding avenues were set with pillars and benches which led past a five-foot concrete scarab beetle, a huge Sphinx with an African face, a museum of Black History, and boulevard lined with eight-foot animal-headed Egyptian deities. The most startling artifact of all was a black Jesus crucified on an Ankh crowned with the feathered headdress of the Plains Indian—a testament

---

[1]   Julius H. Bailey makes this interesting point in his paper, "The Final Frontier: Secrecy, Identity, and the Media in the Rise and Fall of the United Nuwaubian Nation of Moors," *Journal of the American Academy of Religion* (Volume 74, Number 2, June 2006), 302-23.

[2]   Frank Ford discovered a Nuwaubian newsletter on his doorstep that made this claim. See Bill Osinski, *Ungodly: A True Story of Unprecedented Evil* (Macon: Indigo Publishing Group), 122.

to the group's syncretistic creativity. Tama Re was built by voluntary laborers, by its residents and the visiting disciples over the summer months, between 1993 and 2000. By 2002, Tama Re's residents numbered around 400.

Tama Re was designed as an Egyptian theme park, as a money-making enterprise open for visitors, black or white, during the summer. But for York's disciples and American Black nationalists, it was a pilgrimage shrine, an American version of Mecca. As one Nuwaubian explained, "Dad wanted to build a Mecca in the West, a *Hadj* for people who couldn't afford it, who didn't have the money to travel all the way to the Mecca in the East."[3]

Tama Re was also known as "Wahanee," the sacred land of the Yamassee tribe. The Nuwaubians referred to it among themselves as "the Land," home to all Nubians in America, and a safe haven in the impending apocalypse. York declared the property a "Sovereign Nation," and on entering the gate, the visitor would enter the gift shop and purchase an "egiptian passport" and change U.S. currency into "egiptian" coins.[4]

Tama Re was also a showcase for Dr. Malachi Z. York; it supported his charismatic claims as a Black messiah. A week-long "Savior's Day" festival was held every summer to celebrate his 26 June birthday. (The celebration of Savior's Day was originally a Nation of Islam custom, but it had been appropriated by Dr. York).[5] The utopian appeal and symbolic importance of Tama Re for York's devotees was eloquently conveyed by a young woman I interviewed:

> I got the call to go to the Land early in the 1990s—my husband went first, and I stayed because my father was ill. Finally I got to go! We all drove to Georgia in a big van. The van was driving past…I didn't know this was the Land, but I put my hands on the window—and suddenly I felt them tingle! I felt I was home! The van suddenly turned left—and it was The Land! There was a big party going on, and I was invited to sing for Dad's Birthday. After the party, late at night, everyone sat around in a circle in chairs, and he made me feel so welcome! The sun was going down, and I felt so happy! It was like I was back home, he made me feel so welcome! We all wore cowboy hats. He spoke. I got everything he said, I felt I was levitating. Then, after a while, it didn't make any sense at all what he said—because I felt so light, like I was floating. After, we talked in the van, going back to the hotel, we talked—and we all felt the same thing![6]

---

[3]   Interview with Prescott at Tama Re, June 24, 2003.

[4]   Ellen Barry, "His Dream became their nightmare," *Los Angeles Times*, 22 January 2004.

[5]   In the Nation of Islam, Savior's Day was to commemorate Wallace Fard, the messianic founder, not Elijah Muhammad, His Messenger.

[6]   Interview with Aisha in June 2003, conducted in Brooklyn while waiting outside the bookstore for the bus transporting Nuwaubian pilgrims to Tama Re (it was delayed by three hours).

Tama Re was also a "Noah's Ark" imbued with apocalyptic significance. In 1993 York had revealed himself to be as an extraterrestrial from another planet come to rescue the 144,000 Chosen Ones from an impending cataclysmic destruction:

> I, YAANUWN, Am An ANUNNAQI Or What You Would Call An Extra-Terrestrial.... I Am What You Would Call An Angelic Being [from] ILLYUWN [a tri-solar system with 38 moons and 19 planets].... I Have Incarnated Here in This Form To Act As A Human Being For The Sole Purpose Of Saving The Children of The ELOHEEM (ANUNNAQI).... The Chosen 144,000.... I YAANUWN, Have Come To Save The Children Of The ELOHEEM (ANUNNAQI) From Being Killed As You Bring Your Planet Near To What Could Be Its Total Destruction.[7]

York's disciples understood that a "Mothership" from the planet Rizq, bearing the angelic Anunnaqi, would descend on Tama Re's 40-foot pyramid on 5 May 2003 to carry away 144,000 Nuwaubians before the destruction of the world.[8] Thus, there was a sense of urgent millenarian expectation among many of the pilgrims who converged on Tama Re. This was confirmed by a registered nurse from Brixton, U.K. with whom I conversed during the June 2004 Saviour's Day festival.

> I had heard about The Land, a place where all black people were welcome and would be safe. I had the feeling something bad was going to happen, so I saved up to come out here. I took time off—and as soon as I saw the pyramids from the bus window—I knew I belonged here, I felt I was home, it was *my* Land.

The Savior's Day festival attracted many African-Americans. The ranks of pilgrims swelled from 2000 to 5000 between 1999 and 2001. They came from the West Indies, the Southern states, Canada, and as far away as Brixton, U.K. to converge on the tiny town of Shady Dale, Georgia. Many of York's followers uprooted their lives and relocated to Georgia, finding work and lodging in the nearby towns. But for many of the visitors and pilgrims at the festival, Tama Re was just a family outing to a fantasy

---

[7] *Man from Planet Rizq* no date, circa 1993, 23.

[8] This prediction is quoted widely in the media, and York's disciples don't deny it, but I have not been able to track down its source. It does not appear in any of the scrolls, to my knowledge. The disciples have confirmed the notion that a "Mothership" is expected to arrive and take them away, but those I spoke to disagreed that there was a specific date—certainly 5 May 2001 had passed uneventfully. The roots of this apocalyptic mythology can be traced back to Zechariah Zitchin whose 1976 bestseller provided the framework for the myth of the Anunnaki, an alien race from the planet Niburu who came to earth to mine gold with the aid of a slave race of genetically-modified apes, and commenced to breed with humans and found great civilizations like the Sumerians. In Dr. York's version, the Anunnaki are the ancestors of the Black man. Cross-breeding between extraterrestrials and humans gave rise to the other races on our planet.

theme park that provided an education in Black history for their children—and an opportunity to dabble in esoteric philosophy and ufological lore.[9]

The Escalating Conflict

The AAC had become a familiar sight in New York City, where eccentricity reigns and the Nuwaubians were not much stranger than Rastafarians or NOI brothers. But in the Southern Bible Belt, in Middle Georgia, where the confederate flag was still flying in many of their neighbor's yards, they were a startling anomaly. Articles soon appeared in the local newspapers that described the group as a "quasi-religious sect"; as a gang of weird black guys with Brooklyn accents, who dressed up as cowboys, and pretended to be Indians, who were building huge pyramids out on a cow pasture. "The Nuwaubians: who are these people?" *The Macon Telegraph* asked.[10]

The first news reports portrayed the Nuwaubians in a light-hearted fashion, as simply bizarre. But as the construction of Tama Re progressed, the Nuwaubians began to experience a series of legal and bureaucratic obstacles to their utopian enterprise—and the media began to present them in a more threatening light.[11]

The Building and Zoning Conflicts

Howard Sills took office as the sheriff of Putnam County in 1997. When I conversed with Sheriff Sills on Thursday, 14 August 2003 in his office in Eatonton, he said,

---

[9]   This was my impression, based on my conversations with many pilgrims, when I attended the Savior's Day festival at Tama Re for ten days in June 2004. I was unable to get any cooperation in conducting a membership survey, but it was my initial impression that Dr. York's following were "upwardly mobile." The older disciples who joined in the 1970s during the Ansaaru Allah days tended to lack formal education; they might be described as blue-collar workers or street peddlers and some had a criminal history. In contrast, the younger members, the "propagators" (missionaries) and administrative leaders were more likely to have university degrees and professional status; to be lawyers, accountants, notaries, computer programmers, teachers, and engineers. Their politics tended to be Republican. In response to my opening question, "What first attracted you to The Knowledge?" some of the older disciples described traumatic experiences of racial discrimination from their childhood. The younger disciples, raised in the post-civil rights culture, tended to express a more general *malaise* towards/ disillusionment with the U.S. government and its post-9/11 anti-Muslim propaganda.

[10]   Matthew Pinzur, "The Nuwaubians: who are these people?" *The Macon Telegraph*, 15 May 2000.

[11]   Vicky Eckenrode, "Mystery Circles Georgia's Clan of Nuwaubians," *Atlanta Chronicle*, 25 February 2001. See also Rob Peecher, "Reaction to Nuwaubians mixed in Putnam County," *Macon Telegraph*, 8 August 1999.

"Dwight York came into my life seven years ago. I could talk for a whole month about what has happened." He then described his first impressions of York:

> The first time we met I didn't know who he was. This was when I went to the compound with the building inspector. I accompanied the building inspector (with my gun on). We told the guard who we were, then waited 30 minutes. Finally, we saw a group of men start to walk towards us down the driveway. There was one man in the center and half a dozen surrounding him, they had this big mean look. The man in the middle wore black pajamas with gold embroidery and gold chains. He was a small, thin man and when he came up to us he broke into a diatribe and proceeded to curse the building inspector. "No good son of a bitch!" he said. His entourage were bad ass-looking guys and just stood there, staring. Then, he suddenly broke off his diatribe and turned around and left. The building Inspector came back the next day and was eventually allowed in so he could do his job. Then, a week later, the police of the Atlanta crime division sent me a tape of York speaking, and I said, "Hell! That was York I met!"
>
> After that we were besieged with calls about the criminal activities of some of the members. We get a lot of calls from prisons because of the Nuwaubian outreach. They have their literature in prison libraries, they have missionaries go in... . I asked to meet with him several times, I spoke with him [after the raid] when he was in my jail, but he and I have never had a conversation without counsel about criminal matters. I have always found York to be pleasant with me—of course his flunkeys call me a "racist."

Sheriff Sills explained how the first conflict between the Nuwaubians and Georgian officials began in 1997, when the guards who manned the obelisk-flanked gates to Tama Re refused entry to local building inspector "Dizzy" Adams, who had been sent to inspect their construction projects:

> I got a court order and went out there. "Let the building inspector on your property! Do not interfere," I told them. Here we were, facing the guards who were wearing guns and saying, "No, you can't come on our land, we are a Sovereign Nation." What was I supposed to do? They had guns, and my job was to disarm them. I had the choice of going from conversation to deadly force—and there was no in-between! They were begging for a Waco! So, I just withdrew with the building inspector and came back the next day. I could not let them wilfully disobey the law... . I became aware of what a volatile situation I had been dragged into... when I heard them say, "we are not subject to your laws!"[12]

This conflict was resolved peacefully, but the next year, in March 1998, a local television show sparked a new conflict over zoning. Sills was watching an Atlanta

---

[12]   Interview with Sheriff Howard Sills in his office in Eatonton, GA, 14 August 2003.

TV news report featuring the lively dance parties taking place in the "Ramses Social Club" out at Tama Re:

> They were on TV—the network showed the nightclub, in a 100-foot storage building—it had been turned into a disco, multilevel, with a stage, restrooms, a gift shop, a bar. The area was not zoned for commercial use; they had no license to sell alcohol.

Dizzy Adams, the building inspector, had given Victor Greig (the Nuwaubian administrator in charge of building matters) a permit to use the 100 x 50-foot metal storage building on the premises. But the Nuwaubians had enlarged it, added bathrooms, extensive lighting and sound equipment, and an Egyptian façade—and it became known as the "Ramses nightclub." A fire marshal was sent out to inspect the building, but he was turned away at the gate. Sheriff Sills then decided to accompany him the next day, bringing along a booklet on fire regulations to show to the Nuwaubians:

> He told them it was unsafe because of wires, generators, the stove. "You can't occupy it!" he told them. But they kept right on. Finally, the inspector came in and padlocked the building. Legal inspection gave them the opportunity to get it rezoned, but they did not succeed. Then the injunction became permanent. The nightclub was locked up.[13]

Greig was charged by Sills and the fire marshal for violating building codes. In April 1998 Grieg was fined $45,750 by Judge Sylvia Huskins.[14] In May 1998, Sheriff Sills sought an injunction to prevent the use of the Ramses club, and the same month the Nuwaubians applied for a zoning permit to build an Egyptian theme park (which was refused). The Nuwaubians' perspective on the zoning controversy was expressed by one of the administrators of Tama Re:

> We bring too much consciousness and awareness focus on Egypt. Our money was not going into the town folk who try to monopolize on different venues inside the city limits. To avoid trouble with the Sheriff, you must use Horton Homes (mobile homes), but our constructions are Native American or African. Egypt is in Africa. If we had used *their* constructions and supported local trade, they would have helped us. Down South there's the good old boys' circuit![15]

Another Nuwaubian protested, "It was *never* a nightclub—I don't know why they called it a "nightclub." It was just our *social club* where we could sit comfortably

---

13   Interview with Sheriff Howard Sills.
14   This amount was reduced later to $2500 at the Georgia Court of Appeals.
15   Interview with Khunsu Hotep, 25 June 2003 at Tama Re.

with our kids and watch a show, have a meeting—you know we don't drink alcohol."[16]

The Savior's Day Showdown

Huge crowds of York's black supporters would converge on the sparsely populated farmland of the Eatonton area for the week-long festivals that, in June 1997 and 1998, attracted as many as 4000 to 5000 people and brought in around $500,000 a year. The festival also brought in business for the local townspeople, but it was feared that the sheer numbers of pilgrims posed a security risk. Moreover, the adulation expressed for Dr. York raised the usual fears about "cults" and cult leaders who "brainwash." Sherriff Sills noted this in our interview:

> When they started to talk about the Mothership coming to take away·144,000 chosen ones to the planet Risq…well, that's when people saw them as an alien cult, like Heaven's Gate. I began to receive calls asking if they were a cult and if they were going to commit mass suicide.[17]

A local white woman was quoted in the *New York Times* saying, "this man was going to take over the county. He was going to take it over!"[18] Local journalists characterized the UNNM as a "racist" organization, and the townspeople began referring to the Nuwaubians as "the Waubs."

In February 1999 Dr York transferred the ownership of his Tama Re property to Tama Re Enterprises, and in June 1999 to nine of his followers, with Al Woodall acting as the manager of the trust.[19] But, according to Osinski, no money ever changed hands. Around the same time, York purchased a $285,000 building in Athens for his private residence. In February 2000 the land of Tama Re was temporarily put up for sale.[20]

On June 22, 1999 Dr. York ignored Superior Court Judge Hugh V. Wingfield III's order to appear in the Putnam County court on a contempt motion filed by the

---

[16] Conversation with Prescott, 24 June 2003 at Tama Re.

[17] Ellen Barry, "His dream became their nightmare,"*Los Angeles Times*, 22 January 2004.

[18] Tom Lassete, "Tensions simmer around a black sect in Georgia," *New York Times*, 29 June 1999.

[19] Their names are; Nathaniel Washington, Yvonne Powell, Vincent Powell, Ethel Roberston, Anthony Evans, Donald McIntyre, Patrice Evans, Althea Shine, and Michelle Mitchell (see Mattthew Pinzur, "Nuwaubians, Who are these people?" *Macon Telegraph*, 15 May 2000).

[20] Rob Peecher, "The talk of the town here Thursday wasn't really the talk of the town at all," *Macon Telegraph*, 4 February 2000. (It is not clear to me why the land was temporarily put up for sale.)

county. In retaliation, the judge sent Sheriff Sills to padlock several buildings. As thousands of visitors arrived to celebrate Saviour's Day, they were forced to hold their festival out of doors. They stood chanting defiantly, "We love sunshine!" Racial tension rose to a peak when hundreds of York's supporters remained in the area after the June 1999 festival to protest the next hearing in Eatonton. The hearing had to do with zoning disputes, and Dr. York was under threat of going to jail for refusing to appear in court. One hundred state troopers and GBI agents[21] were secretly dispatched to the Eatonton armoury in case of trouble.

But this time Dr. York conceded to take the witness stand, "sombrely resplendent in a black fez and an all-black outfit accented by a bucketful of jewellery." He explained why he hadn't bothered to show up for the previous hearings, as follows: "I move around because I want to stay out of somebody's focus...I move from place to place." The case was dismissed, since it turned out that the summons had been sent to the wrong address. York had moved to his new home in Athens in March 1999.[22]

Deviance Labels in the Media

The Nuwaubians sought to correct their deviant image in the mass media by creating their own newsprint media, hoping to make their voices heard. In December 1999 they printed and distributed their own newspaper—*The Putnam News*—which, on first glance, might easily be mistaken for a mainstream newspaper. It accused the local media of racial discrimination and expressed the Nuwaubians' frustration at being denied a voice in the Press. It featured unflattering articles on the officials on the Putman Commission who had voted against their building permit. The African-Americans who worked for the local authorities were denounced in this publication as "house niggers."

Allies, Reputable and Disreputable

A far more effective self-defensive strategy was adopted in September 1999, when the Nuwaubians decided to try to de-escalate the conflict by inviting distinguished black leaders to visit Tama Re and speak up on their behalf. Al Sharpton of the National Action Network spoke up, and so did Tyrone Brooks, who was the Atlanta State Representative and President of the Georgia Association of Black Elected Officials. Brooks regularly intervened in racially-sensitive cases as a veteran legislator and had already visited Tama-Re three times. He came to Putnam County to mediate in the dispute between the Nuwaubians and local officials, testifying as character witness for Dr. York, and writing opinion letters that supported the

---

[21]   GBI stands for Georgia Bureau of Investigation.

[22]   Osinski, 197.

Nuwaubian cause. In 1999 Brooks warned Governor Barnes that "Dwight York and his group were being targeted for Waco-like racial violence."[23]

Journalists covered the visits of Sharpton and Brooks and, for the first time, a few relatively sympathetic articles on the people of Tama Re appeared in the news.[24] Dr. York, however, may have undermined these efforts when he held a press conference on September 15, 1999 in which he called white people "the Devil" and suggested they "go home to Europe."[25]

Tyrone Brooks' reputation was suddenly compromised when he was tricked into sending in a group of armed, unlicensed private security guards called the Georgia Rangers to Putnam County for an "investigation" of the Sheriff's office.[26] Sills described this fascinating episode to me in some detail:

> Then there were the "Georgia Rangers." They were just hoodlums, black and white guys who drove around town in unmarked white cars and went into offices, flashing their fake badges. They would knock on doors, beat people up and seize their computers and sound equipment that was never returned. One day, two individuals came into my office in uniform, flashed their badges, and said they were sent by the Governor's executive assistant, Roy Barnes. They had a letter from Tyrone Brooks and said he had sent them here. I handed over their credentials to my secretary and asked her to make copies. Then there was a knock on the door and my deputy said there was a group in the parking lot across the street from my office, but they appeared to be unarmed. I looked out my window. There were cars, video-cameras—a group of Nuwaubians, wearing black pajamas and the black and gold braid fezes were filming my office. There were 10-12 Nuwaubians with cameras on tripods filming with a vehicle that said, "Georgia Federal Ranger Service"—they had marked cars. They were forbidden to come onto my property—as civilians, they needed a permit. The Georgia Rangers gave me a citizen's arrest statute, and then I looked more closely at the badges, and saw "MLKPOA"—that means "Martin Luther King Property Owners' Association." Then I realized it was a set up! It was a provocation. I took away their guns and ordered them off the precincts. Two days later, they were rounded up and put in jail for "impersonating officers." They were charged with a little-known Georgia statute—"unauthorized militia." Some of them were convicted felons, the head man, Phoenix Ali, was a white guy, who was on probation in North Carolina. I did some research on the Georgia Rangers. They turned out to be hoodlums, marauders—thugs! They *took* things, they raided private homes. They were an unlicensed private security group with blue lights

---

[23] Bill Osinski, "Legislator Intervened in Nuwaubian Case," *Atlanta Journal-Constitution*, 31 August 2002.

[24] Bill Osinski, "Legislator intervened in Nuwaubian case." *Atlanta Journal-Constitution*, 31 August 2002.

[25] Personal communication.

[26] Osinski, "Legislator Intervened in Nuwaubian Case."

on their cars. They were unlawful militia. Later, I talked to Tyrone Brooks. He said, 'But I thought they were federal marshals!'[27]

The next disreputable ally arrived from quite an unexpected quarter. In mid June, 1999, several Montana Freemen came to town. The Montana Freemen were the anti-government Patriot group that had been besieged at their headquarters in Montana in 1996 by the FBI. One of them, Everett Leon Stout, introduced himself to the Nuwaubians as a "common law judge." He moved into Tama Re to work with them. First, he called on the county coroner to arrest the sheriff, and showed the Nuwaubians how to sue various county officials for $1 million in a "common law" court. He then helped them draw up a lien on Sheriff Sills' property.[28]

Stout filed a complaint against the Sheriff in federal court that was signed by 200-odd people listing their address as 404 Shady Dale Road (the address of Tama Re). Stout also issued arrest warrants for a Superior Court judge, for two deputies, and for York's former attorney, Frank Ford (who was complaining that he never got paid), and for Sheriff Sills. He also filed a million-dollar lawsuit against several officials, including a black commissioner. He then left the area. Sheriff Sills commented on the situation as follows:

> Everett Leon Stout…was the guy who moved in with them at the compound and attempted to serve me with one of those *ridiculous* common law statutes, putting a lien on my property. I immediately contacted the Arkansas state police for intelligence on Stout. It turned out he used to belong to the Montana Freeman, and he had recently volunteered his services to the Nuwaubians. When I contacted the FBI, they said 'you must be mistaken!' This Stout character, being a Freeman, was a *racist*, a *white separatist*—while the Nuwaubians are *black supremacists*. It didn't make sense…. What was *he* doing with the Nuwaubians? But, it seems he came to teach them Common Law…. So, they filed a lien on my property. That means, if I go to sell, I first have to get the lien cleared up. It's not a forged document, it's just a false legal document, but it's a nuisance, and costs time and money to clear up.[29]

Republican Sentiments

The Nuwaubians have always officially endorsed the Republican Party, and many of them carry around a small booklet containing the American Constitution, called *The Guidebook for Nuwaubians*. One Nuwaubian explained their political affiliation as a way to distance themselves from issues such as gay rights and abortion. "At least Republicans have a respect for religion," he noted. Many

---

27   Interview with Sheriff Sills.

28   Rob Peecher, "Arrest Nuwaubians' latest trouble" *Macon Telegraph*, 9 May 2002.

29   Interview with Sheriff Sills.

devout Nuwaubians have served in various branches of the U.S. military and several joined the Macon police force. Others work in the U.S. prison system as wardens.[30] Nevertheless, despite their Republican sentiments, the Nuwaubians were very excited when Obama won the election, and many had voted for him. A photograph of Obama, captioned "HOPE" is posted on a website advertising the *All Eyes on Egipt* bookstore in Toronto.[31] It is interesting to note that when a major schism in the movement formed during Dr. York's 2004 trial, it was over the issue of whether the Nuwaubians should network with the ultra-Right anti-government groups who practice Common Law.[32]

The Voting Fraud

In 2000 the Nuwaubians attempted to increase their influence in Putnam County in order to better facilitate their religious aims. In June 2000 they presented several of their own Republican candidates for the elections, and soon had a candidate running for sheriff. But the Putnam County Board of Registrars began purging Nuwaubians from its voters' rolls, challenging the residency of 196 of their members. Journalist Rob Peecher of the *Macon Telegraph* claimed, "In Putnam County 90% of the Nuwaubians showed up in this area right before the 2001 election. It was a voting fraud."[33]

The Nuwaubians, in turn, claimed this was an instance of racial discrimination, and filed a federal lawsuit that threatened to hold up the 18 July primary election. A three-judge panel sided with the county and dozens of Nuwaubians were removed from the voter rolls, and the election took place. Despite a strong lobby for the Nuwaubians' candidate, Sheriff Sills won 72 percent of the vote.[34]

On 27 June the Nuwaubians held a rally to protest the discrimination they believed was preventing them from voting. The Putnam County Board of Registrars had just purged 36 Nuwubians from the voters' rolls and challenged another 36, while another 72 cases were still pending. Between 700–800 Nuwaubians circled the courthouse in Eatonton chanting, "Amun Ma-at." A spokesperson explained it meant "hidden justice" in ancient Egyptian.

---

[30] Paul Greenhouse pointed this out to me.

[31] profile.myspace.com/index.cfm?fuseaction=user.viewprofile&friendID=6706795 5 - 193k-.

[32] www.experiencefestival.com/yamassee_-_relation_to_the_washitaw_nation - 73k -.

[33] Interview with Rob Peecher in *The Nuwaubian Story*, documentary film in progress by Paul Greenhouse, screened at the American Academy of Religion (AAR-EIR), Eastern International *Regional Meeting*, at McGill University Faculty of Religious Studies, in *Montreal*, Canada, 6-7 May 2005.

[34] "Nuwaubian voting suit dismissed," *Augusta Chronicle*, 11 April 2001.

Rob Peecher, a journalist with the *Macon Telegraph,* quoted a Putnam County resident saying, "Dwight York's purpose was to take over the state of Georgia politically, by moving in all his followers—just like the Rajneesh in Oregon."[35]

Mounting Hostilities

By 2001, the Nuwaubians had been the target of hundreds of unflattering, stigmatizing stories in the local newspapers. Rob Peecher quoted officials saying that the Nuwaubians posed a political threat. He quoted commissioner Sandra Adams as saying, "I have a problem with them trying to take over." Several Nuwaubians began to behave in a threatening manner towards Rob Peecher, who had been covering the Nuwaubian story since 1992 in the *Eatonton Messenger* and the *Macon Telegraph*—and he began to fear reprisals:

> I started to get death threats—anonymous phone calls…"Rob Peecher, if you don't start printing the truth I'm going to hunt you down and kill you!" In the fall of 2000 I was in the grocery store in Engels, and I saw two Nuwaubians. They followed me around. They started to yell things at me. They called me a liar, a racist…one was holding a beer bottle. As I was standing at the cash trying to buy my groceries, he reaches around, bangs on the counter and threatens to knock my teeth out. The cashier doesn't say a word. I walked out, not hurrying, until I was close to the car, and then they started to run towards me. I drove away, but as I left, I saw Rufus (another journalist) there, getting out of his car and going into the store. He was my replacement at the *Eatonton Messenger*. The Nuwaubians attacked him, beat him up. His wife was waiting in the car, drove up, honked—and he jumped into the car and escaped. After that, he started to carry a gun when he went out shopping. It was very difficult for me not being able to take my children places. The FBI found out about a plot to kill the Sheriff, and there was a threat against Sill's child. There were flyers circulating saying bad stuff about me. All it took was one lone, crazy Waub to decide he was going to be the Nuwaubian of the Year and take me out… . For example, at Savior's Day 2000 there was a guy out there who was apparently too crazy for even the Nuwaubians, so they kicked him off their property—and he pulled his car around to the front of the compound and set his own person and his car on fire! I was concerned some crazy like that might attack me or my family.[36]

When I asked a Nuwaubian leader what he thought of Peecher, he replied, "Peecher tries to sway the public to believe that we are a bunch of partying, law-disrespecting negroids. They don't want black, educated people doing powerful things!"[37]

---

[35]   Paul Greenhouse, "The Nuwaubian Story."

[36]   Interview with Rob Peecher in documentary film, *The Nuwaubian Story*.

[37]   Interview with a Nuwaubian on 25 June 2004 during the Savior's Day festival.

By this time, relations between the Nuwaubians and Putnam County officials were strained. Commissioner Sandra Adams (no relation to Dorothy) complained that she had been insultingly referred to as a "house nigger" in a Nuwaubian publication. One Nuwaubian slashed the attorney, Frank Ford's tires while he was in a grocery store. Sheriff Sills complained that the "so-called Nuwaubians" had labelled him a "demon" and a "racist," and were stalking him, his wife and son in a threatening manner. Meanwhile, the Nuwaubians were passing out flyers offering a $500 reward to anyone who could provide them with negative information on Sills.

In June 2001 Dr. York was ordered to appear in court again on contempt charges. The court day of 29 June fell right in middle of the week of the festival. There was a record crowd of 5000 Nuwaubians at Tama Re that year. Around 700 black-clad Nuwaubians, dressed in Moorish black tunics with embroidered fezes, surrounded the courthouse in Eatonton and organized themselves in patrols as sentries. A U-haul truck circled filled with Nuwaubians circled the square "ready to be deployed if their Savior was taken into custody."[38]

But this time York arrived punctually at the courthouse, dressed in an elegant blue suit, with a procession of body guards and attorneys. He bounded up the courtroom steps, greeting each local journalist cheerfully by name. Inside the courthouse, photo journalists, Nuwaubians and townspeople elbowed each other for space as spectators. The judge ordered the court cleared, just as a Georgia thunderstorm erupted outside, soaking everyone as both sides reached an agreement that they hoped would end the zoning conflict.

Famous Black Supporters of 2001

On 27 April 2001, Jesse Jackson, the Rainbow/PUSH Coalition leader spoke at Tama Re. He called it "the American Dream" and pledged his solidarity with the Nuwaubians in their ongoing zoning and building disputes.

Another ally appeared unexpectedly in the person of Rudy Snipes, the brother of the famous African-American Hollywood actor, Wesley Snipes. In May 2001, Rudy Snipes expressed an interest in purchasing the 350 acres of land adjacent to Tama Re for his security company, the *Royal Guard of Amen Ra* that provided security for movie stars. Snipes told the press that he hoped to use the land as a "paramilitary training camp." Osinski wrote: "to the sheriff, it would created a migraine of nuclear proportions to have a military-style training camp next door to a group that he suspected would be willing and able to provide foot soldiers for an armed insurrection."[39]

---

[38]   Bob Moser, "'Savior' in a Strange Land," *Southern Poverty Law Center: Intelligence Report* (Fall 2002) http://www.splcenter.org/intel/intelreport/article.jsp?pid=88, accessed 9/28/2005, 10:42 AM.

[39]   Osinski, 221.

But in the end, Snipes was unable to get zoning clearance, so the camp project never materialized.[40] The spokespersons for Tama Re capitalized on this glamorous connection, but Wesley Snipes' public relations team assured the press that the distinguished Hollywood actor was not involved with the Nuwaubians in any way.[41]

Meanwhile, a new source of conflict was secretly gathering force. A network of ex-members had formed, and they went to the FBI with their complaints. It suddenly turned out that a case against York on multiple counts of child molestation had been secretly building since 1997.

A Network of Ex-Nuwaubians

It is not unusual to find a high rate of defection in communal, "high demand" utopian movements.[42] A wave of defection occurred after the group's move to Georgia, during the building of Tama Re. The defectors voiced the standard complaints of unpaid labor, wretched and unsanitary living conditions, a gap between the executive leaders *versus* the rank and file members' living conditions, and financial and sexual exploitation. In 1999 there were a series of defections. Interviews with some of these defectors are featured in Osinski's book; two mothers who left with their children and sued York for child support; and four second-generation female members, some of whom had been York's groupies, called the "backstreet girls," who assisted in the Passion recording studio.[43]

Each member had his/her particular reason to resent the revered "Master Teacher." Several of York's former concubines or "Muslim" wives, mothers of his 200-odd children, had left the movement feeling neglected and embittered because he had discarded them for new lovers and refused to pay child support. By 2001 a network of ex-members had formed, under the leadership of Dr. York's disaffected son, Jacob York.

Jacob York (b.1973) was raised in the Ansaar Allah Community, but had left in 1990 at the age of 16 with his mother, Dorothy "Dhubayda" Johnson (1945-95)

[40]   Rob Peecher, "Snipes' company may buy property," *Macon Telegraph*, 11 May, 2000. "Amen Ra" sounds very Nuwaubian, but Snipes denied he was a member of the group. Nevertheless, the Nuwaubians interpreted the event as enhancing their social legitimacy.

[41]   Rob Peecher, "Snipes' company may buy property," *Macon Telegraph*, 11 May 2000.

[42]   See Eileen Barker, *The Making of a Moonie: Choice or Brainwashing?* (London: Blackwells, 1984).

[43]   Osinski, 203-14. Paul Greenhouse claimed that "backstreet girls" referred to women who worked in the publishing office.

and his three siblings.[44] His mother, who had served as the head administer in the AAC, had left on very bad terms with her husband.

Jacob lived for a while with his sister in Philadelphia, until his father found out and threatened to evict the tenants and deprive her of this income unless she cut off all contact with her brother.[45] Then Jacob enrolled at Columbia University, where he began organizing big dance parties for the students, inviting the new and promising hip-hop bands to play. By 1994 he had become a successful music producer and agent with his own company, "Untertainment."[46] He became the manager for Li'l Kim, a rap singer and outrageous feminist erotic dancer, one of the first women to break into an all-male art form. She was flamboyant, creative and *avant garde* and became so fashionable she even performed at the Museum of Modern Art. She called herself "Queen B#*&#."

Jacob then became the executive producer of a successful Hip Hop band, "Junior Mafia" (founded by Biggy Smalls, a.k.a. "Notorious B.I.G." who died under mysterious circumstance). Jacob admitted to Osinski that he had relied on "burglars" and criminal connections at one phase of his career: "As a budding entrepreneur, he looked for venture capital wherever he could find it, sometimes in not-so-legal directions"—but that he had distanced himself from them "knowing he'd either wind up in jail or dead."[47]

Once his career was established, Jacob severed all ties to his father's empire. But one day he was approached by an FBI agent seeking information about

---

[44]　According to the "Conspiracy And [sic] Conspirators" article, his mother died of a brain aneurysm in 1995, and his older brother, Yadullahi Muhammad, was shot through the heart at a party in 1998.

[45]　Osinski, 224.

[46]　The "Conspiracy And Conspirators" article offers the following account of Jacob York's career: "In 1999, the NBA filed a law suit against Jacob York's company Untertainment Records. An article in LAUNCH NEWSPAPER dated May 17, 1999 A.D. tilted Activists And The NBA Shoot Down Cam'Ron Campaign, stated that, 'The brain trust behind the marketing campaign for popular New York-based rapper Cam'Ron had no idea of the firestorm that it was getting into when it appropriated a version of the National Basketball Association's logo in a national advertising campaign to promote the artist's upcoming album Sports, Drugs, & Entertainment. The ad featured a silhouette of a man holding a gun dribbling a basketball, which was practically identical to the NBA logo-except that the NBA's silhouetted figure was unarmed. Untertainment's problems began when they put a huge billboard on Malcolm X Boulevard in Harlem on April 19. Mistakenly thinking that the album was sponsored by the NBA, a loose collective of community activists, church leaders, and school officials complained to the NBA and demanded action... . According to frustrated Untertainment Records President Jacob York, the litigation was unnecessary. York, who had been fending off angry calls from the Rev. Al Sharpton and New York Mayor Rudy Giuliani's office, said that the ad was a chronology of Cam'Ron's personal history. The controversy began because the Billboard was placed right across the street from a boy's and girl's high school.

[47]　Osinski, 225.

Dr. York. On hearing of the controversy surrounding Tama Re on the news, Jacob decided to re-establish contact:

> The last time I saw my Dad was in 1995. I was sitting in New York, watching television and this program came on about the trouble with Tama Re about zoning and illegal nightclubs. It was right after Waco, and I already knew about his zoning conflicts, but I thought, 'if this is stuff is starting to appear on national television, then he really is heading for disaster!' I called up my brother in Atlanta and he agreed with me, so I flew out to Atlanta, and we went out to the Land to warn him. He didn't listen to us. He talked of aliens, UFOs, how the Mothership was coming.... Then I realized how crazy he was—but he was funny! He made me laugh, even then.[48]

York's supporters explain that Jacob turned against his father because he refused to lend him money for his music business, but Jacob tells quite a different story: "He asked *me* for money!" [for a donation to the Nuwaubian movement].

Jacob claimed he first became aware of his father's alleged malfeasance when he met an ex-member who showed him a video of a young girl dancing naked who had been his childhood sweetheart when he was in the AAC. He decided at that point to set up an "underground railroad" to help members escape. He opened up an email account so that members of the group who needed help and "wanted out" could write to him. He moved to Atlanta, rented a house in the suburbs, and set up a "halfway house" for defectors. His sister left Philadelphia, moved in with him, and opened a beauty salon.[49] Jacob manned a rescue operation:

> I would drive up to the Land, and arrange a rendezvous point. People would walk out with their belongings in garbage bags, as if they were coming out to dump the garbage, and I would be waiting to pick them up in my car and bring them to Atlanta. I would find them a job, get them resumés, show them how to open a bank account, find a place for them to stay, introduce them to the network of ex-members.[50]

As part of the "deprogramming" process, Jacob would show the ex-members videotapes: documentaries or news clips on violent and dangerous "cults" ("I wanted [them] to see the parallels—that we lived like those people did").

The York siblings made it their mission to "rehabilitate" the second generation members who had grown up in a commune. They showed them how to survive in a secular society; how to get a driver's license, open a bank account, write a CV,

---

[48]   This interview took place on 19 August 2003, at Jacob York's boutique, next door to the Roxy Theatre in the Buckhead district of Atlanta, GA.

[49]   Osinski, 227.

[50]   Interview with Jacob York, 19 August 2003.

and fill out a job application. Jacob even helped a 50-year-old mother of five, to buy a house by giving her the down payment:

> She had two girls, twins that were turned over to the Land… . I co-signed [a mortgage loan] for a house. She had five kids, two from him, one has Down's syndrome, and her three kids were sodomized by that man! And she was fifty years old! I have two half sisters from her—so I thought I should help her out. So they could all live in a home.[51]

In March 2001, Jacob heard through the ex-members' circuit that one of the top administrators at Tama Re had just defected—an 18-year-old second generation member named Abigail ("Habibah") Washington. A pretty girl, dubbed "Habibah the dwarf" by her friends (due to her small stature), she had been one of York's long-term concubines and had borne a child by him. After a quarrel with him, she left Tama Re in February 2001 and moved to New York were she was living with her family. Jacob York had been one of her childhood friends during the Ansaaru Allah days. He invited her to go on a weekend trip to Florida where they "would hang out with girls and boys, ex-members, and have fun." (It is interesting that Jacob formed the ex-members into a coalition through organizing a party, which was his *forte* at University.) Abigail traveled to Georgia and met him at his house in Atlanta, where he introduced her to a group of ex-Nuwaubians.

Jacob told me in our interview that he had at first distrusted white law enforcement. He even feared his dad had infiltrated the government. But after seeing the Nuwaubian flyers attacking Sheriff Sills' reputation, he decided he could trust him.

The Raid on Tama Re

On 8 May 2002 the FBI executed a military raid on the Egyptian village of Tama Re. Sheriff Sills described the raid as "a joint operation planned between the FBI and my office—and I provided the jail for Dwight York!"

Sheriff Sills explained in our interview, that Jacob York only helped provide objective proof for a situation that he was already well aware of:

> I knew about the child molestation long before Jacob York contacted me. In December 1997 I received my first inkling that something was afoot when a woman came and told me that young underage girls were getting pregnant by York out at the compound. Did I launch an investigation? No, I had nothing substantial to go on. But we started to get anonymous phone calls complaining about child molestation. Then, in the Spring of 1998 I received an anonymous

---

[51]   The Nuwaubian website, "Conspiracy And [sic]Conspirators" claims that the house was a bribe, since two of Barbara Noel's children testified against Dr. York.

letter claiming that York was molesting kids. In September we opened an investigation and began to gathered information. In September 1998 we got another anonymous letter with a diagram of the compound which showed which buildings the boys, the girls slept in—this was obviously someone who knew. So we continued our investigation, but we had no names yet. I interviewed ex-members who called me who told me about illegal acts involving children. Then Jacob York came forward, putting me in touch with 12 people who were willing to come forth and tell their story. We found we had the biggest case of child molestation in the history of the United States; big in terms of the number of victims, but also in terms of the timeframe. According to the allegations, York's molestations went back for three generations—with kids, with their mothers and even with their grandmothers when they were young back in the Ansaaru Allah Community days in Brooklyn.

The Planning of the Raid

For a whole year before the raid, Sheriff Sills had been working closely with the FBI, one of the consequences of 9/11 which weakened the boundaries between local law enforcement and the FBI. The Homeland Security initiatives and the Patriot Act brought about a closer cooperation between local police forces, state police, and federal law enforcement agencies, as part of President Bush's "war or terrorism." Sills was involved in the FBI's secret preparations for the raid, scheduled for 8 May 2002. Osinski notes, "there were significant logistical barriers to making a case against York. [Federal agent Tom] Diehl complained of receiving very little support from federal bureaucracy. He complained in a 2006 interview that the group was practically impossible to penetrate with informants, and its isolated location on a large tract of private land made it difficult to set up surveillance."[52]

Thus the FBI relied on Sherrif Sills, who began to conduct surveillance on Tama Re, accompanied by his friend, Rob Peecher, the journalist.

Rob Peecher described their surveillance activities in a filmed interview with Paul Greenhouse:

> Right before the raid, the Sheriff was conducting surveillance across the street. The Sheriff got the frequency of the radio the guards were using. I went down with him one night and sat there in the cold mud watching them for six hours.... We used a scanner and wire tapped the guards' walkie-talkie so we could hear them. Sills camped out in the woods across from the gate for one or two months, picking up their frequencies.[53]

---

[52]   Osinski, 215.

[53]   Interview with Rob Peecher in *The Nuwaubian Story,* documentary film in progress by Paul Greenhouse, screened at the American Academy of Religion (AAR-EIR) Eastern

Peecher's articles relied heavily on the opinions of Sheriff Sills, as did those of Bill Osinski and other journalists. Sills soon became the leading interpreter of events in the escalating conflict, and virtually the only source of knowledge regarding Nuwaubian religious culture. Peecher could not interview any Nuwaubians, since they were antagonistic towards him—as the story he told illustrates:

> One night they delivered a stack of flyers to the gate. The guard...said, 'that's a good photo, we need to blow it up and use it for target practice.' Who's the photo of? It was *me*! That's a little unnerving...that people are using photos of you for target practice![55]

Peecher overheard this conversation between the guards while he and his buddy, Sheriff Sills, were camped out on the hill across the street conducting surveillance on the "Nuwaubian compound" at night.

Sheriff Sills described the suspenseful preparations for the raid, as follows:

> What we didn't want was a Waco-like situation. We had planned the raid for a whole year, and came in with a federal and a state search warrant for the compound, and with a federal and a state arrest warrant for York. There was a psychological factor. We timed it when the least number of people would be there. We wanted to arrest York off the compound. We did have the element of surprise. We knew we would have to keep it a secret. This was difficult, so no one was involved other than my own personnel (six people) and a handful of FBI officers. By the time we moved in, we had to muster massive resources to do the raid, so the closer we got to D-Day, the greater the risk. Three to four law enforcement agents were moved into rural Georgia country and kept secret.

Tom Diehl, a federal law enforcement official stationed in Macon, had obtained two search warrants for York's property and had brought in eight FBI profilers for a search of Tama Re. Dwight York's name was on the search warrant, but it turned out that York was not the legal owner of the property. Tama Re was co-owned by a group of Nuwaubian leaders.[54]

The raid was planned as a spectacular show of force. Armoured vehicles filled with over 300 agents from the FBI, ATF, and the local county Sheriff's department rammed through the flimsy painted obelisks that flanked the gates of Tama Re. The FBI's SWAT team made a "dynamic entry" armed with machine guns, Glocks, hand grenades, head masks, body shields and tear gas. Agents leaped out of helicopters, kicked in doors and threw tear gas in windows.

International Regional Meeting, at McGill University Faculty of Religious Studies, in Montreal, Canada, May 6-7, 2005.

[54]   Interview with Rob Peecher in *The Nuwaubian Story.*

The FBI were careful to maintain the element of surprise. They had learned this lesson the hard way from their disastrous assault on Waco on 19 April 1993, which had resulted in the deaths of 85 adults and children through fire, tear gas, suffocation and bullets. This time they came in fully prepared for casualties—with fire trucks, ambulances, body bags and refrigerator trucks at the ready. Nevertheless, despite the strong objections raised to violations of the *posse comitatus* act at Waco where they had employed military weapons against U.S. citizens, they arrived at the gates of Tama Re with armoured vehicles, tear gas, and helicopters with mounted guns.

There were no casualties this time, because the residents of Tama Re (unlike the Branch Davidians) did not shoot back. They lay face down on the ground, their hands on their heads and put up no resistance. Only 65 adults were present, and only 25 of them were men, mostly elderly. Sills reports they found "twenty-five men, forty women, and the rest kids—around sixty of them." The FBI did not open fire on them. Thus, the raid was "successful" in that no one was killed—but the results proved to be disappointing. The FBI agents reported seeing "people who were like zombies," but their searches failed to uncover any illegal caches of weapons, or any children showing signs of abuse. Sheriff Sills, however, described the raid as an unmitigated success:

> It was impressive! We had three armoured vehicles that were brought in on the day of the raid carrying the SWAT personnel, and these armoured trucks rammed the gates—and within three minutes we had control of the situation. We had control of the perimeters and held the ground in three minutes. We already knew where most of the men and the weapons were, and we had everybody on the ground in three minutes! We had 80 FBI agents, 69 Deputy Sheriffs, we had snipers and a rifle team, and two helicopters. 80 SWAT personnel and lightly armoured vehicles that could not be penetrated if shot with small arms. We were up to 11 to 12 at night. I went to hospital with severe dehydration and had to be put on IV. That was the closest thing to an injury that happened that day!

The BATF participated in the raid, hoping to find the suspected stash of illegal weapons. But there was no mention of finding a stockpile of machine guns or illegal weapons in the news reports that covered the raid

The Charges

On the same morning, just before the raid was launched, Dr. York had already been arrested in nearby Millidgeville, in the parking lot of a supermarket where he was shopping in the company of his "main wife" Kathy Johnson. York's $528,000 house in Athens was searched and the FBI seized $400,000 cash found in his home.[55]

When first arrested on 8 May 2002, York was charged with 116-counts related to child molestation.[56] But within weeks of the arrest, the Putnam County Grand Jury reduced the number to 74 counts of child molestation, 29 counts of aggravated molestation, four counts of statutory rape, two counts of sexual exploitation of a minor, and five counts of enticing a child for sexual purposes, amounting to 114 charges in all. Osinski comments that "state prosecutors literally had to cut back the number of counts listed — from well beyond 1000 to slightly more than 200 — because they feared a jury simply wouldn't believe the magnitude of York's evil." He described the case as "the nation's largest child molestation prosecution ever directed at a single person, in terms of number of victims and number of alleged criminal acts."

Kathy Johnson, York's "main wife" had been arrested with him outside a supermarket on the morning of the raid of 8 May 2002, and she was implicated in both the federal and state charges of molestation. She was accused of assisting Dr. York in taking the children of Tama Re to Disney World in Orlando, Florida for the express purpose of having sex with them in a Walt Disney fantasy ambience. Three of York's other wives were also indicted. Kathy Johnson was charged with four counts of child molestation, one aggravated; Istytir Cole with one count of child molestation; and Chandra Lampkin and Kadijah Meritt were each charged with three counts of child molestation, and two aggravated.

Five of the 50-odd "children" (ranging in age from 14 to 16) were taken into protective custody on the day of the raid, and were examined by doctors, social workers and psychologists. Four tested positive for STDs.[57] There was no evidence that any of them had had any sexual contact with Dr. York, however. The residents of Tama Re explained that some of the teens had flouted the rules and sneaked off to the barn at night where they consumed alcohol, listened to decadent Hip Hop music, and "partied" with each other.

Sheriff Sills was quoted by Rob Peecher in the *Macon Telegraph* explaining why the five children were taken into protective custody: "We received information about these five children that was corroborated by others that caused us to seek out the protective order. We had an order from the Juvenile court signed [by a judge] prior to going on the compound. The children, we suspect, are victims of child molestation."[58]

---

[55]   Rob Peecher, "Lawyers argue details in York case," *Macon Telegraph*, 18 January 2003.

[56]   "Nuwaubians Indictments allege more than 100 criminal acts," *Macon Telegraph*, 1 September 2002.

[57]   Dr. York was never charged with molestation of those particular children.

[58]   Rob Peecher, "DFACS takes custody of 5 Nuwaubian children," *Macon Telegraph*, 10 May 2002.

The Nuwaubian website (www.unnm.com) complained of a press conference held two days after the raid "where Rev. Malachi Z. York's Presumption of Innocence was dismantled with the aid of the media when Sheriff Sills maliciously labelled Rev. York a 'serial pedophile.'" After the children had received medical and psychological examinations, and after the weapons were counted and labelled, no charges were laid against York—either for molesting those particular children or for the possession of illegal firearms. These details were not considered sufficiently newsworthy by the local mass media to generate a story.

Deviance Amplification

The Nuwaubian's conflict with secular authorities might be better "overstood" if we apply Leslie Wilkins' useful sociological tool, "deviance amplification."[59] This theory, from the sociology of deviance, was first applied to a NRM by the Irish sociologist, Roy Wallis. In his 1976 book, *The Road to Total Freedom*, he analyzed the worsening relationship between Scientology and its host society in the 1960s as a widening spiral of "deviance amplification." Wallis notes that sociologists who have explored the relationship between deviance and societal reaction, have come up with three models.[60]

The first, "classic" model, relates deviance and societal reaction as a simple matter of unidirectional causation. Punitive reprisals are the natural and inevitable consequence when social norms are violated. This "official" view, typically held by law enforcement agents, was certainly held by the county zoning officials and the sheriff who opposed the Nuwuabian enterprise in Georgia.

The second, "labelling," model" reverses the causal direction and defines "deviance" as *socially constructed*. As Howard S. Becker notes: "Social groups create deviance by defining the rules. Breaking the rules constitutes deviance." Those rules are applied to particular persons or groups who are then labelled as outsiders. Deviant behaviour, therefore, is "behaviour that people so label."[61] The Nuwaubians were labelled as "black militants" and a "cult."

The third model of "deviance amplification" was formulated by Leslie Wilkins to explain gang delinquency (real and/or perceived) in Britain.[62] Roy Wallis sums up Wilkins' model, comparing it to a spiral:

---

[59]   Leslie T. Wilkins, "Social Deviance" in *Crime and Delinquency in Britain* edited by W.G. Carson and Paul Wiles (Martin Robertson and Co. London 1971), 209-26.

[60]   Roy Wallis, *The Road to Total Freedom: A Sociological Analysis of Scientology* (London: Heinemann, 1976), 87-9.

[61]   Howard S. Becker, *Outsiders: Studies in the Sociology of Deviance* (New York: Free Press, 1963), 9.

[62]   Leslie T. Wilkins, *Social Deviance: Social Policy, Action and Research* (London: Tavistock, 1964).

> A party's initial deviation from valued norms leads to a punitive reaction. This
> leads to a further alienation of the deviant(s) from social norms, which in turn
> leads to an increased punitive reaction from social control agents, which results
> in further alienation, possibly resulting in violence.[63]

In a manner consistent with the deviance amplification model, the actual *nature* of
Nuwaubian deviance keeps shifting. We can discern six "loops" in a widening spiral
of deviance. In the 1980s in Brooklyn, they were branded as arsonists. Then they
were suspects in a murder case. Next, they were feared as paramilitary "racists,"
who stockpiled illegal weapons and were connected to the Black Panthers. After
moving to Georgia in 1993, they were feared as "Waubs," a quasi-religious sect,"
that was trying to "take over" the county. Next, York was exposed as a "pedophile"
of gargantuan proportions, then finally slapped with a RICO racketeering charge,
which put him in the same criminal class as Mafia bosses like Al Capone.

Many of the news reports are written in the disjointed style of *bricolage*,
where York's shocking depredations are itemized, then juxtaposed with snippets
of the Nuwaubians' most bizarre beliefs:

> They say they are descendants of ancient Egyptians and American Indians,
> even aliens from another galaxy, but they came from Brooklyn, New York.
> Their leader once called himself the "Supreme Being" but he was actually an
> ex-convict and is in jail facing dozens of child molestation charges. The black
> supremacist sect…talked about a spaceship that would take them away.[64]

"Moral Panic" and a Network of Interest Groups

An important dynamic that is part of the process of deviance amplification is
the networking of different interest groups, each bringing their own agendas
to the network where information on the common foe is shared. The sheriff's
professional concern was to enforce law and order. The journalists' concern was to
produce entertaining stories that would sell newspapers. The zoning officials' job
was to impose rules and limitations on local building projects. The FBI were on
the outlook for "apocalyptic cults acting up" around the time of the millennium.[65]
Each of these groups collected and shared their own negative portraits with the

---

[63] Roy Wallis, "Societal reactions to Scientology" in *Sectarianism*, edited by Roy
Wallis (London: Peter Owen, 1975).

[64] Robert Stacey McCain, "Nuwaubian Nightmare," *Washington Times*, 2 June 2002.
(It should be noted that even mainstream religious beliefs can sound absurd and irrational
when presented out of context, but journalists effectively conveyed the message that here
was a "cult," a "quasi-religion" as opposed to a *bona fide* religion.)

[65] See *FBI Report: Project Megiddo* (www.religioustolerance.org/megiddo.htm).

network, and the final product was an image of the Nuwaubians as a threatening, "evil," "black-militant" "cult." The media broadcast this image to the public.

Stuart Wright, in his 1995 edited book, *Armageddon in Waco*, analyzes the events leading up to the 1993 BATF raid on the Branch Davidian "compound" in Waco, Texas, and argues that a network of interest groups collaborated in creating a negative and stigmatizing portrait of "cult."[66] He claims this media-generated portrait may have influenced the BATF and the FBI in planning their assaults of 28 February and 17 April 1993—an assault that Wright deems "a massive over-reaction" to "a perceived cult threat." I would argue that we find a similar pattern in the Nuwaubian case in Georgia, where the local journalists cooperated closely with law enforcement and actually played a major role in "bringing down the cult leader" and in the eventual destruction of the Tama Re.

Sociologist Stanley Cohen, in his 1972 book, *Folk Devils and Moral Panics* argues that deviance labelling can be a response to a collective sense of social anomie and chaos, which he terms "moral panic."[67] This he defines as "a condition defined as a threat to societal values and interests; its nature is presented in a stylized and stereotypical fashion by the mass media." Cohen was struck by public officials' inappropriate over-reaction to relatively minor events involving youth gangs in Britain; events which were defined as a "social problem" and became the focus of exaggerated attention from media, politicians, and law enforcement.

In Neil Smelser's discussion of "moral panic," he suggests that it is an effective strategy for opposing groups that some find offensive, for it invokes "a collective sense of immediate, powerful, ambiguous threat to deeply held norms or values, the preservation of which it is seen as urgent to take some action."[68]

Goode and Ben-Yehuda expand upon Cohen's notion of "folk devils." All moral panics, they argue, by their very nature, attempt to identify, denounce and root out "folk devils" (perceived as wrongdoers harmful to society, whose selfish and evil actions must be stopped). Goode and Ben-Yehuda also trace the development of moral panics through networks of interest groups.[69]

It is clear that the media painted a portrait of Dr. York as a kind of "folk devil." The sheriff was quoted twice condemning York as "one of the most heinous criminals in the history of this nation."[70] Sheriff Sills also stated in our interview, "Dwight York is one of the most diabolical people I have ever met in my life.

---

[66]   Stuart A. Wright, *Armageddon in Waco: Critical Perspectives On The Branch Davidian Conflict* (Chicago: The University of Chicago Press, 1995).

[67]   Stanley Cohen, *Folk Devils and Moral Panics* (London: MacGibbon and Kee, 1962).

[68]   Neil Smelser, *Theory of Collective Behaviour* (London: Routledge & Kegan Paul, 1962).

[69]   Erich Goode and Nachman Ben-Yehuda, *The Social Constructions of Deviance* (Oxford: Blackwell, 1994).

[70]   Terry Dickson, "Nuwaubian leader guilty," *Athens Banner-Herald*, 4 January 2004.

I can't think of an animal who has had a bigger impact on more victims!" He called York "the embodiment of real evil."[71] Osinski labels York as "ungodly" and "evil" in the title of his book.

York's followers have also been cast as "folk devils." Dorothy Adams, the attorney who had opposed the use of the Ramses club was quoted in the *Macon Telegraph* describing the Nuwaubians as "a group of black separatists who believe that white people are genetically inferior mutants." Sheriff Sills, the leading interpreter of Nuwaubian culture for the public, called Tama Re as "a dirty little theme park" where "most of living structures…were filthy and crowded."[72] The inevitable result of this close collaboration between journalists and officials is that the public received a distorted image of the group as a bizarre, dangerous, paramilitary, racist "cult."

Throughout the conflict, one finds there was a close cooperation between county officials, ex-members, the media and law enforcement long before the child molestation allegations surfaced. This fluctuating portrait of deviance was the result of collaboration between different interest groups, each with their own agenda for opposing the "cult's" utopian enterprise. While the Nuwaubians might exaggerate in calling it a "white conspiracy," it does seem fair to call it a symbiotic relationship, and in Beckford's terms, a rather "cosy" one.[73] Thus, it is fair to say that the media may have influenced the decisions made by public officials, and paved the way for the public's unquestioning acceptance of the government's draconian social control measures and overreaction to a perceived threat. It is also very likely that negative news reports may have had an impact on the jury during the trials. This over-dramatization of an ambiguous situation by the media raised the public's fears, and pressured government agents to act quickly and forcefully.[74]

This symbiotic relationship is shown in the media's staunch support of the government's quite unnecessary (and expensive) show of military force, in the raid and at the trial. The rationale for the FBI raid, the (disappointing) results of the search for a stockpile of weapons, and the (negative) results of the children's tests were only mentioned briefly in the news. Instead, journalists focused on the sheer multitude and shock value of the child molestation charges laid against Dr. York. This broadcast the message that Dr. Malachi York was a very dangerous criminal indeed, and implied that the government's excessive social control efforts were justified.

---

[71]   *AP* 27 January 2003.

[72]   "Sect leader trial setting officials on edge," *Associated Press*, 5 January 2004.

[73]   James Beckford, "Media treatment of new religions" (Paper presented at the CESNUR meeting, London, 1992).

[74]   See Stuart Wright's analysis of the role of ex-members and the media in bringing about the tragedy at Waco in his chapter "Construction and Escalation of a Cult Threat: Dissecting Moral Panic and Official Reaction to the Branch Davidians" in *Armageddon in Waco*, edited by Stuart Wright (University of Chicago, 1995).

Since deviance amplification describes an interactive and dynamic process, the responsibility for the conflict cannot rest exclusively on the shoulders of York's cultural opponents. One must scrutinize the Nuawuabian responses to social control, and analyze their part in this process. When attacked, the Nuwaubians fought back. A local Georgian told a journalist, "I've got the idea that when you got the King Bee taken aside, it might scatter the ants."

But the Nuwaubians did not scatter. They rallied around to defend their Master Teacher. But they did it in such a way as to amplify their deviant image.

Figure 4   Concerned Nuwaubians wait outside courtroom

Chapter 5

Dr. York's Trials

Dr. York's legal process might be described as a long-drawn-out epic battle, marked by dramatic reversals of fortune on both sides.

The state charges of child molestation were compounded by new federal charges when the Mann Act was slapped on. The Mann Act of 1910 is a federal law that makes it illegal to transport minors across state lines for purposes of sexual exploitation.[1] A federal grand jury indicted York and his "main wife," Kathy Johnson, for four counts of moving children across state borders nine years earlier, for (alleged) sexual purposes. This referred to the move in the Spring of 1993, when the whole Holy Tabernacle Ministries community moved from Brooklyn, New York to Georgia, and many of the families living at the Jazzir Abba camp in Sullivan County, N.Y. drove south to Georgia in March 1993, and again in April 1993. The third and fourth counts charged York with taking children from Georgia to Florida for a trip to Disney World, again for alleged sexual purposes.

Once the federal charges were added to the state charges, the FBI entered the case, and Dr. York's trial was moved up to a federal court. Dr. York was denied bail, and Johnson was given a $75,000 bond by feds, but it was later denied so she remained in jail. Two of his other wives, Chandra Lampkin and Khadijah Merritt, were held without bond in Putnam County jail, and a fourth wife, Isytir Cole, was released on a $25,000 bond.

In April 2003 Kathy Johnson pleaded guilty to a "misprision of a felony" in the U.S. District Court in Macon, GA. Attorney Pam Lightsey explained to the Press that this meant "she knew a felony was taking place and she didn't do anything about it."[2] As part of a plea bargain, Johnson made this admission in exchange for the more serious charge of crossing state lines with a minor for sexual purposes being dropped.

The Plea Bargain

On 25 October 2002 York was led into Putnam County court, shackled and handcuffed. It was his first appearance in six months since his arrest. Dressed in a sober blue business suit, standing in front of around 200 supporters, he pleaded

---

[1]   18 U.S.C. 2423(a).

[2]   "York's wife pleads guilty," *Athens Banner-Herald*, 1 April 2003, by Stephen Gurr.

"not guilty."[3] But York's attorney, Ed Garland, seemed to consider his client's case to be hopeless, for he persuaded York to assent to a plea bargain.

Thus, on 23 January 2003, in a shocking *volte face*, York pleaded guilty in federal court to one count of transporting children across state lines for illegal sex, and to one count of illegally structuring financial transactions. He reappeared the next day and pleaded guilty to 77 counts of child molestation, 40 counts of aggravated child molestation, 34 counts of child molestation, one count of child exploitation, and two counts of influencing witnesses.

As part of the plea bargain, both federal and state officials had already agreed that the defendant should be given a sentence that would make him eligible for parole in fifteen years. In an unexpected move, however, the U.S. District Judge, Hugh Lawson, rejected the plea bargain on 25 June 2003. Attorney Manny Arora, a lawyer on York's defence team, protested, "Everybody knows he pled guilty. It's going to be hard for him to get a fair trial."[4]

Ed Garland's reason for this strategy of capitulation remains unclear. If he were convinced of York's culpability, presumably he would wish to avoid the prospect of having the court listen to many young witnesses recount their appalling stories of sexual abuse. Predictably, the Nuwaubians explained Garland's actions by calling him a "racist" who conspired with the "racist" judge.

But once the judge rejected the plea bargain agreement, Garland stood up for his client. He told Judge Lawson that he had "tainted his appearance of impartiality in this case" when he told both sides what prison sentence he would find acceptable—should both sides come up with a new plea bargain to replace the one he had rejected on 25 June. Garland was referring to the 28 May informal meeting in Lawson's chambers, when the Judge had said that 15 years was "too lenient" and had suggested "20 years." Garland objected to this, saying: "when a judge becomes a participant in the plea bargaining process, he brings the full majesty and power of his office. Your majesty and power has created an impact and there is a prejudice against the defendant." Garland then made a motion for Lawson to recuse himself, which the judge, in fact, accepted.[5]

"Not Guilty"—the Pretrials of 2003

As might be expected, Dr. York's guilty plea had a demoralizing effect on his followers. For many, it signified a loss of charisma, and it resulted in conflict, confusion and infighting among his people.[6] But York suddenly rallied and reversed

---

3   "York pleads innocent in Putnam case," *Atlanta Journal-Constitution*, 26 October 2002, by Bill Osinski.

4   Judge rejects plea deal for Nuwaubian sect leader," WSBTV, 27 June 2003.

5   "Nuwaubians Religious Sect Leader's Trial Date Set for January," *Athens Banner-Herald*, 10 September 2003, by Joe Johnson.

6   Personal communication.

his position. It seems reasonable to assume that Dr. York realized the importance of re-establishing his charismatic persona and restoring the group's morale. This may be why, at his pre-trial hearing in January 2003, Dr. York behaved in what the media called an "irrational" fashion.

He appeared in court dressed as a Moor, wearing a red fez with a black tassel and made an apparently "nonsensical statement" in front of Superior Court Judge William A. Prior. He stood up said, "I am secured and do not give permission to use my name. If you proceed, it will cost you $500,000." Then he warned, "all deals are off if Prior continues to use my name."[7] York's followers showed up in court, also dressed as Moors, and handed out fliers declaring that, "Dr. York had copyrighted his name, and "all his aliases and unauthorized use of his name would be liable to fines."[8] The fliers were stamped, "Clerk of Federal Moorish Cherokee Consular Court, USA."[9]

At his next trial, on 1 July 2003, Dr. York resorted to another shape-shifting tactic. He appeared in court dressed as a Plains Indian, in buckskin and a feathered headdress, and announced he was "Chief Black Eagle." He stated that, due to his American Indian heritage, the United States Government had no jurisdiction over him. "I would like to be transferred to members of my tribe," declared York. "All I am asking is that the court recognize that I am an indigenous person. I am a Moorish Cherokee, and I cannot get a fair trial if I am being tried by settlers or Confederates."[10] He then demanded to be turned over to the "Yamassee Native American Government."[11]

York was once again resorting to "Common Law"—an antiquated people's law, still used by anti-government, Patriot and paramilitary groups in the U.S. such as the *Posse Comitatus*.[12] York and his supporters chanted legal phrases from Common Law, almost as a kind of ritual magic to escape what they saw as an illegitimate court. York was resorting to the same strategy the Montana Freemen had adopted before they were arrested by the FBI in 1995, when they denied the authority of the federal government—and York added to this the

---

[7] "Lawyers argue details in York case," *Macon Telegraph*, 18 January 2003 by Rob Peecher.

[8] "Maku is a Secured Party," *We the People* (flyer put out by the Yamassee Native American Moors of the Creek Nation).

[9] "Lawyers argue details in York case," *Macon Telegraph*, 18 January 2003 by Rob Peecher.

[10] "Officials are doing all they can to keep the courtroom from being turned into a circus," *Associated Press*, 5 January 2004.

[11] "York Claims Immunity as Indian," *Macon Telegraph*, 1 September 2002 by Rob Peecher.

[12] For a description of this subculture, see Stuart A. Wright, *Patriots, Politics, and the Oklahoma City Bombing* (Cambridge University Press, 2007).

Native American claim to be a representative of a "sovereign nation."[13] Three hundred Nuwaubians stood outside the courthouse beating tom-toms and handing out anti-government flyers. They wore American Indian clothing with beaded headbands and feathers.[14]

York revoked his guilty plea before the federal judge, explaining that he had been "under duress" when he admitted guilt: "I was in a two-man cell with rats. After being tortured and being told that I would get 1000 years, they made it look like a racial issue. I was on the cross."[15] He demanded to be tried in a non-white court, by his "peers."

It is likely that York was familiar with this Black Panther strategy from the 1960s. The Panthers argued that, since the early explorers from Spain were Moors and had arrived in America before the white colonists, all Black Panthers and African-Americans should demand to be tried in a court of their own peers. A similar strategy had been adopted by Noble Drew Ali in dealing with legal matters involving the Moorish Temple. Needless to say, these tactics were counter-productive. York's behaviour was ridiculed by journalists, it enhanced the public image of York as a "crazy cult leader," and York's refusal, on several occasions, to rise and stand when the judge entered the room may have antagonized the men and women of the court.[16]

The Birth of a Schism

Unbeknownst to York at the time, a hot debate over the issue of employing the quasi-legal strategies of Common Law was facilitating a schism inside the ranks of the United Nuwaubian Nation. One of York's disciples, Derrick Sanders, had stepped into the power vacuum in the wake of his Master Teacher's arrest.[17] He had filed papers with various government officials that asserted Patriot sovereignty issues, using Common Law procedures. While York was asking the court to recognize him as a Native American Moor who should be returned to

---

[13]   For an explanation of Common Law as applied by the Montana Freemen, see Catherine Wessinger (ed.), *How the Millennium Comes Violently* (New York: Seven Bridges Press, 2000). Dr. York may also have been influenced by a Moorish Temple strategy invented by Noble Drew Ali for dealing with legal matters, according to a source who wishes to remain anonymous.

[14]   "York Claims Immunity as Indian," *Macon Telegraph*, 1 July 2003, by Rob Peecher.

[15]   "York Claims Immunity as Indian," *Macon Telegraph*, 1 July 2003, by Rob Peecher.

[16]   "York trial opens with jury selection amid tight security," *Macon Telegraph*, 6 January 2004 by Wayne Crenshaw.

[17]   This schism was later called the Mt. Arafat Embassy Clan.

the jurisdiction of his tribe, Sanders was simultaneously filing his own rogue arguments, based on the Patriots' mythologized version of American history.

Sheriff Sills told a journalist that his office had received a packet of documents ordering York's release. One document, bearing an Egyptian-style hieroglyphic watermark, was sent by the "Yamassee Native American Government" and the "Mt. Arafat Embassy." It charged that "diplomats" of the government and embassy were "being inconvenienced by U.S. Governmental and private employees." A six-page "Exparte Order for Release" was signed by a certain "Dr. Derrick H. Sanders El, Elder, Grand Master Consul for Mt. Arafat Embassy of The Yamassee Native American Government, Original Cherokee, Siminole, Creek, Shushuni, Washita Mound Builders." Sanders claimed in this document that "Dwight York was not a legal 'person' born or naturalized in the federal 'United States' and was therefore not subject to the jurisdiction of the legislative democracy of the federal 'United States.'" He demanded that York be released 'instanter' [sic] to the custody of Mt. Arafat Embassy, to be secured by the Yamassee Native Americans."[18] Included in the packet was a document purportedly signed by Governor Sonny Perdue and a facsimile of the State of Georgia seal.

Ms. Kimberly King, a spokeswoman for Governor Perdue, told Rob Peecher of the *Macon Telegraph*, "these documents appear to be fake." Sheriff Sills noted that the Derrick Sanders' documents resembled other documents previously sent to him by the Montana Freeman, Leon Everett Stout, ordering the county coroner to arrest the sheriff.[19] He dismissed Sanders' missive as an "elaborate package of ridiculous documents" and predicted more "foolishness" if the case proceeded to trial.[20]

Two years later, Sanders appeared in the U.S. District Court of the Northern District of Georgia on 21 August 2005, charged with "engaging in conduct that substantially interfered with the administration and enforcement of the Internal Revenue laws." He had been involved in a tax fraud scheme involving 36 clients, to whom he supplied a Substitute IRS Form W-8BEN that he had claimed would allow them to be exempt from federal taxes. He was at the same time spearheading a schism in the Nuwaubian movement, by claiming that he was the Grand Master Consul of the Yamassee Native Americans of Eatonton Georgia (also known as the "Mt. Arafat Embassy Clan").[21]

---

[18] "Judge rejects York's plea deal: Nuwaubian expected to announce Monday whether he wants trial," *Macon Telegraph*, 28 June 2003 by Rob Peecher.

[19] It is possible that Derrick Sanders may have been influenced by Leon Stout, the Montana Freeman who introduced Common Law strategies to the Nuwaubians (see Chapter 4).

[20] "Judge rejects York's plea deal: Nuwaubian expected to announce Monday whether he wants trial," *Macon Telegraph*, 28 June 2003 by Rob Peecher.

[21] Although there is an entry on Derrick Sanders on *Wikipedia*, I was unable to find out whether or not the Mt. Arafat Embassy Clan is still operating as a viable NRM.

Derrick Sanders' "Common Law" strategy was attacked fiercely by York's loyal followers on the www.unnm.com website: One author ("TheWatchers") queries, "why this Wachita nation crap? If you research the Wachita nation headed by Emperess [sic] Verdiacee, you will find they signed a treaty with the republic of texas [sic], which is an anti-government group that links to the Freeman. Do research!"

Prophetic Responses from Prison

On 24 July 2003, Judge Royal asked that York be sent for a psychological evaluation in New York.[22] The psychologist who examined Dr. York diagnosed him as of sound mind. In the meantime, however, York's followers were witnessing an anomalous event which they interpreted in apocalyptic terms—as a fulfillment of prophecy.

On 14 August 2003 the major electrical blackout, referred to in the media as the "Outage," occurred on the east coast. It happened to occur at exactly the same time that Dr. York was being transported to New York City for his psychiatric evaluation. Several years ago, Dr. York had predicted that on 12 August 2003, "the Vortex would open" and that "beings from other dimensions would be able to slip through into our world and walk among us." These beings were the "twelve avatars," and York was among them. Thus, the Outage was understood by Nuwaubians as a confirmation of prophecy, despite the two-day delay.[23]

While awaiting his next trial, Dr. York was shunted from prison to prison over the next five years, and continued to direct his movement over the telephone. He began dictating a series of audio CDs called "Maku Speaks from the Isle of Patmos" in which he criticizes the way his trial was handled, complains of his prison conditions, and expounds his apocalyptic, dualistic interpretation of his conflict with the government.

The Jury Selection and a Change of Venue

Originally scheduled for 4 August 2003, the trial was delayed until January 2004. This was due to three factors: York's psychiatric testing, the recusal of a judge, and the change of venue from Macon to Brunswick, Georgia, due to a tainted jury pool.

In October 2003 the jury selection process was held at the courthouse in Macon. Hundreds of Nuwaubians turned out. They were dressed as Indians, were beating tom toms and handed out anti-government fliers. Judge Ashley Royal ruled that

---

[22]   "Nuwaubian sect leader will undergo psychological evaluation," *Athens Banner-Herald*, 13August 2003 by Joe Johnson.

[23]   See Chapter 6 for a full account of this prophetic event.

they could not demonstrate outside the courthouse, and expressed his concern about their attempt to influence the jury. The Nuwaubians complained on their website that "in the arraignment hearing of 25 October 2003, Sheriff Sills attempts to push Rev. Malachi Z. York down the courtroom steps while he is shackled in leg irons."[24]

In late December, around 200 Nuwaubians dressed up as Native Americans, Egyptian pharaohs and Shriners and marched in the Christmas Parade in Brunswick, where the trial was to be held. They were described as "dressed in Egyptian costumes of mummies and birds, claiming to be Freemasons...bizarre costumes protesting the persecution of their leader."[25] One Native American named Gary Spotted Wolf complained to the Brunswick officials that York's group were a bunch of "wannabes" who were besmirching Indian traditions: "If he's a Native American, then I'm a Red Chinese!"[26]

At the December 2003 pre-trial hearing, York's disciples stood around the courtroom giving journalists a "copyright notice," which stated that the unauthorized use of the name "Dwight York" would be liable to fines. Again, Judge Ashley Royal chastised them for attempting to influence the outcome of the trial.[27]

The Nuwaubians expressed conflicting views on www.unnm.com concerning the efficacy of these theatrical demonstrations. "Bustin Ya Bubble" asks, "Did you really think protesting would free him? Did you think it would make them say, 'Damn, I can't take those drums any longer! Let them have their chief back!'"[28] Some claimed these tactics had backfired—for when the federal trial opened in January 2004, the Nuwaubians were banned from the courtroom and were only allowed to watch the trial on closed-circuit TV on an upstairs floor of the courthouse. "All you did was give them a reason to close the courtroom!" Bustin Ya Bubble complained, placing the blame on Nuwaubian leader, Tshaka Malik Al-Kush, who (according to Bustin Ya Bubble) "weaseled his way into power" by organizing hundreds of Nuwaubians to come out and march in the Brunswick Christmas parade for a demonstration.

Filtering the News: Chomsky's "Worthy Victims"

While York was still awaiting trial, a series of news stories appeared between February and June 2003, based on interviews with the alleged victims who would

---

[24] "Timeline of the unjust case against Dr. Malach Z. York," Nuwaubian flyer, n.d.

[25] Posted Jan 8, 2004 at 5:34 p.m on www.unnm.com

[26] "York trial hits third week," *Atlanta Journal-Constitution*, 19 January 2004 by Bill Torpy.

[27] "Prosecutor: Nuwaubians Tainting Leader's Jury Pool, Molestation Trial," *Associated Press*, 27 December 2003.

[28] Posted Sat 10 January 2004, 4:43 p.m. on www.unnm.com

be the star witnesses for the prosecution. Reporters Bill Osinski, Joe Johnson, and Rob Peecher had made a point of seeking out these key witnesses, travelling to different cities to interview them, and each wrote stories focusing on the lurid sexual details of their (alleged) abuse at the hands of York.[29] These news stories were designed to evoke the emotions of Aristotelian Greek tragedy—of horror and pity. York was portrayed as a sort of pedophilic Bluebeard, and this bad press heavily indicted him to the general public. These journalists did not bother to insert the word "alleged" into any of their stories, and they exhibited a strong empathy for their informants, and for the prosecution's star witness in particular, a pretty young apostate named Abigail Washington. Journalist Rob Peecher expressed strong emotions on meeting York's presumed victims:

> I traveled to New York and met with one of his victims, and with another in Atlanta. They were both still just children, the sweetest, nicest little girls you'd ever want to meet. What sick, twisted perverted bastard would want to hurt them? Prison is not good enough for him! It consumed my life! All of us who were involved, it consumed our lives. We ate, drank, slept Nuwaubians! Through all of it I kind of got to hate the Nuwaubians. It was hard to maintain my objectivity.[30]

On 7 February 2003, the star witness for the prosecution, Abigail Washington appeared on television, interviewed by talk show hostess, Sarah Wallace on Eyewitness News.[31]

The sympathetic portrayal of these alleged victims by journalists corresponds to a pattern that Hermann and Chomsky describe, of "filtering the news" by choosing who are to become the "worthy victims."[32] In their 1988 book, *Manufacturing Consent*, the authors expose the power alliances of the media and argue that news stories often "dichotomize" or simplify subject matter, so that stories are developed within an overarching frame that reduces subjects to black or white. A strong pressure is placed on journalists to conform to an overarching ideology that vetoes controversial stances and interpretations of events, they argue.[33] In a crime or abuse story, this dichotomization process will divide the players into two camps: the "worthy" and the "unworthy" victims. "Worthy" victims are prominent in the story, rendered fully human so as to generate sympathy and emotion in

---

[29] "Former Nuwaubian says leader abused her for years. Innocence lost during life in sect," *OnlineAthens*, 26 July 2003 by Joe Johnson.

[30] Interview with Rob Peecher in *The Nuwaubian Story*, a documentary film by Paul Greenhouse.

[31] "Survivors Speak out about Bizarre Sect Leader, Sentenced to Prison," *New York-WABC*, 7 February 2003.

[32] Edward Herman and Noam Chomsky, *Manufacturing Consent: The Political Economy of the Mass Media* (New York: Pantheon Books, 1988), 31-5.

[33] Herman and Chomsky, 1988.

the readers, whereas "unworthy victims merit only slight detail…with minimal humanization and little context that will excite or outrage."[34]

Rob Peecher, in his articles, makes it quite clear who the worthy victims are, and who is the villain. One headline reads "York's accusers describe years of sexual abuse," and the reader is plunged into a nightmarish world of "quasi-religious" pedophilia and sexual enslavement.[35]

The media reports also claimed "sex props" and videos of children engaged in sexual acts with York were found in York's house, and child pornography literature and photographs—"evidence" that proved York's guilt. Attorney Adrian Patrick, his defence lawyer, however, insisted that these items were never submitted to the court, despite clear statements by various authorities to journalists that such objects had been found in York's house during the raid.[36]

During the weeks preceding the trial—a period when Dr. York should have enjoyed the right of presumption of innocence—these articles conveyed a clear message to the public—that here was an evil, depraved and guilty person. The possibility that Dr. York might *also* be a "worthy victim"—as a falsely accused religious leader—is never entertained.

The result of these news stories was that on 21 November 2003, Judge Royal declared that Macon's jury pool was "tainted." He stated in the pre-trial hearings, "the court is satisfied that without change of venue for the trial in this case the Defendant cannot obtain a fair and impartial trial in Macon Division of Middle district of Georgia."[37] He wrote in the Change of Venue Order, "The Defendant cannot obtain a fair trial in the Macon Division of the Middle District of Georgia…. The Court has grave concerns about trying to select a jury in this case in any division of the Macon and Atlanta media markets."[38]

The case was scheduled to be tried 225 miles away, in the Brunswick division of Southern Georgia. Of the 16 jurors picked, only three were black. Before the case came to court again in January 2004, there was a superseding indictment added. York was reindicted for three counts of evading federal financial reporting requirements, as well as on racketeering (RICO) charges.[39]

---

[34]   Herman and Chomsky, 72-4.

[35]   "York's Accusers Describe Years of Sexual Abuse," *Macon Telegraph*, 1 September 2002 by Rob Peecher.

[36]   Interview with Adrian Patrick by telephone.

[37]   "York Trial Opens with Jury Selection and Tight Security," *Macon Telegraph*, 6 January 2004 by Wayne Crenshaw.

[38]   The court documents can be accessed on the UNN website, www.hesinnocent. com

[39]   The Racketeer-Influenced and Corrupt Organizations (RICO) Act is a 1970 anti-organized crime law designed to fight political corruption and corporate fraud. See Theresa Tedesco, "Black May Face RICO Charges," *National Post*, Canada (13 December 2005), Section A, pp. 1-2. (This was an article about the newspaper magnate, Conrad Black, not "Blacks.")

Because of these new charges, the Brunswick trial was then cancelled, and York was forced to return to Macon where the Grand Jury was located—despite the fact that the Judge had found a "judicially recognized tainted jury pool" in Macon.[40]

Once again, Judge Ashley Royal expressed his worry over the possibility of a tainted jury pool: "This has been a trial involving extraordinary pre-trial publicity," he noted. When he asked the jury how many of them had prior knowledge of the case, "about 35 jurors stood up." It took him three hours to select the jury from those remaining. While the judge told them they would not be sequestered until the trial started, he did caution them strongly against following any media coverage of this high profile case.[41]

The Nuwaubians expressed their outrage at the notion of a tainted jury pool. Neb Hakum Re complained, "out of the 40 or 50 people the Judge brought in… they all admitted they heard something about the case, and the Judge still put them on the jury panel." He points out that "not one of these people…heard of the case from the fliers passed out by Nuwaubians!"[42]

York then called his (white) chief counsel Ed Garland a "racist," and accused him of colluding with the prosecutors in a white conspiracy against his own client. On 29 December 2003 he terminated Ed Garland's contract, and fired all five of his lawyers. One of them, Jonathan Marks, complained to the Press, "York has had 13 different attorneys since his arrest in 2002."[43]

On 12 December 2003, York hired an African-American lawyer, Adrian Patrick. Patrick found himself in the difficult position of taking on the role of Chief Counsel for York's case only six days before the federal trial. He applied for a "continuance" or postponement of the trial so as to allow time to prepare the case. This request was denied.

By January 2004, the initial 116-count indictment of 2002 had been whittled down to 13 counts of racketeering and molestation.

The January 2004 Trial

The dramatic show of force at the January 2004 trial received considerable media coverage. As described in the *Athens-Banner-Herald*, "the court facility…was ringed by dozens of law enforcement personnel, from black SWAT-outfitted Glynn County police officers to machine gun-toting Federal Protective Service officers."

---

[40]   This was one of Adrian Patrick's key arguments for dismissing the charges against his client, during his September 2005 appeal at the Eleventh Circuit Court.

[41]   "Trial Nears for Sect Leader Facing Child Sex and Racketeering Charges," *Macon Telegraph*, 29 December 2003, by Rob Peecher.

[42]   "He's Innocent—Free Rev. Dr. Malachi York!!!," (flyer) 12 March 2008.

[43]   I was told that Dale Brown, York's sister lives at Tama Re and it was she who found and hired York's lawyer, Ed Garland.

According to the Rick Ross website, the rationale given for these extraordinary security measures was to "thwart possible attempts by York's legion of devout followers to influence jurors."[44]

There was a very high level of security in the town, with snipers stationed on rooftops surrounding the courthouse. The jurors were anonymous, the courthouse surrounded by military guards, and the trial took place in a closed chamber. One Nuwaubian, Frederick Johnson, commented, "this excessive show of force tells the jurors that we're here to protect you from a threat!"[45] Nuwaubian Neb Hakum Re protested, "the heavily guarded courthouse in Brunswick was surrounded by… a military type operation with…weapons only seen in movies by most people. This sight alone…would have a negative effect on potential jurors as well as the general public. The Jury pool (before the 16 were selected) had to walk past the heavily guarded courthouse, and a natural perception for any person would be that whoever was involved in this case…must be dangerous or a threat."[46] An administrator of Tama Re also commented on this situation:

> They were decked out in their gear, snipers on the roof, extra security—so people would think "Gosh! This guy we're about to see in this case must be *that bad* to justify all this security!" They did it to intimidate the jury. Sills was real arrogant—it was a control issue with him. It was as if the Civil War had just ended, and they had just abolished slavery—but no one had told him yet![47]

The *Associated Press* reported, "Officials are doing all they can to keep the courtroom from being turned into a Circus." The same article noted (quite erroneously) that York in his youth had "joined the Black Panther Party."[48]

York's relatives and administrators were barred from the courtroom and watched the trial on closed circuit television. In an eloquent vein, "Etherien999" protested on the www.unnm.com website that, "making our people attend the trial on another floor reminds me of the days of the Old South when the family and friends of a Nubian defendant were segregated and…sat in the tier of the courtroom, or made to sit across the street…and only allowed to get update from a kind white member of the white clergy if the mood struck them to do so…. It's truly disgusting."[49]

Prosecutor Stephanie Thacker argued in her opening statement that "Dwight 'Malachi' York set himself up as a messiah figure who taught his followers that

---

[44]   (http://www.rickross.com/reference/nuwaubians/nuwaubians100.html).

[45]   "This little town didn't back up," *Atlanta Journal-Constitution*, 11 January 2004 by Bill Torpy.

[46]   He's Innocent—Free Rev. Dr. Malachi York!!!, 12 March 2008.

[47]   Interview with Khunsu Hotep at Tama Re, 25 June 2004.

[48]   "Sect leader's trial setting official's teeth on edge," *Associated Press*, 5 January, 2004.

[49]   http://www.unnm.com/phpbb2/viewtopic.php?t=63

he was god, the supreme authority," and that "he violated his followers when they were very young and rewarded them with gold bracelets, candy and trips outside the compound."[50] Adrian Patrick countered her in his opening argument, claiming that here was a case of religious and racial persecution:

> "The government is going to attempt to make you believe that the defendant is guilty because he is different" he said. "This is a sexy case. It's about sex and money. We are depending on you to see beyond the fantasy and sensationalism of the case."[51]

He pointed to the lack of physical evidence in the case, and asked, if abuse had really been going on for years, why had no one ever stepped forward to complain, since Tama Re was home to hundreds of people? He also warned the jury that the allegations were coming from members of four families that had all fallen out of favor with York and were out for revenge. "One of the primary witnesses ran the organization for many years and was ousted in February 2001 because she was out of control," Patrick said. He also blamed that same witness for what the prosecutors alleged were York's attempts to illegally hide monetary transactions. Patrick said York filed tax returns every year and made no attempt to hide his financial dealings. At least three of the government's witnesses, he claimed, are testifying in order to avoid being charged with child molestation themselves.

Patrick motioned to suppress possible evidence that had been found by the FBI when they searched York's house in May 2002. He argued the information used to obtain the search warrants was "stale" since it had been obtained from witnesses who had left the group a year-and-half before the warrants were obtained. These warrants referred to apparently innocuous items, described as "sex props" in the indictment: grass skirts from Disneyland, and an animal bean bag on which children (allegedly) posed for nude photos. The judge denied both Patrick's motions to suppress and to dismiss this "evidence."

The Testimony of the Witnesses

During the three-week hearing, Dr. York did not take the stand, but 14 witnesses delivered their testimonies, some claiming, and others denying, abuse. Exactly half (seven) of the witnesses *changed* their stories while they were on the stand, first asserting, then denying (or first denying, then asserting) abuse. Unfortunately, it is not possible to examine their statements in detail, since the court ordered all the findings of fact and conclusions of law to be filed under seal. One can find a

---

[50]   Summed up in the article of 6 January 2004. "Molestation Trial of Cult leader opens," *Atlanta Journal-Constitution*, 6 January 2004 by Mark Niesse.

[51]   "Molestation Trial of Cult leader opens,' *Atlanta Journal-Constitution*, 6 January 2004 by Mark Niesse.

summary of their statements and of the court proceedings, however, in the *Atlanta Journal-Constitution* and the *Macon Telegraph* by journalists who attended the trial and covered the case.

There are many confusing discrepancies in the coverage of the trial. For example, the number of witnesses who denied being victims are reported as being five, six or seven.[52] The "Pink Panther with a Penis" sidles in and out of the trial like a *leitmotiv* in a Wagner opera. Reports on where this sinister stuffed toy was found—in York's bedroom, in a nearby Jacuzzi hut, or in a storage locker bin—are conflicting, and its relevance to the allegations against Dr. York are never made clear.[53]

Nine middle-aged Nuwaubians who had joined the Ansaaru Allah Community in the 1970s took the stand to testify that York was more like a father-figure than a god; that they were not brainwashed; and that his detractors were "liars." "I severely, wholeheartedly, feel this is a conspiracy," said Elvira Rivera. "They're all liars. I knew them as children. They all lie."[54] A few witnesses claimed they had been molested as long ago as 1988, and some claimed they participated in group orgies involving oral sex with York.[55] Some spoke of being encouraged to procure new victims for his sexual needs.

Adrian Patrick pointed to discrepancies between the court statements and the previous statements given by several of the witnesses. For example, one 18-year-old accuser told the court that York had had sex with her since the age of 8, but had changed her story in terms of the place where, and the age when, York had first allegedly raped her. She also gave contradictory reports of leaving the group with no money, and of leaving with $300 in her pocket. A 16-year-old claimed she had been forced to have sex with York since the age of 12, but also admitted she had denied this in her first interview, because she was "scared." A 17-year-old male witness said York had molested him since the age of 12, but in his first interview, where his father and Attorney Manny Arora and a defense investigator were all present, he had denied ever being molested.[56]

Some interesting speculations on the underlying motivations of York and his accusers were expressed in court. A relative of one of the alleged victims said,

---

[52] Mark Niesse's article ("Cult leader's case goes to jury," *Macon Telegraph*, 22 January 2004) notes, "Seven witnesses said on the stand that York did not molest them."

[53] See "Trial puts an end to York's `regular days,'" *Macon Telegraph*, 24 January 2004 by Wayne Crenshaw.

[54] "Nuwaubian members testify York's accusers are untrustworthy," *Associated Press*, 16 January 2004 by Russ Bynum.

[55] "Alleged victim: York stole childhood," *Macon Telegraph*, 7 January 2004 by Wayne Crenshaw.

[56] "Attorney claims bias by judge in York case," *Macon Telegraph*, 9 January 2004 by Wayne Crenshaw.

"All those young ladies are after money."[57] One of the alleged victims claimed York had once explained to her that "his purpose...was to keep the girls loyal to our culture. He said if you have a girl when she is a virgin, she is more likely to remain loyal to you."[58]

Six of the young women who were listed in the indictment and had received subpoenas to appear in court, insisted that they had never said they were abused.[59] One "victim" listed in the indictment, Suhaila Thomas, refuted the FBI report, claiming she had never once said she had been sexually abused by York. Thomas admitted she had met with FBI agents for four to six hours during their investigation, but denied she had ever told them that she had been molested.[60] The defense then called the next five young women who were named as molestation victims in York's federal indictment. One by one, all these young women denied they had been sexually molested by York. "It seemed [the FBI agent who questioned her] wanted me to say something that didn't happen," said 21-year old Sakina Woods. "They kept asking me over and over and I kept telling them, 'No, no, no.'" Hanaan Merritt, an 18-year old, insisted that investigators "basically told us that he molested us. They kept saying, 'No, you're lying.'"[61] Attorney Richard Moultrie responded to her by waving a document in the air and asking incredulously, "you are telling the jury that two [FBI] ladies you never met before made up this six-page statement of what you told them?" Suhaila Thomas nodded in agreement.[62]

Middle District U.S. Attorney, Max Wood commented on the inconsistencies in the witnesses' statements, saying, "It's not unusual in child molestation cases to have inconsistent evidence, because you are dealing with children."[63]

These inconsistencies and denials were rationalized by a retired FBI agent, Kenneth Lanning, a consultant on child molestation cases across the country. When he took the stand, Lanning said, "their answers are related to the reality of

---

[57]   Family members of alleged York victim testify that they doubt girl's story," *Macon Telegraph*, 20 January 2004 by Wayne Crenshaw.

[58]   "Women say York molested them, fathered children," *Macon Telegraph*, 13 January 2004 by Wayne Crenshaw.

[59]   "Alleged victims deny an abuse by sect leader," *Athens Banner-Herald*, 17 January 2004 by Terry Dickson.

[60]   "Sect leader framed, daughter says: Brother had 'vendetta,' she tells jury," *Atlanta Journal-Constitution*, 21 January 2004 by Bill Torpy.

[61]   "York trial hits third week: Key rulings expected today," *Atlanta Journal-Constitution*, 19 January 2004 by Bill Torpy.

[62]   "Sect leader framed, daughter says: Brother had 'vendetta,' she tells jury," *Atlanta Journal-Constitution*, 21 January 2004 by Bill Torpy.

[63]   "Attorney claims bias by judge in York case," *Macon Telegraph*, 9 January 2004 by Wayne Crenshaw.

being a compliant victim and society's inability to deal with it. The kids feel guilty because they didn't say 'no.'" [64]

An alternative explanation for the discrepancies in these witnesses' stories is found in sociological studies of the "Satanic cult scare" during the 1980s. Researchers designed tests to prove that young children can easily be influenced to describe events that never happened, in response to direct and repeated questioning. Sociologists investigating the persistence of the belief in the reality of satanic ritual abuse, despite the absence of corroborating evidence, have also argued that children, if questioned repeatedly and given cues, will seek to please their adult interrogators by supplying the "right" answers.[65] The results of an empirical study by Goodman, Qin, Bottoms and Shaver (1994), funded by the *National Center on Child Abuse and Neglect* raises serious and disturbing questions about the nature and process of recovering traumatic memories, and about the suggestibility of children to repeated and leading questioning by adults seeking confirmation of their beliefs and fears.[66]

Psychologists Carole Lieberman and William Bernet took the stand and expressed the stereotypical "anticult" view of the "cult leader." Bernet explained, "growing up in isolation...children were indoctrinated and subjected to a form of brainwashing...used by pedophiles known as child sexual abuse accommodation syndrome." Lieberman called York a "manipulator" who could "make people believe he was god."[67]

Defense Attorney Adrian Patrick then accused Judge Ashley Royal of helping the prosecution and asked that the judge recuse himself from the case. "The court is clearly acting *de facto* as a prosecutor," Patrick said. The judge countered by saying he had a duty to protect witnesses from "unnecessary embarrassment."[68]

The RICO Charges

York's accountant, Neil Dukoff, was called to the stand and questioned in connection with the RICO charges of money-structuring. The accountant was

---

[64] This view, of discounting children's denial of abuse was first popularized by Roland Summit in his 1978 paper, "The Child Sexual Abuse Accommodation Syndrome."

[65] Jeffrey Victor, *Satanic Panic: The Creation of a Contemporary Legend*. Chicago: Open Court, 1993.

[66] The interview techniques of Kee MacFarlane of Children's Institute International, for example, has been criticized by researchers. Her agency interviewed hundreds of children involved in the McMartin Preschool investigation, using anatomically detailed dolls and hand puppets.

[67] "Experts see manipulator in sect leader," *Athens Banner-Herald*, 11 January 2004 by Joe Johnson.

[68] "Witness tells of sex abuse, death threat by York," *Macon Telegraph*, 15 January 2004 by Wayne Crenshaw.

called by the defense to refute the government's racketeering charges against York. Those charges accused York of splitting cash deposits in order to avoid depositing more than $10,000 at one time, which would have to be reported to the IRS. Dukoff showed the jury York's federal income tax returns from 1996 to 2001 that indicated a gross income of nearly $6 million over that time period. York's net annual income—the amount after expenses related to operating his businesses are deducted—ranged from $70,000 to $225,000. The income came from four businesses: The Ancient Mystic Order of Melchizedek, Holy Tabernacle Ministries, Holy Tabernacle Stores and various rental properties.[69] It appeared that York had paid his taxes, and Dukoff observed that his client could have paid less in taxes if he had claimed his 100-odd children as dependents. He also noted that York never tried to file for tax-exempt status as a religious organization. "He wanted to call it a business," Dukoff said. But he also stated under cross examination that the tax returns were based on information provided by York's finance office. Therefore, Dukoff could not say whether or not criminal activity relating to York's finances had occurred.[70]

Journalist Bill Torpy makes the point that, although York's organization averaged "more than one million a year," no wages were ever paid out to "employees or followers."[71]

Defense attorney, Adrian Patrick, in his closing arguments asked whether it were physically possible for York, a middle-aged man with a heart condition, to have sex with so many people. On the basis of the court testimony, he counted a total of 11,568 times between 1993-2001. He displayed a chart showing the connections between Jacob York and all the victims who testified in the trial, arguing they had colluded in a conspiracy launched by Jacob who was angry because his father refused to lend him money for his music business.[72] He also attempted to counter the racketeering charges by portraying the Nuwaubian organization as a spiritually uplifting group that cleaned up a crime-infested area in Brooklyn and gave followers new direction in their lives.[73]

A jury of nine men and three women deliberated for seven hours, over two days. On 23 January 2004 they pronounced Dr. York guilty of four counts of racketeering and six child-molestation-related charges.

---

[69] Wayne Crenshaw, "Family members of alleged York victim testify that they doubt girl's story," *Macon Telegraph*, 20 January 2004.

[70] Wayne Crenshaw, "Family members of alleged York victim testify that they doubt girl's story," *Macon Telegraph*, 20 January 2004.

[71] "York reported no wages paid," *Atlanta Journal-Constitution*, 20 January 2004. (Both Max Weber and Rosabeth Moss Kanter have observed that charismatic communities and utopian communes typically rely on donations, voluntary labor and exhibit unconventional economic patterns. Predictably, the Nuwaubian communes conform to this model.)

[72] "Cult leader's case to go to jury," *Macon Telegraph*, 22 January 2004.

[73] "York trial hits third week: Key rulings expected today," *The Atlanta Journal-Constitution*, 19 January 2004 by Bill Torpy.

Prosecutor Richard Moultrie commented, "I am very proud of the victims. I admire them, and I'm very pleased for them. It is their victory."[74] Sheriff Sills' opinion was also solicited by journalists. The Sheriff described York as "one of the most heinous criminals in the history of this nation."[75] Of Tama Re, he commented, "it was like another nation, a nation behind an iron curtain."[76] It was quite clear whose side the media were on, for congratulatory headlines appeared like, "This little town didn't back up"; "Eatonton feels relief as nearby cult wanes"; "His dream became their nightmare." The sentence was rendered on 22 April 2004. Dwight York was condemned by Judge C. Ashley Royal to 135 years in prison.

Critiques of the Trial

On 22 February 2004, Judge Royal had ordered the court transcripts to be sealed. Ahmose Khamose, a Nuwaubian talking on the radio show, *Run Sam, Run!*, reports that he requested the transcripts but was told, "the court records were sealed because for safety of the minors policy, the rationale was to "protect the identities of the minor victims, pursuant to Title 18, United States Code, Section 3509(d).... I was told it was policy—and yet none of the victims in this case who testified were minors."[77]

Dr. York complained that the witnesses had been manipulated by the judge:

> The so-called victims in the indictment…the prosecution never called them! *We* had to call them the so-called victims and put them on the stand. That's when the judge…every time we put a victim on the stand who had something to say, that was valid, the judge said, "Hold on! Get the jury out of the room, I want to hear them privately." They called four witnesses before the court who said, "he never molested me, nothing ever happened"—and they still want to use those things…and put that part in the guilty charge.[78]

---

[74]   "Sect leader guilty of molestation," *Atlanta Journal-Constitution*, 24 January 2004 by Bill Torpy.

[75]   "Nuwaubian leader guilty," *Athens Banner-Herald*, 24 January 2004 by Terry Dickson.

[76]   "York found guilty of child molestation and racketeering," *Associated Press*, 23 January 2004.

[77]   Ahmose Khamose, in "Radio Show Talks About Injustices in Dr. Malachi York's Case" (Georgia community activist online radio show www.runsamrun.com, aired 9 Nov 2007) talks about the injustices and lack of evidence in the case of Dr. Malachi Z. York. (See also www.youtube.com/watch?v=X7rIdeuTSoo). Dr. Frederick Bright also questions the rationale behind the sealed transcripts. See "Interview with Dr. Frederick Bright" (www.youtube.com/watch?v=HFnUoBIajiU).

[78]   www.youtube.com/watch?v=X7rIdeuTSoo

York's daughter pointed out that the allegations had her father committing 11,568 sex acts between 1993 and 2001—even after Dr. York had been diagnosed with hereditary angiodema and put on a medication that lowers the testosterone level.

Tama Re administrator, Al Woodall, protested that the court ignored a jurisdiction issue. Since Chief Black Eagle was a Native American, he argued, the U.S. federal government had no jurisdiction over him or the Sovereign Land. Another Nuwaubian commented on the RICO conviction: "So, he's the Kingpin? RICO is designed to catch the Kingpins, right?—but also to catch the gang. Every individual in jail for RICO had to have accomplices. Every case I know of RICO, the Mafia boss gets locked up *with his whole gang of gangsters.* I don't see nobody else locked up with Maku, he's all alone in there. How can you have a kingpin with no mob to help carry out his criminal activities?"

A thought-provoking critique of the trial was supplied by Dr. Frederick Bright in his interview on *youtube.*[79] He had been contacted by York's family to review the medical information provided by to the defence by the government, as a physician and gynaecologist licensed to practice in the State of Georgia. He submitted a report in December 2002 on the case, and subsequently served as expert witness in the federal trial of January 2004. Dr. Bright pointed to the absence of physical evidence in the trial, particularly the lack of DNA evidence.[80] Victims named in trials have usually undergone medical examinations within 72 hours after the alleged assault has occurred, he noted. He raised the issue of the remarkable absence of pregnancies, considering the overwhelming number of rape allegations by females of childbearing age. He argued the medical histories of the victims were inconsistent with their testimonies; for example there were no signs of scarring in the anal or vaginal region that would be caused by sodomy or rape. "Because there had been no medical examinations of the alleged victims at the time when trauma to their body orifices could be used as evidence," he argues, "the prosecution could say, 'well, it happened just the way were saying it,' and they don't have to be held accountable. There was no forensic evidence of any kind linking the victims to Dr. Malachi in this case."

He also pointed out that none of the alleged victims gave *specific dates* when the alleged acts of molestation had occurred. They referred rather vaguely to the "summer of 1999" or the "Fall of 2000." These dates were important, he argued, because in several cases the alleged victim had her 16th birthday during that period, so that she might not have been a minor at the time the alleged molestation occurred. This "deprived the defendant of using the proper age as a defence against those allegations."

Dr Bright also complained of "certain irregularities in the way trial was conducted." The judge, he noted, "disallowed certain information by defence" and whittled down the range of issues to be discussed. He pointed to the fact that "half

79   Interview with Dr. Frederick Bright (www.youtube.com/watch?v=HFnUoBIajiU).
80   Interview with Dr. Frederick Bright (www.youtube.com/watch?v=HFnUoBIajiU).

of the victims denied under oath, both in court and when they were examined, that they had been molested."

After the trial was moved to the federal court in Brunswick, Dr. Bright observed "a highly irregular military presence—as if Al Capone were on trial. As a witness, I was intimidated by the massive police presence. I saw it as a way of swaying the jury." He strongly objected to the date of the trial, since it overlapped with Martin Luther King Day, a national holiday ("and yet federal court trial proceeded and ignored this day that is highly significant for African-Americans").[81]

The Star Witness Recants

By the end of the week that Dr. York had received his sentence, the Nuwaubians produced a videotape of Abigail Washington, the star witness for the prosecution, in which she recanted her testimony and stated that York was innocent of the charges.[82] She also wrote an affadavit for the court accusing Jacob York, Dr. Malachi York's son, of organizing a conspiracy of ex-members to frame his own father.

Abigail ("Habibah") Washington's 18 April 2004 recant statement ("The Falsely Accused Dr. Malachi Z. York: Government's Key Witness Recants False Testimony") can be viewed on *youtube*, and on the Nuwaubian websites.[83] Abigail is a pretty young woman with braided African hair, wearing a peach-coloured shirt and crystal earrings. She speaks eloquently (despite flawed grammar) and comes across as a straightforward, intelligent person. Abigail's testimony provides glimpses into the relationships between some of the key actors in the case against Dr. York, and into the personal motives of the whistle blowers. She declares in her testimony that she felt intimidated and threatened by both the FBI and Jacob York, and realized she was vulnerable to prosecution because she had been one of the top administrators at Tama Re who handled the financial affairs of the community. She had reason to fear that she might be implicated in some of the RICO/Racketeering charges (such as "money-structuring").

> Before we left [for Florida] I had a conversation with Jacob outside of his house. Jacob was really upset with his father…how he hated him, how he felt his father needed to be in jail. He wanted us to bring a case against his father and told us that some of the boys and girls that had left went to the government about child molestation. I was the main person in charge of finances…I was basically in

[81]   Interview with Dr. Frederick Bright (www.youtube.com/watch?v=HFnUoBIajiU).

[82]   "Recanted Testimony Prompts Delay," *Athens Banner-Herald*, 29 April 2004 by Maryann McNeal; "New Evidence Exonerates Johnson and York," *Eatonton Tribune*, June 2004; See also Sharon Crawford, "York attorneys seeking new trial," *Macon Telegraph*, 25 May 2004.

[83]   www.unnm.com and www.hesinnocent.com

charge. The FBI knew who I was…and he said there were certain things I'd done that could be incriminating. The FBI could come after me and take my kids. I could be incarcerated, put in jail unless I went to them first with information against Malachi [York].

She described a veiled threat: "Jacob said he'd talked to other members and I should really, really talk to them, so I would not be prosecuted and see how I could clear my name." She notes, "Jacob also brought up the fact that I had a child by his father when I was 17… . I was not forced, I consented, there was nothing wrong with it. I was an adult, it was my decision." On the way down to Florida in the car, "Jacob started to talk about going on the Land [to] kidnap other little kids off the Land. He didn't feel they should be living…with his Father. But none of us were interested… . So Jacob said, 'we can do it the legal way.'" After they returned to Georgia, she claims that Jacob applied more pressure and intimidation:

Jacob told me that there were certain children who went to the FBI about certain things with myself, and there was no way I could disprove it. The only way was to go to the FBI and seek immunity. At that point I was afraid. No one really messes with the FBI. So, I went to the FBI the following day with Jacob. He went in and talked for an hour, I sat in the car, and then they called me out. I gave them my name… . They talked about the different kids that I knew… . I told them about my life in the community. There were questions about money charges, because I did deal with the money, how we ran our finances, I felt they already knew about me. I went along, I said, "yes, I did do these things." I had to tell them what they felt that they knew. They asked me if I knew members who would want to talk to them. The only [ex] members I knew were also disgruntled with Malachi. Nicole, Sakinah, Ahmal, Krystal—they all had issues against Malachi. They called in different people, and we all called each other and we discussed how the story should go and backed each other's stories up. That's how the case sort of started.

Abigail discussed the private motives of the whistle blowers:

Nicole had a lot of disgruntled [SIC] issues—she had been kicked out and she felt it was wrong…she spent her whole life in the community, she had nowhere to go, Everybody started venting about different things they dislike—nothing to do with child abuse—things to do with growing up, mostly arguments with Malachi. Jacob brought up the fact that he was in love with Nicole [and that] she was in love with his Father. Jacob fed off of that anger, he felt his father was responsible for his mother's death, his brother's death. Jacob took that anger and said we should go to the government with that anger.

She explains how the finances at Tama Re were handled:

I'm also going to talk about the money situation…a lot of the financial decisions that were made were by me when I was in charge, Kathy also. We collected, separated the money, how it was handled, where it went, He never sat us down and told us about the FBI or IRS. He was very serious about handling money legally. I didn't really understand the structure charges; they explained that any time you try to avoid filling out that report—that is a serious charge.[84] Malachi never told us not to file those reports. He never told us not to follow through or talk to any one. He had nothing to do with finance.

She claimed the ex-members all supported each other's stories:

If Nicole did an interview, she would call us, we would back her up…make her story sound more real, more believable. If we all prosecuted [incriminated] ourselves, then what we said about Malachi would sound believable. If we all back each other up, we can make it sound more believable.

Besides receiving threats, she claims she was offered bribes:

Jacob said we would have a class action lawsuit worth millions of dollars. We would make movies, there would be books…everybody fed off of that idea. Prior to going to Florida, he showed us movies…Charles Manson, the guy in Watergate [Heaven's Gate?] and leaders of other cults. He made us look at the documentary and compare it to his father, to the way we lived, where parents would live with parents, children with children, brothers together, mothers together—not a normal way to live, a cult. Yes, we were in a cult—that type of mind-frame. Added onto the anger, "so this is how we grew up!"

Abigail regrets that she did not seek legal counsel before going to the FBI:

In my initial interview I made some statements. I did not have my personal attorney to represent me, to explain...what immunity really meant. I thought it meant I would be protected, that what I said could not be used against me… . I was afraid of going to jail…afraid my children would be taken away from me. I spoke to different agents and they said, "You know, Habibah, you can be incarcerated for certain things!" Being reminded of that, I felt compelled to go ahead with the story. By breaking the agreement, I could be prosecuted, because I had given certain statements already. We had an attorney representing all the victims, but I did not have my personal attorney… . I felt compelled to go ahead with the story. I didn't really know my rights.

---

[84]   Adrian Patrick gave an example of "money structuring" as follows: " If you have a cheque for $10,000 and you put it in a financial institution, it is a requirement that you must report it to the IRS. If you don't then that is money structuring."

She explains her personal reasons for recanting:

> Why I want to come out with the truth now? It's really, really important for me
> that I tell the truth! I don't sleep at night knowing two people will spend the rest
> of their lives in jail as I speak because of disgruntled issues that me and a whole
> bunch of ex-members came out with.... I feel totally guilty bringing this case
> against Malachi. I don't feel that it's right that he is in jail right now because all
> of us were angry and got together and agreed to this case and we went ahead
> with it.... Nobody should be sent to jail because of a bunch of lies! What was
> said on the stand was a bunch of lies. I just feel the Truth had to come out. There
> is no way a person can go on living their life knowing they sent someone to jail
> for life...no way!

York's attorneys demanded a new trial in light of this new evidence. The Nuwaubians
held a series of press conferences at the end of April to broadcast the good news
of the recant, and triumphantly distributed DVDs of Abigail's testimony to their
contacts in the media. They printed a less-than-convincing replica of the *Eatonton
Tribune* in June of 2004. The headlines announced, "Second Nuwaubian Recants
Testimony: Witnesses Say York Never Molested Them!"

But they were bitterly disappointed by the lack of response.[85] Only two
journalists chose to cover the story.[86] And they were even more discouraged when
Abigail Washington took the stand in August 2004 and rescinded her recantation.
She explained to the court that her recant had been motivated by pity; she had felt
"he deserved a second chance."[87]

The Seizure and Sale of the "Land"

On 22 April 2004, Dr. Malachi Z. York had been sentenced by Judge C. Ashley
Royal to 135 years in federal prison. Now that York was found guilty of RICO
and no retrial was in the offing, the government moved to claim the 450 acres of
Tama Re.[88]

The Triad protested in vain that York did not legally own the property, for
in February 1999 he had deeded it in a trust to nine people, now listed as the

---

[85]   I describe this meeting at the National Black Theatre in Harlem in my Preface.

[86]   "York's Supporters say Tape Proves his Innocence," *Macon Telegraph*, 23 April
2004 by Sharon Crawford.

[87]   "Witness in York Case Maintains her Original Testimony was True," *Associated
Press*, 14 August 2004.

[88]   "Nuwaubian Leader Likely to Face New Charges, Including Racketeering," *Macon
Telegraph*, 25 October 2003 by Rob Peecher (this article is the only one that goes into any
detail concerning the RICO charges).

legitimate owners.[89] Judge Ashley Royal, nevertheless, issued an order on 14 July 2004 to seize the land of Tama Re, a property worth $1.7 million. The Egyptian temples were demolished, the gods were smashed and the Nuwaubians' "Mecca in the West," was sold at auction.[90]

Sheriff Sills was spotted personally driving one of the bulldozers that tore down the "compound." "It feels good to tear down the SOB myself," he told journalist Bill Torpy.[91] By this time most journalists had given up all pretence of objectivity. Joe Johnson of the *Augusta Chronicle* described Dr. York's mansion in unbridled purple prose—and he mistakenly tacked on two years to York's already draconian jail sentence:

> The mansion's rank odor is as foul as the unspeakable deeds done there when occupied by a religious sect leader now serving a 137-year prison sentence on federal molestation and racketeering charges.[92]

A Conspiracy?

An article called "Conspiracy And [sic] Conspirators" appeared on the Nuwaubian websites in April 2004. It claimed that Jacob York had "masterminded a conspiracy" by forming a network of ex-members "with disgruntled issues" [sic] to put Dr. Malachi Z. York in jail for life and seize the Land belonging to the Yamassee Nation:

> It is time to reveal the conspiracy and the conspirators that have caused the illegal incarceration of Maku: Chief Black Thunderbird "Eagle," Dr. Malachi Z. York. For more than a year and a half Maku: Chief Black Thunderbird "Eagle," AN INNOCENT MAN, has been tortured mentally and physically, unjustly held without bond, deceived by the officers of the court, held under duress, enduring violation after violation of his human rights, granted by the creator. The question that you must ask is FOR WHAT?!! Now it is time that we pull all the pieces together and expose the conspiracy and the leaders behind it. The demonic forces behind this evil scheme is none other than JACOB YORK aka YAQUWB ABDULLAH MUHAMMAD the son of Dr. Malachi Z. York.

The authors also note that, on 17 February 2003 A.D., Abigail Washington had appeared on the Sarah Wallace show and announced that it was during a reunion

---

[89]   "The Talk of the Town," *Macon Telegraph*, 4 February 2000 by Rob Peecher.

[90]   "Former Nuwaubian property sold; demolition begins." *Associated Press*, 10 June 2005.

[91]   "Demolition begins on land seized from Nuwaubian sect," *The Atlanta Journal-Constitution*, 11 June 2005 by Bill Torpy.

[92]   "Nuwaubian Manor goes up for auction, "*Augusta Chronicle*, 18 August 2005 by Joe Johnson.

with several ex-followers that they had all agreed to tell their story to the authorities, and that had been the "turning point." The Nuwaubian author concludes:

> This is confirmation of the plot. Abigail Washington thought that after the bogus plea agreement this case was over all the liars and conspirators would collect their portion of the $414,000 that was stolen off of the 404 Shady Dale Rd. property and the house in Athens, to simply move on with their lives.

The prose is vituperative, hysterical in tone, and riddled with errors in spelling, grammar and diction. It is also full of teen gossip about who was having sex with whom. This is unfortunate, since the subjective, immature tone of the narrator(s) tends to undermine its serious underlying message. But it does invite us to examine the grievance claims of a handful of ex-members who defected during different tumultuous phases of the Nuwaubian movement and came together to complain about their leader.

One of these apostates is Pauline who had three children by York and who claims she was "kicked out" of the AAC because she was sick and unable to work.[93] She had left home when she was 16, joined the AAC in Philadelphia, and was called by Dr. York to New York where she worked as a writer and editor in their publications office. She described how she became Dr. York's concubine in an interview over the telephone:

> I found him very charismatic, he took my breath away. I was 18 or 19 when we got together. I wanted to go to college, but women were not allowed to go to college—they were too easily influenced, he said. I was under a lot of brain power control at the time. It wasn't rape, it was consensual, but it was terrible the first few times. I wanted to hide! I was a virgin. But then I was glad to be his wife and stayed with York for years. I had prestige in the community as one of his wives and mother of his children. But then he put me out. I was pregnant with my third child…I was very ill and couldn't work. He saw I was of no use to him and put me out—no money, no milk for the children, no pampers. I had to go on medical assistance. I was suffering from stress. We were living in Liberty, N.Y. (That was while he was "The Lamb")…. I had a nervous breakdown.[94]

The Montel Williams Show

Pauline and two other ex-wives (who were among the original whistle blowers to the FBI) revealed themselves years later on the Montel Williams Show, "Cult

---

[93] Interview with Pauline over the telephone, 25 May 2007. She identified herself and told the same story on the *Montel Williams Show*, although Osinski refers to her as "Nasira."

[94] Interview with Pauline, 25 May 2007.

Survivors Speak Out," aired on 10 February 2007. The ebullient African-American host, Montel Williams, opens the show by announcing, "Over 3000 cults exist in America today, with over three million members" [later in the show he repeats this statement, but substitutes "four million" members]. "The amount of pain that these people suffer is unimaginable!" he concludes. Images of the mass suicides in Jonestown and Heaven's Gate flash by, and a woman announces "30% who die in cults are children. Despite the damage caused by cults, few organizations exist to help prevent the damage."

Montel first brings on Pauline, who complains she was treated like a "second-hand citizen" in the "cult." She is a tall, attractive woman, and talks about how, a year and a half after leaving the cult, she wrote the very first letter to Sheriff Sills alerting him of sexual abuse "out at the compound." Montel reads out her letter that complains of "the sick, theocratic hold Dwight York has over the thoughts of his followers...Dwight has been exercising more divine rule...to do anything he wants to girls under 16 years of age and boys of the same age, and a [handful] of concubines." While Pauline admits she never actually "saw with my own eyes anything happening with the children," she affirms that she "heard rumours." Sick and pregnant at the time with her third child who had congenital defects, she states she saw little kids coming out of his room late at night and felt a sick feeling in her stomach: "I just knew he was messing with those kids."

Two other pretty young women, Nicole and Sakinah, tell their stories (punctuated by interruptions and prompting from Montel). Both were brought into the AAC by their mothers as children, and each bore a child by York. Both girls were over the age of 17 when they gave birth, but they claimed Dr. York had molested them when they were still under the legal age.

Next, Montel introduces Bill Osinski, author of the 2007 book, *Ungodly: The True Story of Unprecedented Evil.* [95] Osinski sums up Dr. York's religious mission in one sentence: "York was a young ex-con who figured out a great way to get all the sex and money he wanted; it was to declare himself a god, all this religion stuff was a façade!"

Montel then introduces a Sergeant Tracey Bowen who speaks of the anonymous letters received by Sheriff Sills. One letter, received in September 1998, included a diagram of the "compound," showing the sleeping quarters of the girls and women next to York's apartment, and the men's sleeping quarters in the barn after the tribal system of segregating members by age and sex. The Sergeant spoke of the number of children fathered by York: "When we did the raid on the compound we located a yellow notebook that we had been told about...with pictures of the mothers and a record of the children he had fathered by them. We counted 89 children, and were able to verify 20 more." She claimed they figured Dr. York had fathered "close to 200 or more" children.

Sakinah was the author of this diagram of the "compound," according to the authors of "Conspiracy And [sic] Conspirators": "Sakinah Parham came to

---

[95]   Interviews with Pauline, Sakinah and Nicole are featured in Osinski's book.

the 404 Shady Dale Rd. property days before the 8 May 2002 A.D. raid. She was the one who walked through every building and gave the FBI items to place in their affidavit to get the illegal search warrant." (Damon Prior, an ex-member, claims the girls were promised money, cars, and told they would be put on the FBI payroll: "They trusted Jacob because he was Dr. York's son, so they followed him.")

The Eleventh Circuit Appeal

On 14 September 2005, York's Attorney, Adrian Patrick appeared before the 11th Circuit Appeal court in Atlanta to argue that York's conviction should be overturned.[96]

Patrick pointed out many errors in law throughout York's legal process. He argued that the state charges and the federal charges had been "improperly combined." He claimed that the charges of interstate transport of minors for unlawful sexual activity in violation of the Mann Act had been slapped on "opportunistically," so as to allow the federal agents to be involved in the case. He challenged the assumption that the United Nuwaubuan Nations[97] was an organized crime syndicate, and pointed out that the application of RICO was "based on the belief that a State of Georgia-recognized church ministry and Native American tribe constitutes an enterprise for illegal activities."

Patrick's second argument focused on the problem of the media's influence on the outcome of the trial. He claimed the grand jury was tainted by pre-trial publicity, for after the trial had been moved from Macon to Brunswick, GA (due to all the negative pre-trial publicity that had appeared in the Macon newspapers), the federal prosecutors "improperly" sought an enlarged indictment against York. This new indictment moved the trial back to Macon so that Dr. York could appear before the grand jury. "There is no way in fairness that they should have gone back to that [tainted] jury pool!" Adrian Patrick insisted.[98]

Patrick's third argument concerns a "conspiracy of ex-members."[99] He claims that the allegations of child molestation had been "hatched up by individuals ousted from the organization for one reason or another." These individuals were invited by Jacob York to go on a trip to South Beach, Florida during the Memorial Day weekend, 26-30 May 2001. "Jacob York had a grudge against his father and organized all of the members who were ousted. They went to South Beach, a

---

[96] "Nuwaubian leader's case back in court," *First Coast News*, 15 September 2005 by Tenikka Smith.

[97] By this time the group had dropped the "of Moors" in their title, so that the United Nuwaubian Nation of Moors (UNNM) became the United Nuwaubian Nation (UNN).

[98] "Attorneys argue Nuwaubian leader's appeal in court," *Associated Press*, 14 September 2005 by Daniel Yee.

[99] www.youtube.com/watch?v=Pqssxu3QxCo

resort area—an expensive resort area—to have fun. This occurred immediately prior to going to the FBI to report. Within a day or two, that's when they went to the FBI.[100]

Patrick complains that "the court ruled against us…as if we were reaching for a theory. But we had hard evidence to support our theory."

But despite Adrian Patrick's well-prepared appeal and compelling arguments, Dr. Malachi York's conviction was upheld.

Interview with Adrian Patrick, Attorney at Law

I interviewed Adrian Patrick on two occasions over the telephone. I had read his arguments at the Eleventh Circuit Appeal, and I was surprised they were rejected, so I asked him to explain some of the puzzling aspects of the case.

Palmer: "What was the purpose of the May 8, 2002 raid on Tama Re? Did they find any illegal weapons?"

Patrick: "Weapons in Tama Re? It's like Bush in Iraq, looking for weapons of mass destruction. It was extension of his fantasy about stockpiling weapons, based on faulty information. There were over 300 officers that went in. Here, in Georgia, we have a raid based on spiteful rumors, on faulty information and an overuse of force. Guns pointed at children. It was pretty brutal. They came in with masks on, but after several days of interrogation there was no evidence of molestation. There was an extreme use of force, it was violent, ridiculous, unnecessary. Their pretext was to protect the children—by pulling guns on kids? There were allegations of stockpiles of weapons. Any act of the Nuwaubians was seen as extreme. Now, you can put anything you want in an affidavit, but this one had no information—there was nothing specific—they were prepared for anything! More important, they had established that Dr. York would not be in the premises."

Palmer: "What about the media's stories about finding child pornography?"

Patrick: "They were looking for child pornography, but it was never found. No videos, no nude photos. Nothing! But the whole scenario was troublesome, because the nature of the allegations kept changing. The news articles lied about the child porn videos. These were never found nor produced. They made it all up. There never was one picture, not one porn video, no nothing! Not in his house, not on the Tama Re property."

Palmer: "What about the Pink Panther story?"

Patrick: "Now there was another building that was a storage unit full of bins with…junk, and they found a toy pink panther with a penis. The journalists said he kept it beside his bed and he used it to initiate kids into sex. But it was just somebody's…junk, probably a silly joke. It never found its way into his house."

Palmer: "If they found nothing incriminating in the raid, then why was he convicted?"

---

[100]   www.youtube.com/watch?v=Pqssxu3QxCo

Patrick: "Part of the problem from the beginning was that the media had already colored him so bad! He was found guilty of some charges that were unfounded. The plea bargain—it compounded the problem, it influenced the judge and the jury. After several months of pre-trial negativity, we had to go against 20 jurors who were struck from the jury pool. At the 2004 criminal trial federal level, there were two 'not guiltys.' Half the children said he didn't, half of them say he did—and they kept switching sides. We almost had a hung jury. One juror said she did not believe them, and then there was a request to remove this one juror who was 'not listening to evidence.' It is a very rare situation for the other jurors to complain that one of them 'isn't listening to evidence'! Then they went back in to deliberate. And after lunch she changed her mind—so there must have been some strong-arming going on."

Palmer: "Can you explain the charges?"

Patrick: "Initially there were only four charges. He pleaded guilty to them in federal court—and the judge was part of the decision-making. Six months later, the judge rejects his plea bargain. On November 16, 2002 they added RICO—six months *after* the initial charges. RICO is extremely easy to prove in the federal court."

Palmer: "Why is RICO so 'easy to prove'?"

Patrick: "Once you slap a RICO charge on someone, you're almost guaranteed winning. RICO is extremely easy to prove because you can cite the testimonies of 'unindicted co-conspirators.' That means there are some witnesses who could not go on the stand because of conflicts at the state and federal level. If the prosecution had simply gone with 'child molestation' I think he would have been acquitted—because there were so many children who said he didn't do it. Those kids were so confused! They kept accusing each other, changing their stories…. No jury would have found him guilty on the basis of those kids' testimonies.

"But if they go with 'conspiracy to molest,' then other people are brought into the trial as evidence—the 'unindicted co-conspirators.' When I would ask to cross examine the witnesses, I was told I could not because, 'they are unindicted co-conspirators.' It was like coming up against a brick wall. Who are these people? We don't know. They are simply 'unindicted co-conspirators.'

"The state of Georgia had an anonymous tip in 1997. If they truly believed that children were being abused, they would have acted sooner, not waited three and a half years to investigate. I am convinced the prosecution's concern was not to protect the children, but it was a cloak to get him out of the county and to get the land. They use one premise for another premise."

[Patrick also explained that the seizure of the Land was an illegal act, since Dr. York's conviction was still under appeal. "During that period of time between the conviction and the sentencing of the person, there was a motion that the evidence was insufficient, a motion for a new trial, and a motion to stay forfeiture proceedings." If property is seized before an appellate court hearing, he explained, it is prior to judgment, and is based on an assumption of what the judgment will be.]

Palmer: "What about the witnesses, the alleged victims?"

Patrick: "The children kept telling social workers, 'nothing ever happened!'"

"One child complained he kept telling and telling them it never happened to him—then finally he got tired and said, 'ok, ok, it did happen!' Now there were 42 witnesses on the stand, and one witness was named who was never even interviewed. On the stand he claimed they never took his statement [which was] 'Dr. York never touched me!'

"There was a lot wrong with this case, in the techniques of questioning the kids, in the way they combined the different charges... . There was no data, no physical evidence. They alleged he had sex with 3, 4, 5 year-olds, but there was no evidence—no scarring, bleeding, etc. The doctors said everything was normal. There was no history of trauma.

"But it seems when you have a child molestation charge, all you need is an allegation, and then the onus is on the accused to try to prove his innocence. There is nothing to counter, nothing to tackle. I tell my clients, 'be very careful when you are alone with female children!'"

Palmer: "Do you think the jury was prejudiced against Dr. York because he was a 'cult leader'?"

Patrick: "It was a complex case for the jury. They were faced with an uncommon culture. We're from rural GA, the southern Bible Belt, and a lot of people are uncomfortable with a group that is not...orthodox, not going to church on Sunday, if you understand my meaning. But the whole purpose of the clause in the Constitution on Freedom of Religion—it is to *protect* freedom of religious minorities. The way I see it is, the whole purpose of the prosecution was to get rid of a culture, a new religion they felt uncomfortable with in the Bible Belt."

Palmer: "Do you think it is possible that Dr. York may have molested children?"

Patrick: "I cannot go back and say what did or did not happen ten years ago in the privacy of his bedroom. But, I *can* say that there were state allegations that were not suitable for prosecution in a federal case."

Palmer: "What about the charges of transporting minors across state lines?"

Patrick: "The charges of interstate transport of minors were ridiculous! It was a pretext to turn it into a federal case, because it was alleged he had transported children across state lines from New York to Georgia strictly for purposes of sexual molestation. They finally admitted in court that there was no sexual molestation going on when he took the kids to Disneyland. I got them to drop the Disneyland charges, but they kept the charges of interstate transport of minors when the whole group moved from New York to Brooklyn. Then you had whole families moving up, driving kids in their cars, finding housing and new jobs. They were saying the entire purpose of Dr. York's decision to buy land in Georgia and construct a theme park and declare the land a sovereign nation was...to move kids around so that he could molest them."

Palmer: "So, how would you sum up the case?"

Patrick: "There were a lot of inconsistencies. It was double jeopardy, a dual prosecution. There was no way out once there was an attack on the federal level—once they decided to use RICO!"

Figure 5   Dr. York escorted down the courtroom steps after his guilty verdict

Chapter 6
Regressing into the Millennium

The United Nuwaubian Nation, as a "world-rejecting" movement, has weathered 25-odd years of conflict with society, but the Nuwaubians have consistently refrained from aggressive reprisals. Rather, they have sought to confound their enemies by adopting evasive tactics. Confronted with external threats and bureaucratic pressures they will stage ritualistic public demonstrations, or they may try to deflect hostility through humor, as in a photograph taken in 2002 which shows Roy Barnes posing with seven Nuwaubians dressed in clown costumes, with wigs and red noses, carrying placards that read: "Violence is no joke!" and "Hate is nothing to clown with!"[1] Often they resort to camouflage; by dressing up as their mythic ancestors and stepping backwards into the mists of time. One finds many examples of these evasive tactics in their short history.

After the move to Georgia, as tension mounted and county officials in Georgia continued to stonewall their zoning and building requirements, the Nuwaubians resorted to quasi-legal strategies of self-defense. First, they tried to stack the voters' rolls and were accused of voting fraud. Then they put forward their own Republican candidates for office, and their own candidate for Sheriff, which the locals interpreted as an attempt to "take over" the State of Georgia. Next, they resorted to Common Law tactics learned from various radical anti-government groups, like the Georgia Rangers and Everett Stout. These colorful incidents were ineffective and served to enhance the public's perception of the Nuwaubians as threatening weirdos.

They also resorted to shape-shifting strategies. When the zoning disputes began, they reacted by reverting from their Wild West cowboy or Amerindian attire to the Moorish fez and high-collared, gold-embroidered black suit. When their lawyers' rational, legal self-defensive measures met with delays or obstacles, Dr. York and his people would suddenly change their color, like chameleons, and hide inside a new racial identity. When their Ramses Social Club was stalled by zoning problems, they redefined it as a "Masonic Lodge." In May, 2001 they made an offer to purchase on the Al Sihad Shrine Temple on Poplar Street in Macon, with a down payment of $50,000, and began to call it the "Al Mahdi Shrine No.19."[2] York then became the "Imperial Grand Potentate of the International Supreme

---

[1]   Bill Osinski, *Ungodly: A True Story of Unprecedented Evil* (Indigo Publishing, 2007), 195.

[2]   "Nuwaubian leader York working on his public image," *Macon Telegraph*, 22 July 2001, by Rob Peecher.

Council of Shriners" and unveiled a whole series of fraternal organizations.[3] (It is unclear whether these were secret, pre-existing brotherhoods that decided to go public, or whether they were new, opportunistic concoctions.)[4]

After Dr. York was arrested and held in prison, his disciples staged theatrical protests, marching in parades dressed as pharaohs or Yamassee Indians. They showed up at the Putman County Dairy Festival to hand out flyers proclaiming, "Putnam County Dairy Festival promotes RACISM!" They posted ungrammatical, *ad hominem* attacks on their enemies on their www.unnm.com website. They distributed flyers at local shopping centers and on car windshields stating that Sills and his "devils" attempted a "Waco-type murder."[5] They even tried to make their voice heard by forging a fairly convincing *simalcrum* of the local paper, the *Macon Messenger*. They forged (or imitated) its masthead and featured fictitious criminal histories of many of Putnam's respectable county officials, including an article on Sheriff Sills ("John Gotti hiding behind a badge").[6]

But these antics were ineffectual, and did not succeed in de-escalating the conflict. They merely reinforced the public perception of the Nuwaubians as a bizarre, unwholesome, sinister "cult." While ritualistic and "irrational" responses to persecution (both actual and/or perceived) might "make sense" within the Nuwaubian mythopoaeic worldview, they were interpreted as "cult-like" behavior by journalists, and as a threat to public order by law enforcement officials. In this way, the Nuwaubians contributed to the widening spiral of "deviance amplification," and invited aggressive reprisals from their enemies.

Race and Deviance

Race is an important issue throughout the history of Nuwaubian controversy. The word "racist" was slung as ammunition by both sides. The Southern Poverty Law Center placed the Nuwaubians on their list of hate groups ("It's definitely a black supremacist group, a mirror image of white hate groups").[7] *The Macon Telegraph* called them "a group of black separatists who believe white people are genetically inferior mutants."[8] The Nuwaubians, in turn, branded their African-

---

[3]   William A. Muraskin, *Middle-Class Blacks in a White Society* (Los Angeles: University of California Press, 1972).

[4]   One explanation I heard was that York was guided in this enterprise by a disciple who was a former member of the Prince Hall Masons, the only black order recognized in American Freemasonry.

[5]   "Prosecutor; Nuwaubians distribute flyers in Newton County," *Macon Telegraph*, 27 December 2002, by Rob Peecher.

[6]   *Online Athens Banner Herald*, 27 December 2002.

[7]   Bill Osinski, "Cult leader ignored his own rules," *Atlanta Journal-Constitution*, 7 July 2002.

[8]   Osinski, 7 July 2002.

American cultural opponents as "house niggers" and since their arrival in Georgia have tended to interpret bureaucratic obstacles to their utopian dream as the result of racial discrimination. Putnam County officials responded by accusing them of "playing the racism card."[9]

Osinski denies that the Nuwaubians were victims of racism; indeed, he argues that they took advantage of their privileged minority status. The only reason York was able to "get away with" his "sexual depredations" for so many years, Osinski claims, was simply *because* he was black—since law enforcement maintained a "hands off policy" limiting investigations into Black Muslim communities, as a "sensitive zone." Osinski complains that even high-ranking state officials "accepted the notion…that York was the victim of racial discrimination by the backwards folks of Putnam County."[10] He wittily describes the public authorities' unwillingness to intervene in York's enterprise as "a rather awkward sociological waltz with twenty-first century political correctness staggering around the floor in the embrace of the skeletal remains of Civil-Rights Era activism."[11]

So, the question remains—was the Nuwaubians' racial minority status a protection or was it a liability? Were the Nuwaubians perceived as deviant because they were a "cult," or because they were *black*?

White "hate" groups can be easily dismissed. White Pride advocates tend to be caricatured as ignorant, bigoted rednecks in the mass media. Black nationalist groups, however, are problematic. They cannot be dismissed in quite the same facile manner because they do, after all, have a compelling historical rationale for desiring separation and resenting whites. They demand respect and tolerance. But, if they begin to cross that thin line between Garvey's "uplift" and unpatriotic "uppityness," if they start to demand *more* than a neutral, secular self-sufficiency, and claim to be a "Sovereign Nation"—then the proverbial "alarm bells" will resound.

The racial issue adds a new wrinkle to the deviance amplification trajectory. Black nationalistic movements play an ambiguous role in American society, because they are the outspoken descendants of a minority group that was once the targeted victim of a socially constructed model of deviance. Today, after 400 years, after a long struggle for racial justice and equality in America, there is "zero tolerance" for the public expression of racist attitudes. But what about historically-based "reverse racism"?

The public's awareness of how deviance labeling works; its educated understanding of the devastating consequences of prejudice, and the suffering of stigmatized groups in our recent history has led to an awareness of labels and positive action. This is seen, for example, in the media's care to refer respectfully to homosexuals as the "gay community," to old people as "senior citizens," to AIDS patients as "PWAs." The constant renaming of America's racially-defined

---

[9] "Accusations of Racism," *Macon Telegraph*, 8 August, 1999, by Hilary Hilliard and Rob Peecher.

[10] Osinski, 270.

[11] Osinski, 272.

marginalized social group—from "Negro" to "Coloured," to "Afro-American," to "Black," to "African-American"—is a visible sign of the struggle to shake off the stigma. Public officials are careful to mince words when dealing with Black nationalist groups—particularly with the Black Panthers, who have responded in a militant fashion to police brutality, particularly after the Chicago Police and the FBI gunned down Fred Hampton and another BPP leader in their sleep in 1969.

Thus, journalists are wary when dealing with Black nationalist, separatist movements—particularly the religious ones. To maintain a "politically correct" tone, they must simultaneously imply their disapproval of racism and mock the "cult's" religious and racialist doctrines—while carefully avoiding any "racist" overtones. One solution to this dilemma is to simply ignore the subtleties and historical realities behind the group's stance on race, and to link the Nuwaubians (quite erroneously) with notorious black militant groups. (We are told, frequently, for example, that York joined the Black Panther party as a youth.)

Black resistance movements can no longer be considered as "deviant" in an age that deplores racism, but a problem arises when their uncompromisingly anti-white racialist mythology and doctrines place them squarely in the middle of a newer category of "deviance"—as "racists." When Farrakhan and his ministers relate the myth of Yacoub of Patmos, creator of white soulless humans ("like white lab rats"); when Dr. York reverses the Christian fundamentalist myth of the curse of Ham, explaining white skin as a consequence of leprosy—then suddenly a dignified "Black Pride" organization will be reclassified as a "hate group," even if its members are perfectly law abiding.

One might compare the social construction of Nuwaubian deviance to a sound system at a rock concert. The slightest amplification—a twiddling of the knob so to speak—can suddenly explode into a cacophonous paroxysm of "static." If one non-white member of a racialist religion breaks the law or commits an act of violence—even if it is an isolated renegade act perpetrated by a disaffected fringe member—suddenly a deafening roar of feedback will fill the public auditorium. Echoes of the old, discarded notions of race will resonate beneath the new un-PC word, "racist"—and this will evoke a strong societal reaction.

Regressing the Millennium

Whereas previous studies of millennialism have defined the phenomenon as essentially linked to an imagined future, I would argue that the Nuwaubian's preoccupation with the past, with their mythic origins, might also be categorized as "millenarian." Like many other, well-documented utopian groups and cargo cults, when confronted with superior force and military technology, the Nuwaubians will look for mythic solutions, for supernatural means to vanquish their enemies and restore their mighty nation. Sometimes the Nuwaubians will look towards the future for such supernatural interventions, but more often they look towards the past, retreating back in time, regressing into myth in order to seek help from, or identify with, their mythic ancestors.

One future-oriented "solution" to their problems was promised in the "Mothership." In 1992, just as the HTM was relocating to Georgia, Dr. York had prophesied that the "Mothership" (a "sham" or UFO) would descend from the sky in May 2003 and hover over Tama Re's great pyramid. The earliest revelation of this prophecy (to my knowledge) appeared in *Man from Planet Rizq* (n.d.) where York reveals himself as "Yanuuwn," an extraterrestrial, incarnate in human form to spiritually prepare his people:

> My assignment is to Re-Spiritually Educate the Beings of the Planet Earth who are the children of the Eloheem (Anunnaqi) who came down to Planet Earth in Sumer at a place called Eridu where Iraq is today.[12]

He predicted a classic "Rapture" type of experience:

> I am here to Prepare the 144,000, Those Chosen to Be Picked Up By A Motherplane, NIBIRU, By Way Of A Mothership...That Will Release Smaller Passenger Crafts.

York was not shy about giving exact dates for this rapture:

> Catastrophes taking place all over the world on May 5, 2000, as the result from the alignment of planets...the Gates of Heaven will be Lined up and Opened. Then, on August 12, 2003 the passenger ships the "Shams" will be released from the Crystal City and reach earth to retrieve the 144,000 Worthy Souls. First pickup will be on August 12, 2003, and the last on June 26, 2030. A.D. These 144,000 "Worthy Souls" will be taken up to the Crystal City and "groomed" for 1000 years, and then will return to earth to "save the planet."[13]

But he warned his "Nubians,"[14] that in order to qualify as a Worthy Soul, each individual must cultivate Black Pride:

> The kind of people who won't make it are liars, cheaters, thieves, etc. ....and you who want to live in the image of the Beast. So what is that telling the...Eloheem, whose image and likeness you were created after, who are olive toned in color and have 9 Ether Hair? You hate the way they look.... You Will Fall To The Way Side.[15]

---

[12]   *Man from Planet Rizq*, n.d., 32.

[13]   *Shambala and Aghaarta: Cities Within the Earth* (pamphlet, n.d. circa 1993).

[14]   Although York's scribes are quite capricious in use of their "Arabic" spelling, "Nubian" seems to refer to all African-Americans who are "asleep," and "Nuwaubian" to those who have been awakened into "Right Knowledge."

[15]   *Shambala and Aghaarta: Cities Within the Earth*, 36.

Moreover, York spoke of cultivating a certain psychological stance or altered state of consciousness in order to enter into a timeless zone of consciousness and board the Mothership:[16]

> "Now" is an actual event that began in the midst of the created nothingness of your time zone. A Time war is truly occurring and will continue to accelerate until "Now" is finally reached and the dimensions can finally interface, Nothing and Something or the… . space between tick and tock…become one again, much like a ship landing at a predetermined Time Moment.[17]

There is little doubt that this prophecy drummed up a greater level of commitment among his disciples, particularly the voluntary workers who spent their holidays toiling in the hot Georgia sun to build the temples and pyramids of Tama Re. Moreover, it inspired Nubians from York's far-flung mission to embark on pilgrimages to The Land. One such pilgrim expressed a sense of urgent millenarian expectation.[18]

> I had heard about The Land, a place where all black people were welcome and would be safe. I had the feeling something bad was going to happen, so I saved up to come out here. I took time off—and as soon as I saw the pyramids from the bus window—I knew I belonged here, I felt I was home, it was *my* Land.

After the raid on Tama Re in May 2002, while their Master Teacher was in prison awaiting trial, the Mothership prophecy became a symbol of unity and a focus of hope. When May 2003 passed uneventfully, however, York's disciples voiced their doubts in a chat room on www.unnm.com. They were evidently coping with what Leon Festinger termed "cognitive dissonance."[19] Years later, four disciples confessed their feelings of disillusionment:[20]

Guest: "Did the elders come and begin rapturing us, not that I know of. If by 2030 we're all still here then I will admit his prediction didn't come true."

AkhenAtun: "You are willing to wait 26 years?...Amazing, this man York has actually made mental illness contagious!"

Ideel: "Ooohh yeeaahh, I forgot about that failed prediction, It was May something 2000 right? Or was it May 23, 2003? Something like that. The shams

---

[16]   This is typical of millenarian movements, where apocalyptic expectation involves an experiential dimension.

[17]   *Shambala and Aghaarta: Cities Within the Earth*, 37.

[18]   Conversation with a registered nurse from Brixton, U.K. at the June 2004 Savior's Day festival.

[19]   Leon Festinger, Riecken, H.W., and Schachter, S., *When Prophecy Fails* (Minneapolis: University of Minnesota, 1956).

[20]   This conversation appeared on the www.unnm.com on 10 January 2004, during the first week of York's trial.

was supposed to land and come get the 144k who had skin the complexion of brown paper bags. I saw more Nuwaubians leave after that failed prediction than at any other time."[21]

Anonymous: "Don't you get it, Sonny? The Sham is over, done. It's a wrap. Nuwaupoo is dead. It was all based on lies, Sham! Oh yeah, ain't he say the SHAM is coming to get ya? LOL! Yea that's one thing he was CORRECT about cuz the sham did come and get ya. YOU WERE ALL TAKEN IN BY LIES (SHAMS)."

(This heated discussion degenerates into *ad hominem* attacks and name-calling. AkhenAtun takes offence when 1dell calls him "Akhen-Nutmeg" and addresses him in turn as *I-Dull*—but this interchange proves that York's disciples took the prophecy quite seriously, and that the failure of the Mothership to materialize resulted in defections, doubt, and mutual recriminations.)

The Triad wisely attempted to forestall the possibility of prophetic disconfirmation by issuing a flyer shortly before the fateful day of 29 May 2003, titled "Prophecy Being Fulfilled." It was distributed at the *All Eyes on Egipt* bookstores.[22] Its text can only be interpreted as a careful revision of prophecy, a prudent attempt to rationalize the possible failure of the expected Mothership. It offers an explicitly apocalyptic interpretation of Dr. York's legal situation during a period when York's followers were confused and demoralized by his guilty plea. This flier is not written in Dr. York's inimitable flamboyant style. Its language is more conventionally Christian and it relies heavily on the Bible. It appears to be the work of Tama Re's theologians, possibly one or more members of the Triad. This revelation states that York's adverse circumstances—his imprisonment and legal battles—were "foretold" and denote better days to come.

> It is evident with world calamities, natural disasters, and wars that we are living in the…times that Yowkhanan…prophesied in the book of Revelation. The prophecies [of] Daniel…produces the real reason for the incarceration of our beloved Master Teacher… . Since the year 1970 A.D. our Master Teacher has been working diligently to break the spell of ignorance that we as a people have been blinded by for countless generations. With over 360 books, Dr. Malachi Z. York has opened the minds and hearts of people all over the world to the true message of…Isa Al Masih, Jesus the Messiah. We, as the true Judahite Negroids of the royal bloodline of Judah are not deceived… . But most may still have doubt [sic] about how and why we are going through our current legal situation, which is a temporary problem we will overcome. …On May 8, 2002 we lived through the attempt of genocide against the Nuwaupian family which, uncoincidentally, coincided with planetary alignment. CHECK IT OUT!!

* * *

---

[21]   http://www.unnm.com/phpbb2/viewtopic.php?t=58

[22]   This flyer bears no date, but I picked it up at the *All Eyes on Egipt* bookstore in Atlanta three weeks before the fateful day.

This flyer refers to an obscure entry in the *Arab News* ("Man arrested for claiming to be promised Messiah").[23] It concludes, "Our Master Teacher was not the only righteous man arrested on 8 May 2002. There was another. On the exact same day!!" Then the authors identify these two imprisoned men as the "Two Witnesses" of Revelations XI, prophesied by Daniel as the "two olive trees," and by Zechariah as the "two brazen pillars" of Solomon's temple. They explain that the Two Witnesses are currently "locked up," and until these witnesses are freed, "the Holy Temple [Mothership] cannot come down out of heaven":

> These are great signs of the times and we are the Angels of Michael who have to beat the devil and his helpers. …It is a must or the crafts will leave and will not return for another 3,400 years and the Devil will gain an extension of time up to 06/06/06 or the next 666…. The Day of Ascension is May 29, 2003…. So the evil reptilian seed knows what they are doing by scheduling the last court date for our Beloved Master Teacher on May 29, 2003. It is no coincidence. …We must continue to fight for our master's release. …Hold on to the rope, for our victory is soon ahead. Words from Our Master Teacher, "Can you Beat Him? Yes or No?"[24]

It appears the authors of this flier are not only seeking to forestall a potential failure of prophecy, but are trying to restore group morale and drum up financial support for the "He is innocent!" initiative.

The Outage as Prophecy Fulfilled

The Mothership failed to materialize, but (for the Nuwubians) supernatural assistance did arrive—exactly three months later. On 14 August 2003 the "Outage" (or "Northeast Blackout of 2003") occurred; a massive widespread power breakdown that occurred throughout parts of the Northeastern and Midwestern United States, and Ontario, Canada. It was the largest blackout in North American history, affecting an estimated 10 million people in Ontario and 40 million people in eight of the eastern states of U.S.A. Outage-related financial losses were estimated at $6 billion.

At the very time of the Outage, Dr. York was being transported to New York City for his psychiatric evaluation. The theologians of the UNN made use of the anomalous event as a "charismatic display" of York's psychic powers—just at he was at his weakest point in his legal process. These theologians linked the Outage to York's prophecy concerning the "Vortex."

---

[23]   www.arabnews.com/print.asp?id=15058ArY=2003&Arm=5&ArD=216

[24]   *Prophecy Being Fulfilled*, flyer found in the Atlanta bookstore, circa February 2003.

Around ten years earlier, York had written in *Man from Planet Rizq* that on 12 August 2003, the "Vortex" would open; that beings from other dimensions would be able to slip through into our world and walk among us. He describes the Vortex as "a whirlpool of time," a "time continuum change" whereby extraterrestrials can enter our planet.[25] The first "Vortex" incident happened at the time of the Philadelphia experiment in 1940. Then, the extraterrestrials built a computer on 12 August 1943 called the Rainbow Project which permitted their entry into our dimension, due to the magnetic pull from the Big Generators that had supplied the energy to the Invisibility project in Philadelphia. Again, on 6 June 1966 the Vortex had opened and permitted malevolent extraterrestrials to arrive on our earth, and 13 sons of the Devil were born on that date.[26]

The theologians of the UNN interpreted the Outage of August 2003 in an opportunistic fashion, as confirmation of York's prophecy of the opening of the Vortex, despite the two-day delay. But, they noted that our human measurement of time is flawed, so that the delay was insignificant. In October 2004 York wrote a letter from prison to one of his followers, confirming that Avatars had indeed visited him at the time of the Outage:[27]

> On August 12, 2004, just days before court, 3 visitors came to me, Crlll, Alomar, and Saad, they healed me. They came from Zeta Reticuli. I had not seen them since I was a child in Teaneck, New Jersey. They don't age at all. Anyway, they told me the game is almost over. Those that truly love you are coming together for you. They are passing the Great Test. I asked them why I could not just walk out? They said, "Because there is an order to the Kosmos that must never be altered".... . Many inmates have seen me float. That is why they keep moving me away. It is because people Canaanites as well are converting inside.[28]

The Outage was discussed two years later at a Question&Answer meeting in August 2005. The presiding minister, Sakinah, referred to it within the context of prophecies in *The Holy Tablets* that were fulfilled when the World Trade Center, and the Twin Towers were bombed.[29] The minister explained that the "Beings" who used the Vortex to slip into our dimension were York's fellow "Avatars," arriving to assist Dr. York at his time of trial. She then gave a speech weaving the Outrage into an elaborate web of conspiracy theories:

> Earth is going into its last resurrection that will happen within our lifetime. This is the final end, we have had multiple lives. Some people are ready to go to the

---

[25]   *Man from Planet Rizq*, 37.

[26]   Leviathan 666 (Brooklyn, *The Original Tents of Kedar*, circa 1983).

[27]   "Pop's Letter To Diane Stevens," *NuWorldOrder Forums*, 17 October 2004.

[28]   Here he is referring to white prisoners among the inmates who are joining his mission.

[29]   Paul Greenhouse attended this meeting and described the discussion to me.

New Jerusalem. This is the time frame that was allotted to us to get our lives together. After 1970 all the children born were new souls. Their job was to be warriors of Melchesidek… . Like Michael Jackson, Mike Jordan, Mike Tyson, incarnations of the Archangel Michael in These Days… . People that came after the Opening of the Seal—where have they gone? Wherever they come from, they go back. One blood type, repercussion equals caution—re-purr –caution. I am hy-po-the-syz-ing… . When the Pope came here in 1966, 13 years later, it was the Year of the Child. In 1979 the children turned 13. The Pope came and kissed the ground where the Demon Seed was born. On National TV it said there were 13 nations behind the Pope. Now the shuffle is going on. The Demon Seed had to go, you have to take off your blindfold. Especially with the polarity shifting, we got no room for error. We talk about the return of the Antichrist. The VORTEX is opening up to let in Angels that can destroy the earth! Any day Raphael can blow his trumpet! They are going strictly to your heart because that's the scales of Ma'at! The Gilgamesh Epics predicts the Bible, it talks about the Flood. The Planet earth is going to be destroyed again, and the Pope tells us it will probably be a nuclear destruction… . We went over to Iraq to look for weapons of mass destruction. But Beings outside the earf [sic] sent holographic images, and they sent a ship more than three times the speed of light, so they never catch them. Yanun (January) is the 19th Elder… . There are other Avatars, but He is our axis.[30]

The Retreat into Myth

The future-oriented expectation of the Mothership is an exception, for York's prophetic revelations tend to focus on the remote past. True to the "here and now" pragmatic materialism of Blackosophy that rejects "pie-in-the-sky" Christianity, Dr. York shows very little interest in the afterlife. But he does show a passionate interest in archaeology, "ancient astronaut" theory, human genetics and physical anthropology. His scrolls are cornucopias of ever-unfurling and overlapping creation myths that address the genetic secrets of the Nuwaubian people. Themes of regression, of a return to roots, greatly outweigh his future-oriented dramas. While the Nuwaubians are as fervently "millennial" as many of the notorious NRMs (Heaven's Gate, Branch Davidians, Aum Shinrikyo) their millenarian activity is more likely to take the form of racial and genealogical revisionism than the expectation of/preparation for a future millennial event. In this way they have succeeded in avoiding confrontation.

When faced with serious opposition, York often responds with a kind of liturgical shape-shifting. He simply revises his genealogical-racialist mythology and wraps it like a cloak around his person and his people. As he himself has declared, "I move around because I want to stay out of somebody's focus…I move from

---

[30]   I have tried to reconstruct this monologue from my scribbled notes.

place to place."[31] This pattern—of self-defensive "regressive millennialism"—might be discerned throughout his charismatic career.

Various scholars in millennial studies have explored the impact of cultural opposition or "persecution" on prophetic traditions in the past.[32] Norman Cohn characterizes millenarian movements as "religions of the oppressed," and shows how their charismatic prophets, when faced with overwhelming opposition from the larger society, will announce the imminent approach of a doomsday.[33] Supernatural intervention, they predict, will destroy their enemies and exalt their people, raising them to the highest rank in society, or leaving them to rule, rebuild and repopulate a barren and blasted world. Grant Underwood, in his study of early Mormonism, calls this the "dream of the great reversal":

> Growing out of a profound discontent with the *status quo* and seeing society and its brokers as evil and antagonistic, it promises that the first will be last and the last will be first. Because the [perceived] forces of sin control their destiny, apocalypticists see very little hope in working through "the system." Divine intervention is expected to come dramatically, even cataclysmically, as superhuman forces square off in the final showdown of good and evil.[34]

Within the framework of these studies, the irrational, puzzling behaviors of Dr. York and his Nuwaubians might be explained as *apocalyptic responses* to cultural opposition, and the frequent revisions and divagations in York's ever-evolving etiology of race appear to be serving this millenarian function. Catherine Wessinger has given many examples of how, when confronted with repeated attacks and ongoing obstacles that jeopardize their "ultimate concern," new religious prophets will respond with a battery of new revelations in which previous predictions are elaborated upon or revised.[35] Just as apocalyptic prophecies must be recast and doled out in increments to hold the attention of the congregation, so the ongoing quest for Nubian racial and spiritual identity must be kept alive. With his new twists and turns in the plot line, Dr. York excites suspense and mystery as he reveals the hidden identity of his people—in installments. This results in

---

[31] He said this in the June 1999 contempt of court hearing, to explaining why he had not shown up to a previous scheduled hearing.

[32] Since the word "persecution" implies a bias and a partisanship, I place it inside quotation marks.

[33] Norman Cohn, *The Pursuit of the Millennium: Revolutionary Millenarians and Mystical Anarchists of the Middle Ages* (New York: Oxford University Press, 1957, 1970, 1990); See also Jeffrey Kaplan, *Radical Religion in America: Millenarian Movements from the Far Right to the Children of Noah* (Syracuse, NY: Syracuse University Press, 1997).

[34] Grant Underwood. *The Millenarian World of Early Mormonism* (Urbana: University of Illinois, 1993).

[35] See Catherine Wessinger, *How the Millennium Comes Violently: From Jonestown to Heaven's Gate* (London: Seven Bridges Press, 2000).

a sense of power and elitism, and a kind of "social implosion" which serves to distance the group from the outside world.[36]

In many respects the Nuwaubian movement fits the classic category of the "cargo cult."[37] For Peter Worsley, the "cargo cult" is a "reaction against...oppression by another class or nationality." People of small stateless societies who lack political institutions and overall unity, who possess no suitable machinery through which they can act politically as a unified force, will embrace "irrational" expectations of supernatural intervention, an apocalyptic "great reversal" that will bring them justice and restore their world to its former state. Thus, cargo cults represent "an escapist, passive trend...principally confined to backwards communities within the wider society."[38]

Worsley extends his analysis of cargo cults to apply to African-American religions: "Negro religious cults...derive from [their] comparatively meager participation...in other institutional forms of American culture."[39] He explains how ("absurd as they may seem when considered as rational solutions") they are creative attempts of a people to reform their own institutions, meet demands, and withstand new pressures: "In a broader sense, their aims are to secure a fuller life."[40]

The psychological function of cargo cults is also explored by Raymond Firth, who argues that although they offer "no real solution," they can provide an "emotional outlet" for the frustration that derives from material and social deprivation. He explains how "new wants...shackle the native more effectively to the European order than any political or legal compulsion, and...the incompatibility between his wants and the means of satisfying them...becomes a particularly powerful source of frustration and resentment, charged with emotion."[41] Firth concludes that cargo cults provide a creative channel for this sense of frustration:

> It is part of the symbolic validation given to the idea that the things wanted are morally justifiable...part of an affirmation of native claims, native community solidarity, native values, in the face of what is conceived to be an impassive, unsympathetic, or hostile outside world.[42]

---

[36]   The notion of "social implosion" is introduced in William Sims Bainbridge's book, *Satan's Power* (Los Angeles: University of California Press, 1978). As he explains it, when the social bonds within the group are intensified and strengthened under the influence of prophecy or charisma, the members' ties with the outside world become attenuated.

[37]   Peter Worsely, *The Trumpet Shall Sound: A Study of Cargo Cults in Melanesia* (New York: Schocken Books, 1968).

[38]   Peter Worsely, 1968.

[39]   Worsely, 233.

[40]   Worsely, 233.

[41]   Raymond Firth, *Elements of Social Organization* (London:Watts & Co., 1951), 247.

[42]   Firth, 113.

Worsley examines the "emotionality" found in millenarian movements; the "motor phenomena...convulsions...twitching, sobbing, hysteria...which spread throughout the community as if by contagion." He proposes that the psychological function of this extraordinary motor behavior is "personal catharsis." The Nuwaubians' trance-like behavior at the Question&Answer meetings might be considered in this light, as examples of "millenarian motor phenomena." Worsley's analysis of the "defiant breaking of taboos" found in cargo cults, might also apply to the Nuwaubian case.[43] He claims the social function of the ritual breaking of taboos is to forge "a new morality":

> The new order cannot continue with the outworn indigenous ethics or code of its former rulers...All prophets stress moral renewal. Deliberate defiance against authority...the extreme expression of this defiance and the most positive rejection of the present way of life is the inversion of the existing social order.[44]

Once this new brotherhood is formed it will adopt "diacritical signs and symbols—songs, badges, dress ornaments—to show they have been reborn." The fraternal orders within the Nuwaubian movement, such as the Ancient Egiptian Order with its exotic costumes and masonic symbols are the "diacritical signs and symbols" of a new order.

Nuwaubians as "Ghost Shirt Dancers"

If one considers the Nuwaubians as a *millenarian movement*, their irrational responses to perceived persecution begin to make sense—as apocalyptic ritual. According to Yonina Talmon, this ritual response to "persecution" is quite typical of "post-political" millenarian movements.[45] Talmon distinguishes between "pre-political" and "post-political" movements as follows. Pre-political movements will form among a people who are socially powerless, struggling to find their voice, whereas "post-political" millenarian movements arise when a group of people have lost all their previous political power and become "dispossessed." The latter does not quite fit the Nuwaubian case, but Talmon also notes that when a people are awarded a *limited* access to legitimate power, frustrated by slow progress in the political arena, they may also form a "post-political millenarian movement." This situation aptly describes the Nuwaubian case.

---

43 See Chapter 2 for many examples of Dr. York's taboo-breaking mode as a "crazy wisdom" teacher.

44 Worsley, 233.

45 Talmon, Yonina, "Millenarism," in *The International Encyclopedia of the Social Sciences*, Vol. 10 (New York: MacMillan, 1968), 351. Yonina Talmon, "Pursuit of the Millennium: the Relation between Religion and Social Change." Reprinted from *Archives Europiennes de Sociologie, III* (1962), 125-48.

Unlike the nineteenth-century Lakota Sioux, African-Americans today enjoy the same constitutional rights as white people. The Nuwaubians, however, reject the post-Civil Rights imperative to promote racial integration, seeing it as offering too little, too late. They are dissatisfied with enforced integration through busing in schools, with "phony" racial harmony and tolerance, as promoted through affirmative action in the media and "tell-lies-vision." They resist assimilation and "cultural imperialism."

The concept of "cultural imperialism" was first defined by the Rastafarian sociologist, Leahcim Semaj, as "when one group imposes its definition of reality, via theories concepts and ideas—metaphysics, epistemology, ethics and even aesthetics—on another."[46]

Ennis Barrington Edmonds applied this concept to race relations in the U.S.: "European values are defined as civilized and desirable...whereas African cultural mores and expressions are perceived as crude and lacking in culture."[47] He observes that white imperialistic cultural had a strong impact in the economic and political realms: "there was a widespread acceptance of the ideas that associate whiteness with beauty, goodness and god, and that associate blackness with ugliness, evil and the devil."[48]

The Nuwaubians have always resisted cultural pressure to integrate into the "Paleman's" culture. Like many nativist movements in the past, they adopted a "quiescent" or "passive" stance towards their oppressors and cling to their identity as a separate, oppressed people striving to preserve and revitalize what they feel is the essence of the urban, underground Black subculture in the U.S.A. Like Talmon's "post-political" millenarian movements, they turn inward, and resort to ritual protest and supernatural agency to effect social change.

The classic example of this behavior (often cited) is the ghost shirt dancers of the Lakota. Cora Du Bois, in her study of this tribe after the defeats of the Modoc war in the early 1870s, shows us how the Lakota Sioux turned to "passivist Christian revivalist cults." She argues that the "accumulating despair of the Indians" drove them to participate in the apocalyptic rituals of the Ghost Shirt dances. These offered a "ready-made escape into supernaturalism from realities which had become intolerable and offered nothing but defeat."[49] Through the ghost dance ritual, Wovoka and his dancers sought to tap into a supernatural source of power that they believed could overcome their oppressors.[50]

---

[46]   Leahcim Semaj, "Race, Identity and Children of the African Diaspora" (*The Caribe* 4/4, 1980), 215.

[47]   Edmonds Ennis Barrington, *Rastafari: from Outcasts to Culture Bearers* (New York: Oxford University Press, 2003), 29.

[48]   Barrington, 31.

[49]   Cora Du Bois, *The 1870 Ghost Dance* (Berkeley, CA: University of California Press, 1939), 150.

[50]   Du Bois, 1939.

Many aspects of Nuwaubian behavior might be explained as a form of "ghost shirt dancing." Whenever Dr. York is overwhelmed by external forces, he will announce a new racialist revelation and his people will don a new mask and costume and follow him into a new tunnel of his labyrinthine quest for "true" racial/spiritual origins.

When the AAC was under investigation by the FBI, and his own life was threatened by a Muslim fanatic, York simply changed shape. He discarded his "Muslim" *persona* and defined his followers as Hebrews. He led his people in an exodus to Georgia and redefined them as the Yamassee tribe of the Creek Nations.

When the zoning disputes in Georgia grew heated, York reacted by discarding Western attire for Moorish garb. Unable to resolve the building permit for the Ramses Social Club, Nuwaubians redefined their club as a Masonic Lodge under Dr. York as "Imperial Grand Potentate of the International Supreme Council of Shriners."[51]

After he was arrested on the very serious charges of child molestation, York's response was—to dress up. At his pre-trial hearing in January 2003, he appeared as a Moor, wearing a red fez with a black tassel, and challenged the Superior Court Judge, saying "I am secured and do not give permission to use my name."[52] York's followers dressed as Moors, and handed out fliers stamped by the "Clerk of Federal Moorish Cherokee Consular Court, USA."[53]

At the 1 July 2003 trial Dr. York appeared in court in full regalia, wearing a feathered headdress and introduced himself as "Chief Black Eagle." He claimed the United States Government had no jurisdiction over him, and asked to be turned over to the Yamassee Native American Government.

After he was convicted and sent to prison for 135 years, Dr. York and his legal team came up with a new strategy.[54] They claimed he was a Consul General of Monrovia and an ambassador for Liberia under appointment from the former President, Charles Taylor, and should therefore be granted diplomatic immunity from legal prosecution and extradited to Liberia. Dr. York explains how his competing claims to be a Moorish Cherokee, a Native American Yamassee Chief and a Liberian diplomat might be reconciled:

> Fact is we called ourselves Native American *Moors* and tell them of *Mali* which is Africa and the Bassa Tribe are from Mali as well as Sudan. So when I stood up in court and stated I was indigerness [sic], that did not in any way state I'm

---

[51] "Nuwaubian leader York working on his public image," *Macon Telegraph*, 22 July 2001, by Rob Peecher.

[52] "Lawyers argue details in York case,"*Macon Telegraph*, 18 January 2003, by Rob Peecher.

[53] "Lawyers argue details in York case," *Macon Telegraph*, 18 January 2003, by Rob Peecher.

[54] I first heard about the Liberian diplomat claim on 27 July 2004 in a speech made by Damon, one of the Triad, when I was attending the Savior's Day festival at Tama Re.

not African and the fact that I wore a fez in court not a Indian head dress shows I favor Africa to America.[55]

These examples show how York and his followers respond to conflict—by recasting their corporate image, by assuming new titles and disguises like ritual masks. This strategy is perfectly consistent with the inner goals of their secret mystery school. York's mission was (and still is) to lead his disciples on a winding journey backwards in time, unpeeling layer after layer of false or incomplete identity, to rediscover their origins as godlike beings, utterly alien and inaccessible to the laws and limitations of the Paleman and the reign of Shaytan.

The Impact of "Ghost Dancing" on York's Legal Process

But what was achieved by this irrational liturgical behavior? In what respects, if any, did York's shape-shifting prove effective? The answer varies depending on which parties in the drama we focus on: the judge and jury, the media and its public, or the Nuwaubian community.

Journalists' response was to portray Dr. York and his followers as unstable lunatics. In journalists' reports, when the Nuwaubians dressed up as mummies, birds and Indians to march in the Brunswick parade, when they wore feathered headdresses and played tom toms outside the courtroom, they were simply "acting silly." Journalists labeled them as "bizarre" or "quasi-religious." Predictably, some journalists interpreted the participation of York's followers in these costume dramas as evidence of "brainwashing." Others saw proof that here was a fake religion. In the Sheriff's view, the transformations in York's spiritual movement were a ploy to wriggle around the law.

This ritual behavior failed to inspire reverence in the public. When Dr. York attempted to defend himself in court by appearing as "Chief Black Eagle," invoking Moorish law and chanting "Common Law" clauses as if they were magical spells, he was portrayed in the media as an unconvincing phony or a madman. However, one might argue that York's irrational antics defused the potential for violence, for York and his followers came across as clowns or madmen rather than as a threatening "Black militants."[56]

For the judges and the juries, this tactic may, in fact, have undermined the efforts of York's attorneys to defend their client. Only one of York's attorneys agreed to use Dr. York's claim to be an "indigenous person" not subject to U.S. laws as part of the defense. But when Frank Rabino challenged the U.S. federal

---

[55]   "360 Reasons to Free Malachi York—Reason No. 3: No Such Person As: Dwight D. York." *A Public Outcry / Nuwaubian Administration of International Affairs.*

[56]   Catherine Wessinger traces the link between external persecution or pressure and the enhanced volatitlity of NRMs in her edited volume, *Millennialism, Persecution, and Violence: Historical Cases* (Syracuse, N.Y.: Syracuse University Press, 1999).

court's jurisdiction over Dr. York as a "Native American," the prosecution refuted it and the motion was denied by the Judge. York's other attorneys were reluctant to pursue this strategy. When Ed Garland asked the judge to indulge him while he read out a statement concerning York's Yamassee tribal affiliation, Judge Lawson responded by asking him if this document was part of his argument for the defense. Garland replied cautiously, "It's not a position that I am making a legal argument about, but I have a client who wants to put on the record his position on certain matters." Then Judge Lawson asked York's other attorney, Manny Arora, if he believed there was any validity to the assertions York was making, threatening him with "serious trouble" if he didn't give a direct answer. Arora replied, "I don't believe, at this point, there is any legal merit."

At the time of his trial, the United Nuwaubian Nation's legal team had filed a letter of intent for federal recognition as Yamassee Native American Moors with the Bureau of Indian Affairs, and were rejected. But the Yamassee Native Americans of the Creek Nation are not recognized by the U.S. Government's Bureau of Indian Affairs. Moreover, American aboriginals are not immune from being prosecuted for RICO or Mann Act violations. The court found "no evidence that the group of followers the defendant purports to lead are in any way a sovereign state worthy of recognition by the United States government or any other government." The judge rejected York's request to be returned for trial to his own tribe.

York's "ghost dancing" in court may have, in fact, slowed down his trial, for it made the court question his sanity. After he appeared in court as a Moorish Cherokee in January, 2003, his lawyer had him evaluated by a forensic psychologist, who diagnosed Dr. York as suffering from delusion, anxiety and depression. He identified several Axis II personality disorders, including "histrionic and self-defeating personality traits and schizotypical personality features."[57] When York appeared in court as "Chief Black Eagle," Judge Royal ordered him to be sent for a psychological evaluation to New York. He wrote in his order of 24 July 2003:

> Because the report provides reasonable cause for the court to believe (York) may presently be suffering from a mental disease or defect rendering him mentally incompetent to the extent that he is unable to…understand the nature and consequences of the proceedings against him or to assist properly in his defense, the court will proceed on its own motion for the determination of (York's) mental competency.[58]

The second psychologist found York to be quite sane, but neither diagnosis helped prove his innocence or reduced his prison term.

---

[57] Matt Robinson, Attachments filed with the 2241 *Habeas Corpus* motion, 27 April 2006.

[58] "Nuwaubian sect leader will undergo psychological evaluation," *Athens Banner-Herald*, 13 August 2003, by Joe Johnson.

For York's disciples, however, these ludic evasions to external threats "succeeded" in the sense that they raised the morale of the group. By participating in this ritual behavior, the Nuwaubians strengthened interpersonal bonds within the Nuwaubian Nation and reinforced their collective vision.

Thus, while this ghost dancing proved ineffective, even counter-productive, as a legal strategy, it did serve an important function—to reunite Dr. York's followers in the secret, exclusive brotherhood of the "Right Knowledge."

Each time York revised his myth of origins, it served the same function as announcing an apocalyptic event; it served to unite his people against a common foe, to forge a new brotherhood, to separate his community from an evil, corrupt, illusory host society, and to test the devotees' commitment to their Prophet, weeding out the faint hearted.

The Nuwaubians' cryptic response to adversity was a dramaturgical expression, an "acting out," of their racialist apocalyptic worldview. Race, for Dr. York, is quintessentially apocalyptic, and the mythic time is measured out in race wars. By dressing up and holding public demonstrations as Egyptians, Moors, Shriners or Yamassee Indians, the Nuwaubians were reaffirming their collective gnostic identity, as an exiled people trapped in a hostile, foreign land. Every time they found themselves threatened by the surrounding white secular society, they reacted in a chameleonesque fashion, by changing color. They redefined their race as black, brown, red and even green—and blended into each new mythic landscape. This ritual behavior was quite consistent with their ongoing quest for roots. It was also a stalling tactic and a way to avoid confrontation by retreating from white society and disappearing into a new mythic landscape forged by Dr. Malachi York's religious imagination.

Figure 6 U.S. Marshall contemplating Egyptian fresco at Tama Re

Chapter 7
Black Messiahs in America:
Religious Leaders or Racketeers?

"But what is the truth?" one must ask. "Is Dwight York guilty, or is he an innocent man who was framed?" The answer to that question varies, depending upon who one listens to.

Just as in Kurosawa's famous 1950 film, *Rashomon*, where events leading to a crime are reconstructed quite differently—by the robber, by the samurai, by the wife and by the passing woodcutter—we find conflicting accounts of Dr. York's story.[1] Lewis Carter comments on the researcher's problem of choosing between different accounts of the same set of events, a problem he encountered in his 1998 study of Bhagwan Shree Rajneesh's community in Oregon. The explanations of the controversial salmonella poisoning incident in the Wasco county salad bars offered by his various informants "differed quite markedly."[2] Carter steps back and comments, "the most interesting thing about such contrasting stories is not always which of them is true. Rather, the remarkable thing in [these] cases is that both sets of stories are true as the 'event' was experienced from different social locations."[3] While this stance might make sense to a sociologist who has read Peter Berger and knows that "reality" is socially constructed, it would not be helpful in a courtroom where a man charged with child molestation (or acts of biological terrorism) is on trial.

In Dr. York's case, the truth may never be known. In one portrait he is an arrogant, over-sexed cult leader, whose multiple wives get younger as he ages; a patriarch presiding over a ring of concubines who, in turn, train pubescent girls (and boys) to cater to his jaded appetites.[4] In the other portrait, he is a respectable

---

[1] I am indebted to Lewis Carter for the *Rashomon* analogy.

[2] In 1984, followers of the Indian guru Bhagwan Shree Rajneesh who resided at the group's utopian commune, Rajneeshpuram in Oregon, went into ten restaurants in the nearby town, The Dalles, and deliberately spiked the salad bars with salmonella, sickening about 750 people, who were afflicted by vomiting and diaorrhea. The rationale behind this act of biological terrorism was to incapacitate so many voters that their own candidates in the county elections would win ("Oregon Town Never Recovered From Scare," *The Associated Press*, 19 October 2001 by Gillian Flaccus).

[3] Lewis Carter, *Charisma and Control in Rajneeshpuram: The Role of Shared Values in the Creation of a Community* (New York: Cambridge University Press, 1998), xx.

[4] On a deeper, esoteric level, there are indications in several of the witnesses' statements that the Master Teacher's aim was to transmit the sacred culture of Nuwaupu—

polygamist following in the footsteps of Muhammad, but no "child molester"—but because he just so happens to be a *Black* religious reformer, he was framed.

Eileen Barker explains the "radically different depictions" of new religious movements in her set of ideal-typical models of "cult-watching groups." These include the "anti-cult" Cult Awareness Groups (CAGs), the religiously-motivated heresiologists who form the Counter-Cult Groups (CCGs), the academic Research-Oriented Groups (ROGs), the Human Rights Groups (HRGs), and the Media (among others). Barker notes that these very different depictions of new religions "have generated a marketplace in which alternative images of reality compete for acceptance by the general populace, particularly by those in positions of power who might be able to enhance or diminish the power of these religions."[5]

The researcher who charts the information field for data on the Nuwaubians will encounter these ideal types; media reports featuring sensationalistic ex-members' stories, available on a CAG website (www.rickross.com/groups/nuwaubians.html); the Southern Poverty Law Center (a HRG) whose Intelligence Report describes the Nuwaubian movement as a "hate group"; the CCG perspective of Bilal Phillips, a Muslim heresiologist, or of Freemasons who challenge York's credentials as a grandmaster. These depictions contrast sharply with the Nuwaubians' charismatic presentations of their Master Teacher.

One can begin to sort out these conflicting portraits by taking into account the motivations and interests of each group. Unfortunately, many of the objective facts are not available. The court transcripts are sealed, the witnesses for the prosecution (the alleged victims) are intimidated, and Dr. York is not receiving visitors (except for his lawyer and sister). Much of the data are privileged to the court or buried in layers of lies and half-truths, recants and retractions. It is difficult to gather the facts, since the crime of child molestation is of a private nature, and there is a significant time-lag between the alleged crime and the complaints of the victims. As Attorney Adrian Patrick aptly put it, "I cannot say what did or did not happen in the privacy of his bedroom ten years ago."

As of this writing, the Nuwaubians regard the incarceration of their Master Teacher as just one more tragedy in the ongoing conspiracy of the White hegemony to silence the great religious or political Blackosophers. For them, Dr. York's fate is just one more depressing example of great black leaders who have been framed, incarcerated, institutionalized or publically humiliated, using pretexts like mail fraud, rape, or draft dodging.[6] One Nuwaubian minister explained his Master Teacher's situation as follows:

---

in a physical, embodied sense—to the next generation.

5   Eileen Barker, "Charting the Information Field: Cult-Watching Groups and the Construction of Images of New Religious Movements," in *Teaching New Religious Movements*, edited by David G. Bromley (New York: Oxford University Press, 2007), 309-29.

6   When Paul Greenhouse and I attended the Afrika Bambaataa meeting at the Black National Theatre in Harlem this feeling became quite clear. One by one, speakers from the

His arrest is a fraud and a set up by a group of people. That's what happens to great leaders, that's the type of persecution inflicted on them. "Know the truth"…but society wants to *tackle* the truth, all Our Master's sayings, and put them in a big box and hide it under the bed. We won't let this ever happen. He's not the sort of person you can shut away![7]

Spokespersons for other Black nationalist congregations have expressed similar opinions. When Clarence 13X ("Allah" of the Five Percent Nation) was assassinated by unidentified gunmen, Louis Farrakhan claimed it was the result of the police and the White power structure inciting and turning black people against each other.[8] When Noble Drew Ali died soon after his release from prison, his followers blamed it on white police brutality. When Yahweh Ben Yahweh (1935-2007) received his 17-year prison sentence, his "worshippers" interpreted this event within the context of the U.S. government's history of targeting its Black spiritual leaders:

> The U.S. Government, using Judas and other false witnesses, secretly plotted and planned the arrest of Yahweh Ben Yahweh in the same manner in which they had attacked other Black organizations and leaders, like the Black Panther Party, the MOVE group of Philadelphia, Martin Luther King, Jr., and others.[9]

The theologians of both the NOI and the NOY trace the origins of the FBI's infiltration of their nations and discrediting of their leaders as a calculated campaign, originally designed by J. Edgar Hoover:

> J. Edgar Hoover March 4 1958 in memo admitted to the government a secret agreement with the media to discredit black leaders. "In every instance, careful attention must be given to the proposal to insure that targeted group is disrupted or discredited through the publicity and not merely publicized." The stated purpose of the slanderous campaign is to prevent sincere black leaders from gaining respectability by discrediting them in "the responsible Negro community…the White Community…and with the followers of the movement."

Prince Hall masons, the Moors and the Nuwaubians stood up and expressed solidarity with the Nuwaubians by introducing themselves as follows: "Good evening, brothers and sisters. My name is…and I am a criminal!" (the idea being that, as African-Americans living in the U.S., they were automatically considered to be "criminals").

[7] Interview with a leader at the Nuwaubian center on 42 Ballspond Road London, U.K. in May 2003.

[8] www.thetalkingdrum.com/nge.html.66k

[9] *The Crucifixion of the Messiah*, PEES Foundation, P.O. Box 1768, Seguin, TX, 1999, 204.

It is tempting to dismiss these statements as conspiracy theories, or as empty anti-white rhetoric. But a survey of the scholarly studies of Black prophets and messiahs in America indicates that they "make sense"—not necessarily as logical explanations of events, but rather as valid expressions of rage. In the biographies of these leaders there is a surprisingly high incidence of trumped-up charges, of prejudicial treatment in the courts, of unfair convictions and unusually heavy sentences, of police brutality and the use of excessive force. One also finds many mysterious disappearances, unsolved murders and unwarranted incarcerations in prisons or mental hospitals. These are some of the outstanding examples.

The Many Martyrs of Blackosophy

Marcus Mosiah Garvey, Jr. (1887-1940) was neither a charismatic prophet nor messiah, in fact he was a fairly conventional Christian, but his philosophical and political writings had an enormous impact on the Rastafarian movement and on the Nation of Islam, among other Black nationalist NRMs. He founded the Universal Negro Improvement Association and African Communities League (UNIA-ACL), dedicated to working for the self-sufficiency and "uplift of his people. He also started the Pan-African ("Back to Africa") movement known as "Garveyism."

* * *

In 1919 the FBI (then named the BOI) launched an undercover investigation into the activities of Marcus Garvey and the UNIA. To this end, the BOI hired its first five African-American agents to infiltrate the organization. Since Garvey was from Jamaica, the aim was to find grounds on which to deport him as "an undesirable alien." A charge of mail fraud was brought against Garvey in connection with stock sales of the Black Star Line (a ship for transporting African-Americans across the Atlantic to resettle in and "redeem" Africa). The U.S. Post Office and the Attorney General soon joined the investigation.[10] Garvey was found guilty of using the mail service to defraud, and sentenced to two years in the Atlanta Federal Penitentiary

---

[10] The accusation was based on the fact that, although a photograph of a ship with the name "Phyllis Wheatley" was featured on the company's stock brochures, it had not yet been purchased. The prosecution produced as evidence a single empty envelope which it claimed had contained the brochure. A witness for the prosecution, Benny Dancy, testified that he didn't remember what was in the envelope, although he regularly received brochures from the Black Star Line. Another witness, Schuyler Cargill, actually perjured himself after admitting to having been told to mention certain dates by the Chief Prosecutor. Moreover, he confessed that Postal Inspector F.E. Shea had told him to state that he mailed letters containing the purportedly fraudulent brochures. While the Black Star Line did own and operate several ships over the course of its history, it was at the time negotiating the purchase of the disputed ship.

where, in February 1925, he wrote his famous "First Message to the Negroes of the World from Atlanta Prison."[11] On his release from prison, he was deported to Jamaica, where he was greeted as a hero by hundreds of his followers.

Marcus Garvey's writings are perhaps the most influential of any Black nationalist writer. His supporters assume his prosecution was a politically-motivated miscarriage of justice. They point to the fact that a witness for the prosecution later admitted to perjury, and that J. Edgar Hoover, in a memo dated 11 October 1919, expressed regret that Garvey had as yet committed no crimes, just before he launched the undercover investigation: "[Garvey] has not as yet violated any federal law whereby he could be proceeded against on the grounds of being an undesirable alien, from the point of view of deportation."

* * *

Leonard P. Howell (1898-1981), an influential dread philosopher during the early Rastafarian movement, proclaimed Haille Selassie as the Second Coming, wrote the six foundations of Rastafari, and set up the Pinnacle Encampment near Kingston where he ruled as "Chief" with his thirty wives. In 1933 he was arrested on charges of sedition while selling photographs of Haille Selassie on the street. He was sentenced to two years in prison, and in 1954 he was committed to the Kingston psychiatric hospital.[12] The Pinnacle was raided repeatedly by the police between 1941-57 on the pretext that the Rastafarians were growing marihuana next to the yam patches, and were selling ganja, as well as vegetables, for profit. The property was seized and sold off by the government, and today there is a movement to reclaim the Pinnacle.

Father Divine (1880-1965) of the Father Divine Peace Mission, launched a successful charitable mission in Harlem in the 1930s, but was sued by two female followers, who wished to recover their donations. The court ruled in favor of one of them, a woman named Verinda Brown. Because Father Divine refused to pay Brown the sum demanded by the court, his movement had to leave New York.[13] The historian William Kephart notes, "I am inclined to believe that the 1942 court decision was a poor one…. Brown's story sounded…contrived, witnesses for the defense were largely ignored, and one of the chief witnesses for the prosecution was none other than Faithful Mary [another disgruntled apostate] who later admitted she had lied under oath."

---

[11] The speech states, "Look for me in the whirlwind or the storm, look for me all around you, for, with God's grace, I shall come and bring with me countless millions of black slaves who have died in America and the West Indies and the millions in Africa to aid you in the fight for Liberty, Freedom and Life."

[12] Helen Lee and Stephen Dare, *The First Rasta* (Chicago: Chicago Review Press, 2005).

[13] William M. Kephart, *Extraordinary Groups; the Sociology of Unconventional Lifestles* (London: St Martin Press 2001), 140.

Father Divine's mission then settled in Sayville, Long Island and attracted busloads of visitors to the Sunday service and free banquets of four-course meals.[14] The conflict started over parking tickets. A female undercover agent was planted to investigate Father Divine's reputed sexual improprieties, and even tried (unsuccessfully) to seduce him. After Father Divine refused a petition by local citizens to leave Sayville, the police arrived on 15 November 1931, and disrupted a Sunday service to arrest him and 80 of his followers on charges of disturbing the peace. Kephart writes, "while the arrest itself was peaceful enough, the entire episode was a shot heard around the Negro world."[15] Despite the flimsiness of the case, Father Divine was indicted by a grand jury and held on $1500 bail for trial.

Kephart points out that the treatment of this Black messiah in court was hardly impartial: "the presiding judge, Lewis J. Smith, was clearly antagonistic in his attitude to the defendant. His first act was to cancel his bail and remand him to prison." The prosecution contended that Father Divine and his followers had disturbed the peace, obstructed traffic and were a public nuisance. After the jury recommended leniency, Judge Smith then imposed "the stiffest sentence the law would permit; one year in prison and a fine of $500." Three days later, Judge Smith died of a heart attack. Father Divine's enigmatic comment from jail was "I hated to do it." The Appellate court then reversed the court's decisions on the grounds of the "prejudicial comments" of the late judge.[16] Thus, the court's unfair treatment of Father Divine is on public record.

Noble Drew Ali (1886-1929) of the Moorish Science Temple was held responsible for shady financial dealings among his followers, although the historian Michael A. Gomez states, "there is no indication that Noble Drew Ali himself was involved in corrupt monetary practices."[17] He was also implicated in an unsolved murder. In 1929, in a struggle over local temple authority, Noble Drew's business manager, Claude Greene, threw his prophet's office furniture into the street at 3140 Indiana Avenue, site of the Unity Club, and declared he was the "Grand Sheik." Greene was shot and stabbed by unknown assailants shortly after this coup.[18] Noble Drew and several of his leaders were arrested, but released when no evidence was found linking them to the murder. Noble Drew died soon after, on 20 July 1929. His Moors believe it was the direct result of police brutality while in jail, but it might have resulted from internecine violence (beatings from supporters of Greene), or from tuberculosis.[19]

Mattias Gardell notes, "the absence of social revolutionary rhetoric did not prevent the Moors from being targeted by the American police. The mere existence

---

[14]   Kephart, 119.

[15]   Kephart, 122.

[16]   "Who is the King of Glory?" *New Yorker*, 13 June 1936, 21.

[17]   Michael A. Gomez, *Black Crescent: The Experience and Legacy of African Muslims in the Americas* (New York: Cambridge University Press, 2005), 271.

[18]   Gomez, 273.

[19]   Gomez, 472.

of organized blacks, no matter how law-abiding, seems to have been sufficient to make security agents alert." The MST was monitored by the FBI whose special agent found a flyer interpreting the Great Depression as a sign of the coming wrath of God. This apocalyptic rhetoric was interpreted as "hostile to the interests of the government."[20] But after decades of government surveillance, no evidence was found of any pro-Japanese or un-American teachings in the MST.[21]

The Nation of Islam has a history of internecine violence. Gardell's study points to the FBI released files which indicate that a number of FBI informants were planted in the NOI. Gardell argues that the FBI deliberately planted "seeds of dissension" which exacerbated the rivalry between different ministers and increased the potential for violence.[22] Author Karl Evanzz[23] and film director Spike Lee both claim that freelancing FOI soldiers were set up to assassinate Malcolm X by someone in the NOI hierarchy acting on behalf of the FBI. This theory is supported by a memo of 7 February 1964 sent within the FBI. It proposes a move to "possibly widen the rift between Muhammad and Little and possibly result in Little's expulsion."[24]

Clarence 13X (1928-69), a former security officer of the Fruit of Islam, formed a schismatic group from the Nation of Islam, called the Five Percent Nation. On 31 May 1965, while holding a rally on the street outside the Hotel Theresa on New York's Seventh Avenue, he was arrested for disorderly conduct and obstructing traffic. At the arraignment he told Judge Francis X. O'Brien that he was "God" or "Allah," and the city would blow up if he were not released. The judge held him in custody under a $9600 bond and the Supreme Court judge sent him to the Psychiatric Unit at Bellevue Hospital. Clarence 13X was transferred to another hospital after he managed to start a small Five Percent cell within the psychiatric ward. In 1967 he was released and returned to New York City, where he was welcomed by his followers in a huge gathering that became the very first "Universal Parliament" in Mount Morris Park.[25]

In 1967 Mayor John V. Lindsay, concerned about the racial tension between blacks and Jews in Crow heights, Brooklyn, sent his aide to speak to Clarence 13X. Clarence requested bus trips to the park and Long Beach for the Fiver Percenters, and funding for a Five Percent school for the inner city youth which was opened on 2122, 7th Avenue. On 4 April 1968, Martin Luther King was assassinated. The Five Percenters launched a peacemaking mission in Harlem thereby diverting a potential

---

[20]   FBI file 62-25889-6 is cited in Mattias Gardell.

[21]   Mattias Gardell, *In the Name of Elijah Muhammad: Louis Farrakhan and the Nation of Islam* (Durham, North Carolina: Duke University Press, 1996).

[22]   See Gardell, who cites the FBI files 105-24822-142 and 05-24822-202.

[23]   Karl Evanzz, *The Judas Factor: the Plot to Kill Malcolm X* (New York: Thunder's Mouth Press, 1993).

[24]   See Gardell, 62.

[25]   Michael Muhammad Knight, *The Five Percenters: Islam, Hip Hop and the Gods of New York* (Oxford: Oneworld, 2007), 132-3.

riot and received a commendation from Mayor Lindsay for their good work, for their peacemaking and their education and vocational training programs for youth.

On 12 June 1969 Clarence 13X was gunned down in an elevator in the Martin Luther King Towers in east Harlem by several assailants.[26] His murder was never solved. It may have been the work of a criminal gang, but the Five Percent Nation suspected it was an assassination plot by the Nation of Islam. Farrakhan, however, denied this allegation and suggested it was the work of the police and the white power structure, inciting black people to fight against and kill each other.[27]

There are more examples, such as the mysterious disappearance of Master Fard, founder of the Nation of Islam, and the murky circumstances behind the assassination of Malcolm X. One of the most infamous cases is that of MOVE. In 1985 the Philadelphia police decided to drop a bomb from a helicopter on the communal home of MOVE, a Black Nationalist group founded by John Africa, killing 11 members and causing a fire which destroyed 61 adjacent houses, leaving hundreds of people homeless. While many of these troubling episodes might be explained as arising "naturally" out of the appalling social conditions in black ghettoes, where poverty and crime prevail, there does appear to be an element of religious persecution. When a Black religious leader inspires his people to transcend their social situation and build a new way of life, he becomes a target. Once his congregation becomes too large, too noisy, too conspicuous, or too influential, he will be arrested and charged with disturbing the peace, obstructing traffic, or on some other pretext. The unconventional religious doctrines and charismatic claims of these "Black Messiahs" will excite derision in the media, and will discredit them in the courts of law.[28]

Black Messiahs are frequently associated with sexual misdemeanors, just as white Christian fundamentalist evangelists are often associated with financial misconduct. A survey of their domestic arrangements, however, suggests the situation is more complex. Some messianic founders of NRMs have preached and practiced polygamy quite openly, as for example Dr. Malachi Z. York, Leonard P. Howell, and Ben Ammi of the Black Hebrews in Israel.[29] Others have practiced it in secret. In the investigation following Noble Drew Ali's death, it was discovered that he had four "wives," whom he married in clandestine Moorish ceremonies.[30]

---

26   Knight, 121.

27   See www.thetalkingdrum.com/nge.html.66k

28   It is important to note that many "white" NRMs have also evoked conflict and controversy. For example, A.J. Ballard, founder of the Great I AM was also found guilty of mail fraud.

29   Merrill Singer, "Symbolic Identity Formation in an African American Sect: Black Hebrew Israelites," in Yvonne Chireau and Nathaniel Deutsch, eds, *Black Zion: African American Religious Encounters with Judaism* (New York: Oxford University Press, 2000), 69.

30   The coroner's inquest into Noble Drew Ali's death discovered that he had been simultaneously sexually involved with a 14 year old, a 16 year old, and a woman over

Elijah Muhammad was married and preached monogamous family values, but was secretly practicing a kind of proto-polygamy with his teenaged secretaries.[31]

But Father Divine is an exception. He appears to have been happily married twice, albeit in celibacy. Yahweh Ben Yahweh was married twice in his youth, but appears to have led a celibate life after he moved to Florida and launched the Nation of Yahweh.[32]

While these case histories do not "prove" that Dr York was framed, they do demonstrate a larger social pattern tending towards the "criminalization" of Black nationalistic movements in America. The responses of Dr. York's disciples to the injustices in his case must be understood in this context, in particular the RICO conviction, which enabled the government to seize and sell the Nuwaubians' sacred land.

New Racialist Religions as "Racketeering Enterprises"

The RICO (Racketeer Influenced and Corrupt Organizations) federal statute was enacted in Congress in 1970. The stated purpose of the federal RICO statute was to stop organized crime's infiltration into legitimate businesses, and to control political corruption and corporate fraud. A private person filing a civil RICO lawsuit must prove that an enterprise has engaged in a "pattern of racketeering," defined in law as the commission of two or more criminal acts. Felonies listed under "racketeering" include murder, kidnapping, arson, extortion, witness tampering, counterfeiting, drug offenses, embezzlement, wire fraud and mail fraud.

RICO gives the U.S. government wider powers and entitles its prosecutors to triple the restitution, fines and penalties of the defendant who is found guilty of RICO (hence the 135 year sentence). RICO sets a minimum guideline of three years for

---

20 while married to Pearl Drew Ali. Mary Foreman Bey (his second wife in polygamy who was pregnant with his child) claimed he had married two "women of tender age" in Moorish-American ceremonies (see Gomez, 474).

[31] A scandal erupted when it became known that Elijah Muhammad had engaged in a number of extramarital affairs with some of his young female secretaries, and at least four girls, Sisters Evelyn, Rosary, Rosella and Lavita, had become pregnant. Sister Evelyn eventually filed a paternity suit against the Messenger. The FBI wrote anonymous letters to his wife, Clara, and to other individuals within the NOI, but to no avail. But when Malcolm X confronted Elijah Muhammad, the latter responded, "I'm David. When you read about how David took another man's wife, I'm that David. You read about Noah who got drunk— that's me. You read about Lot who went and laid up with his own daughters. I had to fulfill all those things." (See *The Autobiography of Malcolm X* as told to Alex Haley (N.Y. Ballyntine Books, 1973), 299.

[32] Yahweh Ben Yahweh was accused by ex-members of seducing under-aged girls, and even of incest. None of these rumors were ever substantiated, however. Nor were they brought up as formal allegations during his trial. See Sydney Freedberg, *Brother Love: Murder, Money and a Messiah* (N.Y.: Pantheon Books, 1994), 175.

each count for defendants with no prior criminal record. RICO allows prosecutors the right to confiscate assets that were "instrumental in the alleged criminal activity." Moreover, RICO charges are often added to a criminal indictment already filed, to assist the prosecutors who might require additional evidence and witnesses.

RICO was initially applied to criminal gangs, but over the years federal prosecutors and private citizens had been using the statute to attack a broadening list of defendants; among them anti-abortion protestors, and a weekly newspaper. But since 1985, RICO had been applied to facilitate the prosecution of leaders of new religious movements. These four RICO cases are the following:

> 1985—James Ellison of the Covenant, the Sword and the Arm of the Lord in Missouri
> 1992—Yahweh Ben Yahweh of the Nation of Yahweh in Florida
> 1995—The leaders of the Justus Freemen in Montana
> 2004—Dr. Malachi York of the United Nuwaubian Nation of Moors in Georgia

It is perhaps significant that all four NRMs might be categorized as "identity" or "racialist" groups (i.e. possessing major doctrines based on a value-laden myth or sacred history of the origin and meaning of race). The Freemen and the CSAL were both called "White separatists." There are remarkable similarities between the two RICO cases involving Yahweh Ben Yahweh and Dr. Malachi Z. York. The initial criminal charges laid against the two leaders by the state were quite different (Yahweh Ben Yahweh was charged with complicity in a series of murders), but both leaders were charged with RICO violations after it became evident that the state charges against them were unlikely to "stick."

Yahweh Ben Yahweh: from Rags to Riches...to RICO!

The Nation of Yahweh's messianic founder was the late Hulon Mitchell Jr. He was born in 1935 in Kingfisher, Oklahoma, and died (or "ascended") on May 7, 2007. In 1979 Mitchell (known at the time as "Father Michal") arrived in Florida and launched his Hebrew Israelite mission and set up the Temple of Love in Miami. By 1986 the membership of the NOY was around 12,000 and the group had bought up and renovated slum housing and established lucrative businesses in Miami, which they claim was worth around $20 million. In 1990 Yahweh Ben Yahweh's remarkable success in establishing a thriving community convinced the Mayor of the City of Miami to proclaim Sunday 7 October 1990 as "Yahweh Ben Yahweh Day."[33]

Yahweh Ben Yahweh (YBY) narrates a mythologized history that makes moral sense out of the African American experience of slavery and oppression in

---

[33]   Sydney Freedberg, *Brother Love: Murder, Money and a Messiah* (N.Y.: Pantheon Books, 1994), 253.

America over the last 400 years.[34] YBY received an overwhelming response from the impoverished and crime-ridden black ghettoes of Miami.[35] He mobilized his followers to live communally, emphasizing ethics of cleanliness, unselfishness, family values and hard work. They pooled their resources and quickly developed a string of businesses, including a convention center, a publishing company, motels, a manufacturing plant, shopping center, apartment buildings, and the University of Yahweh. A journalist in a CBS report in December 1988 reports: "25 years ago, the only blacks allowed on Miami Beach were servants and gardeners who carried special passes. Today Yahweh Ben Yahweh owns part of that beach and that, in Miami, means money and power."[36]

In the 1980s there were a series of homicides perpetrated by NOY members in Miami. These amounted to 15 murders and two attempted murders. The victims ranged from ex-members, dissident current members, innocent bystanders (both white and black), and several homosexuals. The investigation revealed a ritual dimension that involved decapitations and the cutting off of ears, apparently as trophies. The chief perpetrator of these crimes turned out to be Robert Rozier. Rozier was a former professional football player who had served as one of YBY's bodyguards in the "Circle of Ten"—tall, athletic men who would stand holding African staffs to guard their messiah during his sermons. Rozier actually confessed to seven of the murders, but claimed he was following orders from Yahweh Ben Yahweh.[37]

On 7 November 1990, the FBI executed a series of raids in seven states, raids that involved more than 300 FBI agents, drug enforcement agents, SWAT team members, and local law enforcement officers. Yahweh Ben Yahweh and 16 of his followers were arrested on murder charges, arson, fire bombing and extortion, and later charged with conspiracy under RICO.[38] A book issued by the theologians of the NOY after their leader's conviction, *The Crucifixion of the Messiah*, claims that the raid was preceded by and planned in meetings held between U.S. Attorney's office and the State of Florida Attorney's office.[39] As a result of this meeting, the state of Florida ceded its jurisdiction to the feds, who formally indicted YBY with three counts of RICO (murder, arson and extortion). The legal process of Yahweh Ben Yahweh might be analyzed as undergoing three phases. First, he was initially indicted at the federal level, charged with beheadings, killing and cutting off ears,

---

[34]   *You are not a Nigger: Our True History, the World's Best Kept Secret* (Beaconsfield Quebec: PEES Foundation, 1993), 4.

[35]   Yahweh Ben Yahweh addresses his followers in his speeches as former drug dealers, gangsters and prostitutes, and some of them make similar claims in their testimonials. However, Sydney Freedberg notes that, as the Temple of Love grew, middle class businessmen, artists and professionals began to join.

[36]   Uriah David Israel, speaking on *Judicial Murder:"Let the Evidence be heard!"*

[37]   See Freedberg for a full account of these events.

[38]   See *The Persecution of the Yahweh Ben Yahweh*, 6-13, for an account of the FBI raids.

[39]   *The Crucifixion of the Messiah*, 205.

mass murders, fire bombings, extortion. He was found not guilty by the jury. Next, he was rearrested and indicted on two first degree murder charges in the *State of Florida versus Yahweh Ben Yahweh* trial in Miami, before Judge Arthur Snyder. The jury found him not guilty after two hours deliberation on 17 December 1992. Finally, he was reindicted and sent back to trial in federal court on conspiracy (RICO) charges.[40]

On 2 January 1992, the *USA versus Yahweh Ben Yahweh* trial began with the U.S. District Court Judge Norman C. Roettger in Fort Lauderdale. After a five month trial and five and a half days of deliberations, on 27 May 1992 the jury convicted YBY of "conspiracy to commit RICO." He was found "not guilty," however, of the substantive racketeering charge that would have tied him to the murders. The sentence was 18 years in prison and a fine of $20,000. Yahweh Ben Yahweh was incarcerated for 15 years in Fort Leavenworth (the same "Super-max" security prison where Dr. York is imprisoned). Although he had taken a "vow of poverty" in the 1980s and did not legally own any the NOY's property, the government seized the assets and businesses belonging to the whole commune, leaving many of the Hebrew Israelites destitute, deprived of employment, housing and careers. Yahweh Ben Yahweh died on 7 May 2007, shortly after he was released from prison, after being diagnosed with terminal cancer.

A Comparison of the Two Cases

Although these two NRMs and their leaders are very different (in terms of theology, social organization, economic, charismatic and family patterns) they were perceived by the media and law enforcement as almost identical; as a bunch of "racists," as "black supremacists," as a "hate group," as a fake religion hiding a criminal enterprise.

The RICO charges appear to have been applied opportunistically in both cases. An attorney on YBY's defense team, Thomas Buscaglia complains, "What the federal prosecutors did, was to put together a bunch of murder cases and called it a racketeering case. Most judges don't understand it." Boscaglia then describes RICO as if it were a piece of sticky flypaper:

> If you can't prove a specific crime against somebody the best thing to do is to accuse him of 50 crimes, and get people to stand up and say bad things about him, so you are putting the jury in the position of letting this person—who you say is a bad person—go free or charge him with a little bit. It's sad but true that the general technique of a conspiracy or RICO case is to create innuendo and a suggestion of evil.[41]

---

[40]   For a full account of the trial, see Sydney Freedberg, *Brother Love: Murder, Money and a Messiah* (N.Y.: Pantheon Books, 1994).

[41]   See *Judicial Murder* (NOY documentary film).

Another of YBY's lawyers, Attorney Wendell, notes, "RICO…is considered one of the prosecution's favorite strategies. It says, 'you all got together and talked about doing something.' Historically, it is a charge that jurors, when pushed, will convict upon!"[42]

Attorney Adrian Patrick made a similar point in his Eleventh Circuit Appeal. He argued that the federal prosecutors applied RICO improperly, combining racketeering and money structuring charges with the initial child molestation charges. Patrick claimed that the prosecution had "created a hazy aggregation of Mann Act claims, conspiracy claims, and racketeering claims."

Attorney Wende Rush (who, incidentally, is a Hebrew Israelite) asks, "What was the difference between the state case and the federal case? No RICO, no confusion, just the facts…the result? Not guilty!" Journalist Sydney Freedberg also draws attention to the legal anomalies in the case; of how Yahweh Ben Yahweh and some of his leaders were reindicted with federal charges of racketeering immediately after they had been found innocent of the state charges of murder. "The notion of recharging acquitted defendants rubbed some defense attorneys the wrong way," Freedberg observes.

RICO is a difficult concept for lay persons to grasp, as the attorneys cited above note. Attorney McGee says: "RICO is such a complex area of the law. It took…19 lawyers plus the judge…it took us 2 days to fashion a RICO instruction for the jury… . The jury was confused, they pointed out conflicts in the instructions we had given them… . It is impossible for the jury to understand the language that the RICO law is written in." Attorney Boscaglia adds, "[the jury] couldn't agree on what the heck the jury instructions meant!" Journalist Freedberg also makes this point:

> [Judge] Roettger read the jurors 49 pages of baffling instructions on the workings of the federal racketeering laws… . To convict on racketeering [the jury] charges had to agree with the prosecutors' contention that [YBY] had played a role in two crimes listed in the indictment or that he had agreed to crimes that would occur. To convict on a conspiracy charge, they had only to find that the defendant agreed that least two crimes would be committed.[43]

The defense lawyers of both defendants complain of being handicapped by RICO—especially in respect to the waiving of the rules on pre-trial discovery. This hampered them in the preparing of their defense, since they were not permitted to cross-examine the unnamed witnesses, or "un-indicted co-conspirators." Journalist Sydney Freedberg explains this situation as follows:

> Florida's rules on pre-trial "discovery" would make it difficult to convict YBY under state law. "Discovery" is the accused's right to know what evidence the

---

[42] *Judicial Murder.*
[43] Freedberg, 301.

prosecution is planning to introduce in the trial. In a federal trial, however, the accused may be surprised by evidence introduced.[44]

In both cases, the punishment was unusually severe. Although neither leader was found guilty of murder, each received what amounted to a life sentence. Both were consigned to the "Super-max" prison with the worst reputation in the USA—Fort Leavenworth, a prison usually reserved for serial killers, mobsters and terrorists.

It would appear reasonable to argue that RICO was applied opportunistically by the government as a new social control strategy, that turned out to be effective in quelling unconventional religions that appear to pose a threat as highly-organized "black supremacist" groups posing as "Nations." Journalist, Sydney Freeberg, who covered the trial of Yahweh Ben Yahweh, lists three reasons "why the feds took [Yahweh Ben Yahweh's] case": First, they could make use of the IRS to track where the NOY got its funds. Second, they could offer witnesses for the prosecution federal witness protection programs, making it easier to convict YBY. Third, they could side-step Florida's rules on pre-trial "discovery."

RICO, in its formidable punitive power, does not distinguish between the leader and the congregation. Thousands of innocent people were punished in these two communities when their leaders were convicted for "conspiracy to commit RICO." As it turns out, neither leader actually owned the property that was confiscated. Dr. York had transferred the ownership of the land on which Tama Re was constructed to nine of his executive leaders several years before his arrest. Nevertheless, on 14 July 2004 Judge Ashley Royal issued an order allowing federal officials to seize the land, a property of $1.7 million. By 10 June 2005 demolition of the sacred architecture and statues had begun. Adrian Patrick noted in the Eleventh Circuit Court that the law enforcement agencies had profited nicely from the seizure of the 478-acre tract of land on which Tama-Re was constructed. The Putman County's Sheriff's Office had received a check for almost $546,000 for the sale. The federal department of Internal Revenue Service had received around $99,270, and the FBI had received around $350,000 to reimburse the expenses incurred in the raid.

Adrian Patrick points out the injustice in punishing a whole congregation for the alleged crimes of one of its members:

> If an individual commits an act, that does not mean the organization as a whole was an enterprise for criminal activity. When Catholic priests were arrested for sexual molestation, they didn't indict the entire Catholic Church for RICO violations.

Yahweh's reindictment and his subsequent RICO conviction left his followers with a strong sense of injustice, of being innocent victims trapped by a conspiracy.

---

44   Freedberg, 244.

As a result of their made up evidence and contrived events, we, the so-called Black people of America have been deprived of our prestigious positions; reduced politically, financially, and our professional careers have been ruined.[45]

The lawyers in both cases strongly objected to the way the prosecution defined what was essentially a *religious* congregation or organization as a "racketeering enterprise." Attorney Adrian Patrick challenged the assumption that the United Nuwaubian Nation of Moors was "an organized crime syndicate." He pointed out that the application of RICO in York's trial was based on "a belief that a State of Georgia-recognized church ministry and Native American tribe constitutes an enterprise for illegal activities." Attorney Thomas Boscaglia, who defended YBY notes: "Because of First Amendment issues—the idea of indicting a religion as a criminal enterprise was, quite frankly...I find it shocking. These are the issues—the fact that that a religion was targeted as a racketeering enterprise. I felt that it was necessary to get in and do what I could."[46] Another attorney on YBY's defense team, Rayfield McGee, noted:

This is the first time to my memory that a religion organization was indicted by way of the RICO statutes... . It does, in fact, represent a very dangerous precedent and who knows who will be the next victim of this particular use of the statute? The law is extremely broad and all the prosecution has to do is fashion some set of facts...allege particular acts that will fall within the four corners of the statute—and you conceivably can be charged![47]

Chief Judge Norman C. Roettger, who presided over the Eleventh Circuit Appeal, made a careful distinction between the "conspirators in this case" and the "general population of the Temple": "We recognize and stress this difference. This case is not about the persecution of a religion."[48] Nevertheless, as a direct consequence of the RICO convictions of a few, thousands of Yahweh's worshippers were indeed punished by the government's seizure and confiscation of their communal property. The theologians of the NOY protested, "To agree that the whole should not be judged by the acts of a few and then to proceed to do just that is unconscionable... . Upholding the indictment of an entire nation and an entire faith as a racketeering enterprise has had the factual result of branding all followers and worshippers as unindicted co-conspirators."[49]

---

[45]   *Crucifixion of the Messiah* (Seguin,Texas: PEES Foundation 1999), 209.

[46]   *Judicial Murder.*

[47]   *Judicial Murder.*

[48]   Chief Judge Norman C. Roettger, *The United States of America vs. Yahweh Ben Yahweh, et al* (Case Number 90-868-Cr-Roettger, Trial Transcript, Volume 74), 16.

[49]   *Operation Word War* (NOY booklet, n.d.), 12.

The "Persecution" of Unconventional Religions

The application of RICO in these four cases poses a dangerous precedent in a nation that values religious freedom. Any "world rejecting" type of NRM could be charged, at least theoretically, with RICO violations. Communal groups based on the utopian ideals of equality, renunciation of private property, brotherly love and sharing have been legally organized in different ways throughout the history of heresy.[50] As Max Weber observed, one of the characteristics of social organizations based on charismatic authority is a rejection of routine economic patterns, deemed as respectable. The followers tend to live communally with the charismatic leader, to renounce outside labor and attachments, and to depend upon gifts, donations, voluntary labor and "booty" for their sustenance.[51] Since utopian, counter-cultural communes do not "fit" into societal norms, conflicts often arise, in terms of labor laws, tax laws, building codes and inheritance. When public officials scrutinize the financial dealings within these alternative, experimental communities, they are likely to find some irregularities. One might ask, why other "cult leaders" who preside over communal movements—the Amish, the Mennonites, the Fundamentalist Mormons, the Unification Church, the Hare Krishna—or even the Shaker villages—have not been charged with RICO?

Millenarian movements, as "religions of the oppressed" offer hope to the poor, the dispossessed and the downtrodden.[52] A messianic communal movement that demands moral reform and shows the poor how to build a better life will presumably attract a certain number of thieves, pimps, gangsters, drug users and dealers—and murderers. It is not unlikely that at least one of them may suffer a moral relapse and resort to violent or unlawful means to achieve his/her personal ends, or even to further collective goals. Once the crime is committed, it can be blamed on the leader who (according to the brainwashing model) exerts "total control" over the minds of the followers. RICO makes the leader responsible— and therefore punishable—for crimes committed by his/her followers. And in the end, thousands of innocent, hard-working families within the congregation are also punished when the government confiscates their communal property, and the media labels their organization a "dangerous cult."

In an eloquent passage from *The Crucifixion of the Messiah*, the theologians of the NOY express their outrage at being treated like a criminal gang:

---

[50]   See Rosabeth Moss Kanter, *Commitment and Community. Communes and Utopias in Sociological Perspective* (Cambridge Mass.: Harvard University Press), 1972.

[51]   Weber, Max, *Max Weber: The Theory of Social and Economic Organization*. Translated by A.M. Henderson & Talcott Parsons (NY: The Free Press, 1947), 362.

[52]   See Yonina Talmon. "Millenarism," in *The International Encyclopedia of the Social Sciences*, Vol. 10. MacMillan, 1968, 351. See also Norman Cohn. "Pursuit of the Millennium: the Relation between Religion and Social Change," Reprinted from *Archives Europiennes de Sociologie, III* (1962), 125-48. See also Grant Underwood, *The Millenarian World of Early Mormonism*, 1993, University of Illinois.

RICO was designed to attack drug empires and not a whole religion. Since the intent, the legislature in passing the RICO statute was to destroy money laundering and to punish persons engaged in a pattern of racketeering activities. The facts in this article alone eliminate all RICO motives as a basis for a case against Yahweh Ben Yahweh, the Yahwehs, the Children of God, and the Temple of Love. All property and assets of the Temple of Love were acquired through the tithes and offerings of its believers and supporters—the same as any church. Only anti-christ Assistant U.S. Attorney Scruggs, calls tithes and offerings a racket and a criminal enterprise. If the court recognizes Yahweh Ben Yahweh's indigent status, then why does the government insist that [he] is a money-hungry religious racketeer?[53]

Finally, they warn us: "Your religion, church, temple and leader are next!"[54]

---

[53]   *The Persecution of YAHWEH BEN YAHWEH. The People for Truth* (Seguin, Texas: PEES Foundation, 1994), 131.

[54]   *The Persecution of YAHWEH BEN YAHWEH*, 131.

Figure 7　Nuwaubian ritual at the Pyramid

Bibliography

Julius H. Bailey, "The Final Frontier: Secrecy, Identity, and the Media in the Rise and Fall of the United Nuwaubian Nation of Moors," in *Journal of the American Academy of Religion* (74/2, 2006), 302-23.

William Sims Bainbridge, *Satan's Power* (Los Angeles: University of California Press, 1978).

Eileen Barker, *The Making of a Moonie: Choice of Brainwashing?* (London: Blackwells, 1984).

Eileen Barker, "Charting the Information Field: Cult-Watching Groups and the Construction of Images of New Religious Movements," in David G. Bromley (ed.), *Teaching New Religious Movements* (New York: Oxford University Press, 2007).

Howard S. Becker, *Outsiders: Studies in the Sociology of Deviance* (New York: Free Press, 1963).

James Beckford, "The Mass Media and New Religious Movements," in Bryan Wilson and Jamie Cresswell (eds.), *New Religious Movements* (London: Routledge, 1999).

Henrik Bogdan, *Western Esotericism and Rituals of Initiation* (forthcoming with SUNY Press).

Colin Campbell, "The Cult, the Cultic Milieu and Secularization," in *A Sociological Yearbook of Religion in Britain* (5/1, 1972), 119-36.

Lewis Carter, *Charisma and Control in Rajneeshpuram. The Role of Shared Values in the Creation of a Community* (New York: Cambridge University Press, 1998).

Jeff Chang, *Can't Stop, Won't Stop: A History of the Hip-Hop Generation* (New York: Picador, 2005).

Stanley Cohen, *Folk Devils and Moral Panics* (London: MacGibbon and Kee, 1962).

Norman Cohn, *The Pursuit of the Millennium: Revolutionary Millenarians and Mystical Anarchists of the Middle Ages* (New York: Oxford University Press, 1957).

Norman Cohn, "Pursuit of the Millennium: the Relation between Religion and Social Change" (Reprinted from *Archives Europiennes de Sociologie III*, 1962).

Harry A. Williamson Ezra A. Cook, *The Prince Hall Primer* (McCoy Publishing and Masonic Supply Co., 1949).

George W. Crawford, *Prince Hall and His Followers: Being a Monograph on the Legitimacy of Negro Masonry* (New York: The Crisis, 1949).

Edward E. Curtis IV, *Islam in Black America: Identity, Liberation and Difference in African-American Thought* (New York: SUNY, 2002).

Harry Davis, *A History of Freemasonry among Negroes in America* (United Supreme Council, Ancient and Accepted Scottish Rite of Freemasonry, Northern Jurisdiction, Prince Hall Affiliation, 1949).

Levi H. Dowling, *The Aquarian Gospel of Jesus the Christ: The Philosophic and Practical Basis of the Religion of the Aquarian Age of the World and of the Church Universal* (New York: DeVorss & Company; New Ed edition, 1972).

Cora A. Du Bois, *The 1870 Ghost Dance* (Berkeley: University of California Press, 1939).

Carl E. Ellis, Jr., *Beyond Liberation: The Gospel in the Black American Experience* (Downers Grove, Illinois: InterVarsity Press, 1983).

Robert S. Ellwood, *Alternative Altars: Unconventional and Eastern Spirituality in America* (Chicago University Press, 1979).

Henry Emmerson, *Negro Masonry: Being a Critical Examination of Objections to the Legitimacy of Masonry Existing* (New York: AMS Press, 1975).

Edmonds Ennis Barrington, *Rastafari: from Outcasts to Culture Bearers* (New York: Oxford University Press, 2003).

E.U. Essien-Udom, *Black Nationalism: A Search for Identity in America* (University of Chicago Press, 1962).

Karl Evanzz, *The Messenger: The Rise and Fall of Elijah Muhammad* (New York: Pantheon Books, 1999).

FBI Report, "The Ansaru Allah Community, also known as The Nubian Islamic Hebrews, The Tents of Kedar" (The United States Department of Justice, Federal Bureau of Investigation, Domestic Security/Terrorism, 1993) (File number deleted).

FBI Report: Project Megiddo (www.religioustolerance.org/megiddo.htm).

Leon Festinger, H.W. Riecken, and S. Schachter, *When Prophecy Fails* (Minneapolis: University of Minnesota Press, 1956).

Georg Feuerstein, *Holy Madness: The Shock Tactics and Radical Teachings of Crazy-Wise Adepts, Holy Fools and Rascal Gurus* (New York: Arkana, 1990).

Raymond Firth, *Elements of Social Organization* (London: C.A. Watts, 1951).

Sydney Freedberg, *Brother Love: Murder, Money and a Messiah* (New York: Pantheon Books, 1994).

Mattias Gardell, *In the Name of Elijah Muhammad: Louis Farrakhan and the Nation of Islam.* (Durham: Duke University Press, 1996).

Mattias Gardell, *Countdown to Armageddon: Louis Farrakhan and the Nation of Islam* (University of Chicago Press, 1999).

Erving Goffman, *The Presentation of Self in Everyday Life* (Chicago University Press, 1959).

Michael Gomez, *Black Crescent, The Experience and Legacy of African Muslims in the Americas* (New York: Cambridge University Press, 2005).

Erich Goode and Nachman Ben-Yehuda, *The Social Constructions of Deviance* (Oxford: Blackwell, 1962).

Alex Haley, *The Autobiography of Malcolm X* (NewYork: Ballyntine Books, 1973).

Edward Herman and Noam Chomsky, *Manufacturing Consent: The Political Economy of the Mass Media* (New York: Pantheon Books, 1988).

Hans Jonas, *The Gnostic Religion* (Boston: Beacon Press, 1963).

Rosabeth Moss Kanter, *Commitment and Community. Communes and Utopias in Sociological Perspective* (Cambridge Mass.: Harvard University Press, 1972).

Jeffrey Kaplan, *Radical Religion in America: Millenarian Movements from the Far Right to the Children of Noah* (Syracuse, NY: Syracuse University Press, 1997).

Jeffrey Kaplan and Helen Lööw, *The Cultic Milieu: Oppositional Subcultures in an Age of Globalization* (Boston: Altamira Press, 2002).

Stephen A. Kent and Theresa Krebs, "When Scholars Know Sin: Alternative Religions and Their Academic Supporters," *Skeptic Magazine* (6/3, 1998).

William M. Kephart, *Extraordinary Groups: the Sociology of Unconventional Lifestyles* (London: St Martin Press, 2001).

Michael Muhammad Knight, *The Five Percenters: Islam, Hip Hop and the Gods of New York* (Oxford, England: Oneworld Publications, 2007).

Helen Lee and Stephen Dare, *The First Rasta* (Chicago: Chicago Review Press, 2005).

Martha Lee, *The Nation of Islam: An American Millenarian Movement* (Syracuse, N.Y.: Syracuse University Press, 1996).

Michael Lieb, *Children of Ezekiel* (Durham and London: Duke University Press, 1998).

Eric Lincoln, *Black Muslims in America* (Boston: Beacon Press, 1961).

Ahmed Gurbi Mahdi, "Muslim organizations in the United States," in Yvonne Haddad (ed.), *The Muslims of America* (New York: Oxford University Press, 1991), 11-24.

Keith Moore, *Moorish Circle 7: The Rise of the Islamic Faith among Blacks in America and its Masonic Origins* (Bloomington, Indiana: AuthorHouse, 2005).

Wilson Jeremiah Moses, *The Golden Age of Black Nationalism* (New York: Oxford University Press, 1988).

William A. Muraskin, *Middle Class Blacks in a White Society: Price Hall Freemasonry in America* (Berkeley: University of California Press, 1972).

Kathleen Malone O'Connor, "The Nubian Islamic Hebrews, Ansaaru Allah Community: Jewish Teachings of an African American Muslim Community," in Yvonne Chireau and Nathaniel Deutsch (eds.), *Black Zion: African American Religious Encounters with Judaism* (New York: OUP, 2000), 118-52.

William Osinski, *Ungodly: The True Story of Unprecedented Evil* (Eatonton G.A.: Indigo Publishing Group, 2007).

Elaine Pagels, *Adam, Eve and the Serpent* (New York: Vintage Books, 1989).

Susan J. Palmer and Stephen Luxton, "The Ansaaru Allah Community: Postmodernist Narration and the Black Jeremiad," in Peter B. Clarke (ed.), *New Trends and Developments in the World of Islam* (London: Luzac Oriental, 1998), 353-70.

Bilal Phillips, *The Ansar Cult in America* (Riyadh, Saudi Arabia: Tawheed Publications, 1988).

Prince-A-Cuba, "Black Gods of the Inner City," *Gnosis Magazine* (Fall, 1992).

A.R. Radclyffe Brown, "On joking relationships" (*Africa* 13, 1950), 195-210.

James T. Richardson, "Social Control of New Religions" in Susan J. Palmer and Charlotte E. Hardman (eds.), *Children in New Religions* (Rutgers University Press, 1998), 172-86.

Kurt Rudolph, *Gnosis: the Nature and History of Gnosticism* (New York: Harper & Row, 1987).

Leahcim Semaj, "Race, Identity and Children of the African Diaspora" (*Caribe*, 4/4, 1980), 211-22.

Ian Simmons, "Mothership Connection," *Fortean Times* (London: Dennis Publishing, February 2009), 30-35.

George Eaton Simpson, *Black Religions in the New World* (New York: Columbia University Press, 1978).

Merrill Singer, "Symbolic Identity Formation in an African American Sect: Black Hebrew Israelites," in Yvonne Chireau and Nathaniel Deutsch (eds.), *Black Zion: African American Religious Encounters with Judaism* (New York: Oxford University Press, 2000), 55-72.

Neil Smelser, *Theory of Collective Behaviour* (London: Routledge & Kegan Paul, 1962).

Theophus H. Smith, *Conjuring Culture: Biblical Formations of Black America* (New York: Oxford University Press, 1994).

Yonina Talmon, "Millenarism," in *The International Encyclopedia of the Social Sciences*, Vol 10 (London: MacMillan, 1968).

Grant Underwood, *The Millenarian World of Early Mormonism* (Urbana-Champaign: University of Illinois, 1993).

William H. Upton, *Negro Masonry: Being a Critical Examination of Objections to the Legitimacy of Masonry Existing* (New York: AMS Press, 1975).

Jeffrey Victor, *Satanic Panic: The Creation of a Contemporary Legend* (Chicago: Open Court, 1993).

Harold Van Buren Voorhis, *Negro Masonry in the United States* (New York City, 1940).

Roy Wallis, *The Road to Total Freedom: A Sociological Analysis of Scientology* (London: Heinemann, 1976).

Roy Wallis, "Societal reactions to Scientology" in Roy Wallis (ed.), *Sectarianism* (London: Peter Owen, 1975).

Max Weber, *The Theory of Social and Economic Organization* (Translated by A.M. Henderson and Talcott Parsons. New York: The Free Press, 1947).

Catherine Wessinger (ed.), *How the Millennium Comes Violently* (New York: Seven Bridges Press, 2000).

Leslie T. Wilkins, "Social Deviance," in W.G. Carson and Paul Wiles (eds.), *Crime and Delinquency in Britain* (Martin Robertson and Co. London 1971), 87-94.

Leslie T. Wilkins, *Social Deviance: Social Policy, Action and Research* (London: Tavistock, 1964).

Peter Worsely, *The Trumpet Shall Sound: A Study of Cargo Cults in Melanesia* (New York: Shocken Books, 1968).

Stuart A. Wright, *Armageddon In Waco: Critical Perspectives On The Branch Davidian Conflict* (The University of Chicago Press, 1995).

Zechariah Zitchin, *The 12th Planet* (New York: Harper, 1976).

The Scrolls of Dr. Malachi Z. York (under various charismatic titles of the author)

Al Mahdi Muhammad Ahmad the Only True Mahdi (Brooklyn, N.Y.: Tents of Kedar 1976).

The Ansar Cult. The Truth about the Ansaruallah Community in America. Rebuttal to the Slanderers (Brooklyn: the Original Tents of Kedar, 1989).

Ansaar's Guide through the Scriptures for Better Living: Bringing Up the Children, Book 5 (Bushwick Ave: The Original Tents of Kedar, 1989).

Are there UFOs in Your Midst? (Eatonton, GA: The Holy Tabernacle Ministries, n.d.).

Be Prepared for the Anti-Christ (Scroll #67, Eatonton, GA: The Holy Tabernacle Ministries, n.d.).

Book of the Five Percenters (Brooklyn, N.Y.: Tents of Kedar, n.d.).

The Call of the Mahdi in America (Brooklyn: the Original Tents of Kedar, 1987).

El Maguraj: The Journey Within (Athens, GA: Tama-Re, Egypt of the West Embassy, n.d.).

Extraterrestrials Amongst Us (Brooklyn, N.Y.: Ansaaru Allah Community, 1996).

The Final Link (Brooklyn, N.Y.: Tents of Kedar, 1978).

Hadrat Fatimah, Part 1&2 (Brooklyn, N.Y.: Tents of Kedar, 1988).

The Holy Koran of the Moorish Holy Temple of Science: Circle Seven (no date, no publisher, no city).

The Holy Tablets (Eatonton, G.A.: The Holy Tabernacle Ministries, n.d.).

I Am Your Chance: I Have Warned You! 1985: 2.

I Don't Claim to Be Who I Am (flier n.d. Edition #116).

Is there Eternal Life after Death? n.d. (Al Mahdi Shrine Temple No. 19, n.d.).

Malachi, I Will Send You Elijah, by the Honourable Elijah Muhammad (The Holy Tabernacle Ministries P.O. Box 4490 Eatonton, GA., n.d.).

Man from Planet Rizq n.d., circa 1993.

A Masonic Prayerbook.

The Mystery Clouds: Are They UFOs? (Scroll#91, Eatonton, GA: The Holy Tabernacle Ministries, n.d.).

The Nuwaupian Masonic Quiz Book; Hidden Symbolism of Freemasonry; Shriners and Freemasons Family Guide.

The Original Handbook for the Order of the Eastern Star As Never Before (n.d.).

The Paleman (Monticello, N.Y.: The Original Tents of Kedar, 1990).

Prayers of the Sons of Light.

Prehistoric Man and Animals—Did They Exist? (Brooklyn, N.Y.: Tents of Kedar, 1980).

Sex Life of a Muslim, Vol. II. (Brooklyn, N.Y.: Ansaaru Allah Community, 1980).

Shambala and Aghaarta: Cities Within the Earth (Scroll #131, n.d.).

The Spell Of Leviathan 666: The Spell Of Kingu. Brooklyn, N.Y.: Ansaaru Allah Community.

The True Story of Noah [PHUH] Part One (Brooklyn, AAC, 1989).

The Universal Lesson of the Masonic Lodge.

Who was Jesus' Father? (Monticello, N.Y.: The Original Tents of Kedar, 1988).

Nation of Yahweh Publications

The Crucifixion of the Messiah (PEES Foundation, P.O. Box 1768, Seguin, TX , 1999).

Judicial Murder: "Let the Evidence be Heard!" (documentary film).

The Persecution of YAHWEH BEN YAHWEH (*The People for Truth,* Seguin, Texas: PEES Foundation, 1994).

Operation Word War (NOY booklet, n.d.).

You Are Not a Nigger: Our True History, the World's Best Kept Secret (Beaconsfield Quebec: PEES Foundation, 1993).

Index